Create Your First Web Page in a Weekend

How To Order:

For information on quantity discounts, contact the publisher: Prima Publishing, P.O. Box 1260BK, Rocklin, CA 95677-1260; (916) 632-4400. Include information concerning how you intend to use the books and the number of books you want to purchase. For individual orders, turn to the back of this book for more information.

Create Your First Web Page in a Weekend

Steven E. Callihan

PRIMA PUBLISHING

Publisher: Don Roche, Jr.

Acquisitions Manager: Alan Harris

Managing Editor: Tad Ringo

Product Marketing Specialist: Julie Barton

Acquisitions Editor: Debbie Abshier

Development Editor: Faithe Wempen

Project Editor: Jeff Ennis

Technical Reviewer: Nanci Jacobs

Interior Design and Layout: Carl Yoshihara

Cover Design: Victor Kongkadee

Indexer: Katherine Stimpson

Prima Publishing and the author have attempted throughout this book to distinguish proprietary trademarks from descriptive terms by following the capitalization style used by the manufacturer.

Information contained in this book has been obtained by Prima Publishing from sources believed to be reliable. However, because of the possibility of human or mechanical error by our sources, Prima Publishing, or others, the publisher does not guarantee the accuracy, adequacy, or completeness of any information and is not responsible for any errors or omissions or the results obtained from use of such information. Readers should be particularly aware of the fact that the Internet is an ever-changing entity. Some facts may have changed since this book went to press.

ISBN: 0-7615-0692-6

Library of Congress Catalog Card Number: 96-68058

Printed in the United States of America

96 97 98 99 BB 10 9 8 7 6 5 4 3 2 1

Acknowledgments

To all the folks at Prima Publishing and elsewhere who have been involved, and have labored long and hard, in bringing this project to fruition, including Alan Harris, Debbie Abshier, Jill Byus, Jeff Ennis, and Faithe Wempen. And to Don Roche, at Prima Publishing, who originally proposed the idea for the book.

To Michael Neubarth at *Internet World* for publishing my article, "Web Site on a Budget," which ultimately led to the writing of this book. To Lisa Bearnson at *WordPerfect* magazine for publishing every article I ever sent her.

To my sister, Darlene Gadley, and my brother, Don Callihan, without whose assistance and backing I never would have made it to the starting line.

Lastly, to all my friends, especially Jerry, Laura, Deborah, Kay, and Holly, who have stood by me through thick and thin.

The Author

Steven E. Callihan is a freelance writer and has published articles about computers, the Internet, and the Web, including an article, "Web Site on a Budget," in the April 1996 issue of *Internet World*. He has worked professionally with computer technology in the areas of document processing and desktop publishing over the last 12 years, in line, lead, and supervisory roles. Over the last three years, he has been exploring the brave new world of electronic publishing on the Web.

Contents

Introduction

You live in a busy world in which time is at a premium. You've surfed the Web and wondered what it would take to start creating your own Web pages, but you think you have to become an expert on HTML (*Hyper Text Markup Language*), and somehow you just never have been able to find the time. But you don't have to wait! Even if you know absolutely nothing about HTML, you *can* create your first Web page—in just one weekend! You don't have to become an HTML expert—Chapters 1 and 2 tell you everything you need to know about HTML. Learn to create Web pages first, worry about becoming an "expert" later.

Anyone who has a basic understanding of HTML and the right tools, and has easy-to-follow instructions on how to use them can easily create the vast majority of pages you see on the web. That's exactly what this book is about. After you create your first Web page, this book also tells you everything you need to know to put your page up on the Web.

Who Should Read This Book?

You don't have to be a "techie" to create a Web page. On the contrary, what is so liberating about the Web is that you don't have to be a computer expert to take advantage of its benefits. The same holds true for the HTML—anybody can learn basic HTML. Most of what some call *advanced* HTML is not all that difficult to learn, either. Anybody should be able not only to *surf,* but also to publish on the Web.

One assumption driving this book is that everyone has absorptions and interests besides computers. The computer is a tool that enables people to do stuff, not an end in itself. So also should be the Web and HTML. The Web, via HTML, should serve as an extension of *your* interests. What tends to get in people's ways is that they think they have to know more than they actually need to know. People make the mistake of thinking HTML is for computer professionals, but in fact, HTML is for everybody.

Consequently, this book, like the Web, is for everybody or at least anybody who wants to get up and running fast right away.

HTML isn't something you learn first and do later. It's more like riding a bicycle. That is, you learn by doing. Don't worry about making mistakes. Mistakes are just experimental results by another name. Play around with it, experiment, and try new and different things. That's the only way you're going to truly learn.

What Can I Do in a Weekend?

I'm not going to promise that you're going to be able to learn HTML and develop a full-blown multi-page Web site in a single weekend. What you can do, reasonably, is learn the most useful features of HTML and how to apply them, then use that knowledge to plan and create a wide range of different types of Web pages.

One of the most common types of pages on the Web is the *personal page*, where you just tell the world about yourself—you know, personal stuff. Or you might want to create a page for your family, your fraternity or sorority, your church, your club, or whatever. If you're interested in getting a job or advancing your career, you might want to create an on-line version of your résumé.

On the other hand, if you have a product or service to offer, you might want to create an online brochure. Or just a business card. You might want to put up a description of your project, organization, or community. You might want to create an informational page, such as a page on which you offer your own special expertise on a subject of interest, or share perspectives with others and get feedback. You could devote this page to a hobby or something you've researched. Basically, the page could be about anything, from any perspective.

If you know quite a bit about a particular subject, you might want to create a glossary or a FAQ (Frequently Asked Questions) page. If you are helping to run an organization or a social club, for instance, you might want to create a calendar of upcoming events. If you're creative, you could put up a page of your poetry, a short story, or a gallery of your drawings, paintings, or photographs. If you're a student, teacher, or professor, you might want to publish an online version of a paper, abstract, thesis, dissertation, or a book review. You could publish your own page of movie reviews, or a newsletter or journal. The point is your options are virtually unlimited.

Now, you couldn't necessarily do any of the above in just one weekend, but you could definitely create the page and get off to a substantial beginning to its development. The idea isn't to create just one and only one Web page, but by the end of the weekend to have enough hands-on experience with HTML to be able to create any kind of page mentioned here, or any other type of page you might dream up.

In helping you to plan and create your first Web page, I'll be focusing on a few basic and generic Web page examples which can be expanded and adopted to fit any of the above projects. One of the virtues of HTML is that it is highly versatile, and yet relatively simple, allowing you to do a very great deal. So, what can you do? Pretty much, whatever you want to do.

What Does This Book Cover?

The book is organized into five "sessions" covering Friday evening, Saturday morning, Saturday afternoon, Sunday morning, and Sunday afternoon. Each session should take no more than two to four hours to complete, but I've tried to take different learning styles into account, for the purpose of building in flexibility as I can. Parts of the Friday Evening session and all of the Saturday Afternoon session are optional, for instance, to do only if you have time (you can always come back and do them later). In other cases, you may only need to do the parts of a session that apply specifically to you, depending on which choices you make. It also depends on how sophisticated you want to get in creating your first Web page. I've also included a number of appendixes, including a resource directory, the CD-ROM contents, a table of special characters, a tables tutorial, a tutorial on creating interlaced and transparent images, information on how to get your page noticed, and instructions on how to put your Web page up on the Web. Here are some details of what's included in the book:

1. **Friday Evening: Getting Started.** Covers essential background information and the minimum requirements necessary to do the two Saturday HTML tutorials. It also includes an optional section on tools and resources that can help you create your Web page.

2. **Saturday Morning: A Basic HTML Tutorial.** A step-by-step tutorial that covers the basic HTML codes most commonly used to create Web pages. Abundantly illustrated to show you what each code does. Organized according to function, to not only teach you what each code does, but also to give you an overall view of HTML and how it works. Although this tutorial is slated for Saturday morning, feel free to go ahead and take all day.

3. **Saturday Afternoon: An Intermediate HTML Tutorial.** Optional tutorial that covers "intermediate" HTML, which is largely composed of codes originally introduced as "Netscape Extensions" but which have since been

incorporated into HTML 3.2. The information here is value-added. You don't need it to be able to plan and create your first Web page on Sunday. Do whatever suits your schedule or interest level.

4. **Sunday Morning: Planning Your First Web Page.** A hands-on session that guides you in planning your Web page, including defining an objective, doing an outline, and assembling or creating the different pieces or components that will make up your page, including writing your text, creating a banner graphic, and gathering any Web addresses you want to use as hypertext links. It also furnishes some models that you can follow in assembling or creating these components.

5. **Sunday Afternoon: Creating Your First Web Page.** Focuses on creating your first Web page based on the decision tree you design during the Sunday morning planning session. You also choose whether to use basic HTML or intermediate HTML to create your page.

Of course, you don't have to do all five sessions over the weekend. If you do follow the schedule, and do put in the time and effort, you can complete the process in a single weekend. You could just as easily do the five sessions over a period of five evenings, Monday evening through Friday evening. Or you could take two weekends. It's entirely up to you.

This book contains considerably more information than most people can absorb in a single weekend. That's so it isn't just a one weekend throwaway book. Anything not essential for you to create your first Web page in a weekend is marked clearly as "optional."

Appendix A, "A Resource Directory," also is an excellent long term resource. It provides pointers to just about everything you might need or want to know to enhance and refine your Web page and get it up on the Web. It references resources, information, and tools available either on the CD-ROM disk, the Web, or the Web site for this book for easy retrieval, download, or viewing, including:

- **General HTML resources,** including tutorials, guides, references, style guides, and sample templates.

- **Advanced HTML resources,** including Netscape and Microsoft extensions, tables, forms, image maps, frames, CGI programming, Java, JavaScript, and other "cutting edge" HTML features.

- **Graphics tips and tricks,** including interlaced and transparent GIFs, background colors and images, low-high resolution trick to "fade in" your logo graphic, Web art libraries and collections, GIF animations, and more.

- **Software tools,** including a comprehensive listing of Web browsers, HTML editors, HTML converters, word processing document templates, graphic editors, graphic converters, FTP and Telnet applications, site management and Web automation tools, and more.

- **Getting your page up on the Web,** including finding an affordable Web host, placing and maintaining your page on a server, and promoting your presence on the Web.

What Do I Need To Use This Book?

The examples furnished and techniques demonstrated in this book have all been tested using Windows 3.1 or Windows 95. You don't absolutely have to be a Microsoft Windows user to use this book—you can create HTML files on any platform—but you do need to find equivalents on your platform for any programs, utilities, or tips and tricks referenced herein.

Although most of the illustrations come from Windows 95, the examples and techniques almost all apply equally to both Windows 3.1 and Windows 95. In the rare instances in which the two platforms diverge, notes and tips are on the scene to let you know accordingly. Also certain software tools and capabilities sometimes are available on one platform, but not the other—again, these cases are pointed out as you go along.

Besides a computer, of course, you need only three things use this book to create a Web page:

1. **A graphical Web browser connected to the Internet.** Most current graphical Web browsers should be fine for doing the basic HTML tutorial and creating a "basic" Web page. For the intermediate HTML tutorial and creating an "intermediate" Web page, you should use the latest version of Netscape Navigator or Microsoft Internet Explorer. The illustrations in this book feature mainly Navigator, NCSA Mosaic, and Internet Explorer. Ultimately, you'll probably want to download and install all three—only by viewing your Web

page in more than one Web browser can you tell whether it works in more than one Web browser. But for right now, the one you already are using will probably do. Just in case, for your convenience we've included Internet Explorer on the CD-ROM. Appendix A also points to sites on the Web from which you can download Navigator, NCSA Mosaic, and many other Web browsers.

NOTE

If you're connected to the Internet through one of the online services (such as CompuServe or America Online), you may not have your choice of browser, and you might not be able to run it offline. Check with your online service to find out whether you have your choice of browser and whether you can run it offline. Even if the answer is no, you still can do the tutorials and exercises in this book—you just have to do them online.

2. **A text editor.** Consider using Notepad, which comes with both Windows 3.1 and Windows 95, rather than a word processor or an HTML editor, to start out. Notepad is perfectly suited for creating HTML files and, in fact, offers several advantages over larger, more cumbersome programs—many professional HTML coders prefer Notepad. A couple other Notepad-like HTML editors, HTML NotePad and Gomer HTML Editor, also are well-suited for HTML coding, and both are included on the CD-ROM. Avoid starting out with one of the WYSIWYG-type HTML editors. Learn some HTML first, then try out some of the fancier tools (a large selection of which also are included on the CD-ROM).

3. **A graphics editor capable of creating GIF graphic files.** Any of the commercial draw or photo-paint programs can create GIF files, but some excellent graphics programs for creating and working with GIF files also are available on the Web. In case you don't already have a graphics editor capable of working with GIF files, *both* LView Pro and Paint Shop Pro are included on the CD-ROM.

What Do I Need To Know?

You don't need to be a "techie" or "computer nerd" to use this book, but you should have a working knowledge of basic Windows operations (3.1 or 95), such as using File Manager or Windows Explorer to create directories or folders or copy, move, and delete files, and so on. You also should know how to switch between Windows applications (although Chapter 2 does provide a rundown on this activity).

The book is written under the assumption that you already know how to use a Web browser and navigate on the Web. It mentions quite a few resources available on the Web, so you should know how to download a file or program from the Web. Because many programs on the Web are in compressed format—ZIP or TAR, for instance—you should you should know how to decompress files using utilities such as PKUnzip or WinZip.

This book doesn't tell you how to use your computer, run Windows, sign up with an ISP (Internet Service Provider), install your Web browser, log on to the Internet, surf the Web, download files, and so on. If you need to learn about these tasks, plenty of other books are available in your local bookstore. This book covers only using HTML to create Web pages.

Do I Need a CD-ROM Drive?

Although a CD-ROM does ship with this book, you don't need to have a CD-ROM drive to use the book. Web addresses (URLs) are provided in the book for all of the software programs, Web art and reference materials are included on the CD-ROM, so you can download them even if you can't use the disc. Sample Web pages and graphics created just for this book are available for downloading at the Web site for this book. Appendix A also provides the Web addresses for any programs, utilities, or Web art collections that are included on the CD-ROM.

What's on the CD-ROM?

If the book mentions a program or utility, every effort has been made to get permission to include it on the CD-ROM. Appendix A also lists many programs and utilities that you can find the CD-ROM, including Web browsers, HTML editors and converters, graphic editors, file viewers, Web art, and much more.

Do You Have a Web Site?

Yes. I have set up the Web Page in a Weekend Web site at http://www.callihan.com/Webpage/. At the Web site you will find a list of affordable Internet presence providers (IPPs) that you can use as a starting point in your search for a server to host your Web page, continually updated lists of Web publishing resources and tools which will be updated on a continuing basis, as well as a section devoted entirely to placing, maintaining, and promoting your Web page or pages on the Web. Additionally, all sample Web pages and graphics used in the book will be available for download.

Friday Evening:
Getting Started

It's Friday evening—at least if you're following the schedule. Yes, for the purposes of this book, Friday evening constitutes part of the weekend. Okay, maybe that is fudging a bit, but if you're going to create your first Web page in a weekend, you need to get this little reading assignment out of the way first.

The Friday evening session is divided into three parts:

1. Background and Overview

2. Running Your Web Browser Offline

3. Filling Your Toolbox

Go ahead and read the first section, "Background and Overview." It includes general background information on the Internet, the World Wide Web, HTML, and Web pages. You really should have some grounding in the "medium" you plan to use before you start the HTML tutorials on Saturday morning or begin to plan and create your first Web page on Sunday. Of course, if you're already familiar with something, feel free to skip it.

The second section, "Running Your Web Browser Offline," shows you how to run Netscape Navigator, Microsoft Internet Explorer, and NCSA Mosaic offline, so you don't have to run up your Internet bill just to edit HTML files on your local hard drive.

The third section, "Filling Your Toolbox," is optional. Read it on a "need to know" or "want to know" basis, or if you have time. It includes sections on Web browsers, HTML editing tools, graphics editing tools, and other tools you might find useful.

> **NOTE**
>
> *If you already have a graphical Web browser connected to the Internet, a text editor (Notepad in Windows 3.1 or Windows 95 is perfectly sufficient), and a graphics program capable of creating or converting graphics to GIF format, then you don't have to read the "Filling Your Toolbox" section before going on to the Saturday morning session. If you lack any of these "prerequisites," you should read the applicable section. But don't burn the midnight oil—you want to be fresh and awake for the basic HTML tutorial tomorrow morning. You can, of course, come back later and read any part that interests you.*

Background and Overview (Recommended Reading)

Before you do the HTML tutorials and create your first Web page, you should know a few things. You need to understand the nature and operation of the Web before you can use it effectively. This section covers the following Web fundamentals:

- The Internet
- The World Wide Web
- Hypertext
- HTML
- URLs
- Web pages

If you've already been surfing the Web for awhile, and only now are deciding to get into Web publishing, you may already be familiar with much of the information covered here. Skip or skim at your discretion.

What Is the Internet?

It could be said that the Internet is the most valuable legacy left over from the Cold War. It originally came into being, as the ARPANet, which was founded by the U.S.

Defense Department's Advanced Research Projects Agency (ARPA), to link academic research centers involved in military research.

Today's Internet is a kind of "metamorphosis" that has grown far beyond its original conception. Originally a system linking just four university research centers, it has become an international and global system consisting of hundreds of thousands of nodes (servers). In many ways, it has become what Marshall McLuhan called "the global village," in that every node is functionally right next door. You can just as easily communicate with someone in Australia as you can with someone two blocks down the street—and if the person down the street isn't on the Internet, it's actually easier to communicate with the bloke in Australia. That was the promise, even if the original founders didn't realize it, and today it has become an increasingly pervasive reality.

NOTE

A client *is a computer that requests something from another computer. A server is a computer that responds to requests for service from clients.*

An *internet* is a network of networks, a kind of meta-network. In the most minimal sense, the Internet is simply a set of protocols (rules) for transmitting and exchanging data between networks. In the most maximal sense, however, it has become a worldwide community, a global village, but also a repository of global information resources.

NOTE

TCP/IP (Transmission Control Protocol/Internet Protocol) is the standard rule set for Internet communication. You don't have to understand TCP/IP on a technical level. The main thing to know is that the essence of the Internet is not the wire, *but the means for sending and receiving information* across *the wire. In other words, it doesn't matter what type of systems are connected to the Internet, be they mainframes, minicomputers, or Unix, Macintosh, or MS-DOS computers. All that matters is that they all use the same protocol, TCP/IP, to communicate between each other.*

What Is the World Wide Web?

The World Wide Web, also called the WWW, W3, or simply the Web, dates back only to 1989, when it was proposed by Tim Berners-Lee, often called "the inventor of the World Wide Web." Many, many others have been critically involved, but Berners-Lee gets the credit for originally proposing and evangelizing the idea as a way to facilitate collaboration between scientists over the Internet.

The Web has been termed "a wide-area hypermedia information retrieval initiative aiming to give universal access to a large universe of documents." What this means is that the Web is a universal medium for the sharing documents and linking documents to one another with cross-references.

Like the Internet, the World Wide Web essentially is defined by a set of protocols, as follows:

- **HTTP (Hypertext Transfer Protocol).** The protocol used to exchange Web documents across the Internet. When you request a Web document from a server, the protocol used for the request is HTTP.

- **HTML (Hypertext Markup Language).** The markup language that enables users to present information over the Web in a structured and uniform fashion. It is used to mark up documents so that a Web browser can interpret and then display them. See "What Is HTML?" later in this chapter for more information.

- **URLs (Uniform Resource Locators).** Addresses that identify, for instance, a server, a directory, or a specific file. HTTP URLs, or Web addresses, are only one type of address on the Web—FTP, Gopher, and WAIS addresses are just a few examples of other types of addresses on the Web. See "What Is a URL?" later in this session for additional related information.

- **CGI (Common Gateway Interface).** Serves as an interface to execute local programs through a gateway between the HTTP server software and the host computer. Thus, you can include a hypertext link in a Web document that will run a Unix program or script, for example, to process input from a customer request form.

Although other mediums of exchange on the Internet share the same cyberspace, the Web has come to epitomize the new paradigm—in fact, Web browsers can access not only Web, or HTML documents, but virtually the entire Internet, including Gopher,

FTP, Archie, Telnet, and WAIS, as well as Mail and News servers. The Web's universality, that is, its tendency to embrace and incorporate all other mediums, is its most radical and revolutionary character.

A Little History

The beginnings of the Internet go back at least as far as 1957, which marks the founding of the Defense Department's Advanced Research Projects Agency (ARPA) in response to the Soviet Union launching Sputnik. In 1963, ARPA asked the Rand Corporation to ponder how to form a command-and-control network capable of surviving attack by atomic bombs. The Rand Corporation's response (made public in 1964) was that the network would "have no central authority" and would be "designed from the beginning to operate while in tatters." These two basic concepts became the defining characteristics of what would eventually become the Internet. The Internet was conceptualized from the beginning as having no central authority, while operating in a condition of assumed unreliability (bombed out cities, downed telephone lines); that is, of having maximum redundancy. All nodes would be coequal in status, each with authority to originate, relay, and receive messages.

What happened between this first military initiative and the Internet we know today? Plenty. Here are some of the highlights:

1969: ARPANet, the forerunner of the Internet, commissioned by the Department of Defense, linking four nodes at UCLA, Stanford, University of California at Santa Barbara, and the University of Utah. Within two years, number of nodes increased to 15, including MIT, Harvard, and NASA/Ames, among others.

1972: Telnet introduced.

1973: First international connections to the ARPANet, to England and Norway. FTP (File Transfer Protocol) introduced.

1977: E-Mail introduced.

1979: News groups (USENET) introduced.

1982: ARPANet adopts TCP/IP (Transmission Control Protocol/Internet Protocol), the real beginning of the Internet.

1984: Domain Name Server (DNS) implemented, allocating addresses between six basic "domains" (gov, mil, edu, com, and org for government, military, educational, commercial, and non-commercial hosts, respectively).

1986: NSFNet formed by the National Science Foundation (NSF) using five super-computing centers to form the first high-speed "backbone," running at 56 Kbps. Unlike ARPANet, which was focused on military or government research, the NSFNet was available to all forms of academic research.

1987: 10,000 hosts.

1988: Backbone upgraded to T1 (1.544 Mbps).

1989: Initial proposal by Tim Berners-Lee ("the inventor of the Web"), which eventually led to creation of the World Wide Web.

1990: End of the ARPANet. Archie introduced. The World (world.std.com) becomes the first commercial provider of dial-up access to the Internet.

1991: Gopher introduced. The World Wide Web released at CERN (Conseil European pour la Recherche Nucleaire) in Switzerland. Backbone upgraded to T3 (44.736 Mbps).

1992: The Internet Society (ISOC) formed. Viola, the first English language graphical Web browser, released. Veronica introduced. 1,000,000 hosts.

1993: Marc Andreesen's Mosaic for X released by NCSA, followed shortly by versions for PC/Windows and Macintosh. The White House comes online. HTML 1.0 draft proposal is published.

1994: Mosaic Communications Corp., later to become Netscape Communications Corp., formed by Marc Andreesen and James Clark, ex-president of Silicon Graphics. The first meeting of the W3 Consortium met at MIT. The first cybermalls formed. HTML 2.0 draft proposal published.

1995: Netscape went public. The NSFNet replaced by a network of providers for carrying U.S. backbone traffic. NSFNet reverts back to a research network.

1996: Bill Gates and Microsoft jumped into the game with the Internet Explorer browser. HTML 3.2, the newest specification for HTML, announced. Rushing toward 10,000,000 hosts.

What Is Hypertext?

You could say the Web is a graphical, platform-independent, distributed, decentralized, multiformatted, interactive, participatory, dynamic, nonlinear, immediate, two-way communication medium. The basic mechanism that enables all of it is actually quite simple—the capability to embed a hypertext link within a document or page and which when clicked on jumps from it to 1) another place in the same document, 2) another document, 3) another place in another document, and 4) other kinds of data objects, such as graphics, audio, video, or even software. A link can connect anything, anywhere, that has an address or URL on the Net. See Figure 1-1 for a diagram that shows how hypertext links work.

Figure 1-2 illustrates some of the different kinds of *data objects* to which you can link from a Web page. Note the difference here between an inline image, which appears as part of the Web page, and other graphics, which your browser or viewer can link to and display separately.

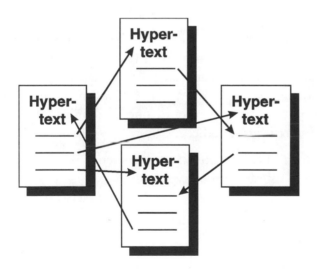

Figure 1-1.
Hypertext links enable you to "jump" from a place on one Web page to another Web page or to a place on the same Web page.

A hypertext link, also referred to as an *anchor*, actually works similarly to the way a cross-reference works in a regular book, except that, instead of having to thumb through the book or go down to the local library to find the reference, you can immediately go to it simply by clicking on the link, whether it's a link within the same "page" or to a page or document halfway around the world. Anything that has an address on the Web can be linked, including not only Web pages, but Gopher documents, FTP files, and Newsgroup articles.

Figure 1-2.
A Web page can link to many other kinds of data objects besides just other Web pages.

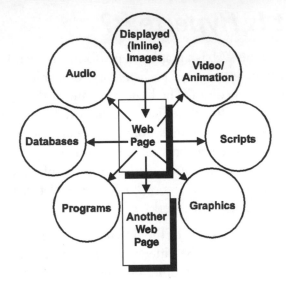

What Is Hypermedia?

Given that *hypertext* is a linking that occurs within and between documents, it makes sense that *hypermedia* is a linking with other nontext (*binary*) media such as graphics, audio, animation, and video. Hypermedia also includes the capability to link with and run software, such as a Java applet. Over time, the Web will naturally evolve from a system predominantly composed of hypertext to one predominantly composed of hypermedia, within which text is just another medium.

For now, though, the Web still mainly consists of documents, or pages, and you can still think of hypermedia as a subcategory of hypertext.

What Is HTML?

HTML (Hypertext Markup Language) is a subset of SGML (Standard Generalized Markup Language). SGML was developed to standardize the markup, or preparation for typesetting, of computer-generated documents. HTML, on the other hand, was specifically developed to mark up, or encode, hypertext documents for display on the World Wide Web.

An HTML document is a plain ASCII (text) file with codes (called *tags*) inserted in the text to define elements in the document. HTML tags generally have two parts, an on-code and an off-code, which contain the text to be defined. Note: A few tags don't require an off-code. You can represent a tag in the following way, where the ellipsis (...) represents the text you want to tag:

```
<Tagname>...</Tagname>
```

For instance, the following is the tag for a level-one heading in a Web document:

```
<H1>This is a level-one heading</H1>
```

The most important thing to keep in mind about HTML is that its purpose isn't to specify the exact formatting or layout of a Web page, but rather, to define and specify the specific elements that make up a page, such as the body of the text, headings, paragraphs, line breaks, text elements, and so on. You use HTML to define the composition of a Web page, not its appearance. The particular Web browser you use to view the page controls the display of the Web page. For instance, you can define a line using the H1../H1 tag, but the browser defines the appearance of an H1 line. One browser might show H1 lines as 18-point Times Roman text, while another might show H1 lines in a totally different font and size.

To understand why this is the way it is, you need to understand how HTML-coded Web pages and Web browsers work together. To display a Web page on your computer, a Web browser must first download it and any graphics displayed on the page to your computer. If the Web page were to specify all the formatting and display details, it would balloon up the size of the file, and therefore, the amount of data to be transmitted. Leaving all the formatting and display details to the Web browser means that the size of HTML documents sent over the Web can remain relatively small, in that they're just regular ASCII text files. It's rare to have an HTML file that exceeds 30 KB (not counting any graphics that it may contain).

However, this means that every Web browser has its own idea about how to best display a particular Web page. Your Web page may appear different in Netscape Navigator than it does in NCSA Mosaic, and different still in Microsoft Explorer. That's why you may want to test your completed page on more than just one browser. Some Web browsers now support the display of tables, which was part of the proposed HTML 3.0 standard and has since been incorporated into HTML 3.2, but some don't. HTML 3.2, by and large, simply standardizes, and gives the official stamp of approval, to most if not all of the Netscape extensions to HTML. However, none of the Microsoft extensions to HTML have been so favored. Still, other than the latest versions of Netscape Navigator and Microsoft Internet Explorer, the vast majority of other Web browsers—NCSA Mosaic, for instance—are best characterized as still being HTML 2.0 compliant, with support for HTML 3.2 tags being sketchy at best.

Thus, not only the Web browser used to view a Web page, but the version of HTML with which it can be said to be compliant and any additional tags it may or may not support are factors in determining how a particular Web browser will display a particular Web page. Tomorrow's exercises (the basic HTML tutorial and, optionally, the intermediate HTML tutorial) include several examples of how the same HTML coding can have quite different results depending on the Web browser used to view it.

NOTE

As HTML has evolved, both officially and in an ad hoc *manner (by browsers having their own extensions), it has become more descriptive, allowing you more freedom to "design" your page rather than simply schematicize it. The more attention you give to designing your page to have a particular appearance, the less likely that all browsers will display your page consistently and accurately. The HTML tutorials in Chapters 2 and 3 show you how different browsers can display the same element differently. Also, many of the "designer" features that have been added to HTML require a Web browser that is up-to-date enough to display them.*

For the purposes of this book, the discussion of HTML falls into three categories: basic HTML, intermediate HTML, and advanced HTML. These divisions are in no way "official"—they're just an attempt to pare down the material into more serviceable "chunks."

Chapter 2, "Saturday Morning: A Basic HTML Tutorial," covers basic HTML. It includes most but not all of the HTML 2.0 tags, and should perhaps be your primary focus as you plan and create your first Web page this weekend. Doing so would guarantee that most Web browsers would display your Web page correctly.

Chapter 3, "Saturday Afternoon: An Intermediate HTML Tutorial," covers intermediate HTML. It includes many, although not all, of the HTML 3.2 tags (previously called Netscape extensions). You can use these tags to create a more "designed" look for your Web pages, including centered text and images, text wrapping around images, font size and color changes, background colors and images, and so on. You can use many of these tags without "breaking" Web browsers that don't support them. The tutorial points out the main pitfalls to try to avoid if you want to use these tags and maintain compatibility with non-supporting Web browsers. Chapter 3 is optional. Do as much of it as you can or want, or skip it entirely if Chapter 2 takes you most or all of the day to complete. You can come back and finish the intermediate tutorial after you create your first Web page.

Advanced HTML includes both HTML 2.0 and HTML 3.2 tags, as well as other tags that originated as extensions to HTML in Netscape Navigator or Microsoft Internet Explorer. These are tags that require considerably more experience to use effectively than a beginning or intermediate Web publisher is likely to have, or simply require more space and time to properly explain them than is available for this book. For instance, this book doesn't cover creating input forms or image maps in this book, even though they're included in HTML 2.0, simply because they're too advanced for a beginning Web publisher to learn to handle without a fairly considerable amount of experience. On the other hand, it excludes any treatment of creating tables, an HTML 3.2 feature, not because tables are that difficult, but simply because to do them justice would involve more time and space than is available (you can, however, do the tables tutorial included in Appendix C after you create your first Web page). Similarly, this book also doesn't deal directly with creating frames or using CGI or other scripts, GIF animations, and so on. Appendix A, "A Resource Directory," does, however, include links and references to resources available on the Web that can assist you in incorporating these more advanced features of HTML into your Web pages.

What Is a URL?

A URL (Uniform Resource Locator) identifies the "address," or location, of a resource on the Internet. Every Web page has its own unique URL. If you know the URL of a Web page and access is not restricted, you can connect to it and view it in your browser. Resources other than Web pages also have URLs, including FTP, Telnet, WAIS, Gopher, and Newsgroups.

A URL may consist of the following parts:

- **Service.** The service designator specifies the service being accessed: http (for WWW), ftp, gopher, wais, telnet, or news.

- **Host.** The host designator specifies the domain name of the server being accessed, such as the following:

  www.myserver.com.

- **Port number.** The port number only needs to be specified if it is a non-standard port number for the service being accessed—most URLs don't require port numbers (the default port number is 80 for WWW servers, 21 for FTP servers, for instance).

- **Resource path.** The resource path specifies the directory path and/or file name of the resource being accessed. At minimum, you should include a "/" here to indicate the root directory of a domain, which, for technical reasons too tedious to explain, will minimize the amount of server cycles your request consumes: http://anywhere.com/ rather than http://anywhere.com, for instance. Both will work, but the second way is the less efficient. You also can exclude the file name here if you use the default file name for index files specified by the server, which usually is INDEX.HTML (INDEX.HTM also is often used). If you don't use the default file name for index files, then you must include the actual file name of the Web page.

Figure 1-3.
A Uniform Resource Locator (URL) is the address of a resource on the Internet.

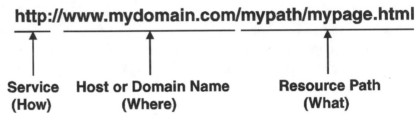

Figure 1-3 shows a diagram of URL. Because most Web addresses don't use port numbers, this illustration leaves out the port number.

A URL actually is an instruction or request made by an agent, such as a Web browser, to a server on the Internet that specifies the following three things:

- **How?** This is the protocol for the transaction. For Web pages, this is HTTP. Essentially, this tells the server what software it needs to run to manage the transaction. More than one "server" can reside on the same computer, for instance—a single computer can function both as an FTP server and as an HTTP (or Web) server.

- **Where?** This is the address where the transaction is to take place. For instance, www.mydomain.com/mypath/ would specify the domain name and location within that domain of what is to be transacted.

- **What?** This is the name of what is to be transacted. For instance, mypage.html would specify the actual HTML document, or Web page, that is the subject of the transaction.

NOTE

If you link to a file or data object that resides within the same directory structure as the referring page, you don't have to supply the full URL for it, just as you don't have to dial the area code for a local phone call. For example, let's say you have two HTML documents in your directory on the server: your main Web page and your resume. You could abbreviate the link from your main Web page to your resume page to reference just the file name, since all the other location information is the same. When a link is local like that, and uses abbreviated information, it's known as a relative URL, while standard (full) URLs are known as absolute URLs.

The advantage of using relative rather than absolute URLs to reference local files is that if later you want to move your Web pages and their attendant files, you don't have to redo your local URLs, as long as the directories in which they reside retain the same names and relations. See Chapter 2, "Saturday Morning: A Basic HTML Tutorial," for a fuller explanation of how to use relative URLs.

CAUTION

Most Web pages reside on Unix servers. Unlike MS-DOS, Unix file paths and file names are case-sensitive. So, if you see a path and file name, like MySite/HOME-PAGE.html, you should type it exactly as it appears.

What Is a Domain Name?

Every Internet server has an IP (Internet Protocol) address, which usually consists of four octets (e.g., 185.35.117.0). Computers like numeric addresses like this because they're precise. Unfortunately, humans have trouble remembering numbers—we prefer meaningful text addresses, like www.mysite.com. That's what a domain name is: a text alternative to an IP address. You usually can use the two interchangeably. The point is that if you know the domain name, you don't have to know anything about the IP address. You will, however, sometimes run into the odd URL on the Web that specifies the IP address rather than the domain name.

Actually, a server can exist on the Web with only an IP address, but without a corresponding domain name. It's not common, though. Most servers have applied for and received a domain name from the Internet Network Information Center (InterNIC), which handles domain name registrations. As long as your Web pages are located on a server that has a domain name, you can use that domain name in the addresses, or URLs, for those Web pages. You don't have to have your own server, however, to have your own domain name. You can set up a Web site on someone else's server, but use your own domain name in what is often referred to as a virtual host arrangement—to the outside world it looks just like you have your own server, when in reality you don't. In fact, nothing stands in the way of a single home page, unlinked to any other pages, from also having its own domain name.

NOTE

Registering domain names used to be free, but this led to a free-for-all somewhat similar to the Oklahoma Land Rush, as companies and individuals scrambled to grab up domain names before anyone else could claim them. And because an organization or individual technically could claim an unlimited number of domain names, speculative trading in, or "scalping" of, domain names evolved. For these reasons, as well as to help fund the costs of registering rapidly increasing domain name requests, the InterNIC started charging a fee of $50 per year for registering and maintaining a domain name, as of September 1995.

A domain name represents a hierarchy, starting with the most general word on the right and moving to the most specific on the left. It can include:

1. A country code.

2. An organization code.

3. A site name.

For instance, myname.com.au, reading from right to left, specifies the name of a site in Australia ("au") in the commercial (com) subcategory "myname." Every country connected to the Internet has its own code, such as "uk" (United Kingdom), "ca" (Canada), "fr" (France), "nz" (New Zealand), and so forth. The country code for the United States is "us." Most sites in the United States don't, however, include the country code because the Internet began in the United States and the country codes were created later, after the Internet went international. The organization codes are:

- **EDU for "education."** Schools and universities, for instance, use the EDU organization code.

- **GOV for "government."** Various governmental departments and agencies use the GOV organization code.

- **MIL for "military."** The Internet was, after all, originally a U.S. Defense Department initiative (the ARPANet).

- **NET for "network."** NET can refer to a network connected to the Internet. In practice, you usually run into NETs with ISPs (Internet Service Providers) that are offering public access to the Internet.

- **COM for "commercial."** This code was created to accommodate commercial usage of the Internet by business enterprises.

- **ORG for "non-profit organization."** This code is for non-commercial, or not-for-profit, organizations.

Figure 1-4 depicts a graphical representation of the domain name system.

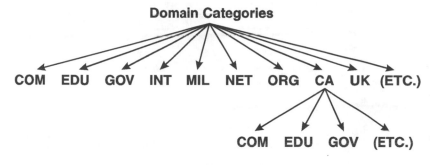

Domain Categories

Figure 1-4.
Internet domains have been organized into categories, such as COM for commercial, EDU for educational, etc. CA and UK are international domains for Canada and the United Kingdom.

What Is a Web Page?

A *Web page* is a hypertext (HTML) document contained in a single file. To have more than one Web page, you must have more than one file. Despite the connotation of the word "page," a Web page can be any length, although most Web pages are at most two or three "screens" in length.

A Web page is simply a plain text document. All codes are entered into the document as ordinary text, unlike, for instance, a word processing document, which has formatting codes embedded in the document on a binary level. When you mark some text as italic in a word processing document, you don't see the actual computer code that causes the text to appear or print in italics. In HTML, though, you would type "<I>" and "</I>" to instruct a browser to turn italics on and off, without any underlying program code, allowing Web pages to remain small but still pack quite a punch.

When a browser displays a Web page, the page may appear to contain special graphical elements like logos or buttons. These graphics don't reside in the HTML file itself; they're separate files that the HTML file references. For instance, you might see a line like this in the HTML file:

```
<IMG SRC="mylogo.gif">
```

The code places the graphic into the version of the page that a browser displays. When a browser displays the page, the reference opens and inserts the graphic in the specified spot. You can include a banner or logo, buttons, icons, separator bars, navigational icons, and more. See Figure 1-5 for a graphical representation of a Web page that contains these different kinds of elements.

Figure 1-5.
Graphic elements, such as a banner or logo, an image, icon bullets, horizontal rules, and navigational buttons actually are separate files linked to and displayed as part of your Web page.

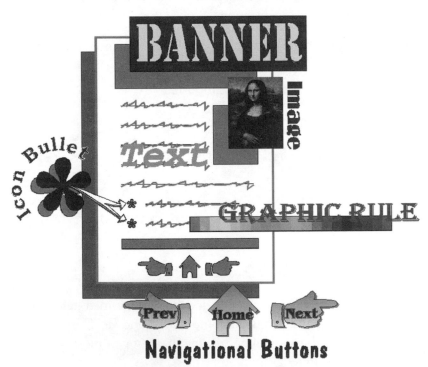

What Is a Web Site?

The term *Web site* has a couple different, although analogous, meanings. Servers often are called Web sites (sites on the Web), but then any grouping of related and linked Web pages sharing a common theme or subject matter may also be called a Web site.

NOTE

I prefer to refer to servers as "Web hosts," and reserve the term Web site for a group or collection of related and linked Web pages.

A personal, non-commercial Web site can often be hosted by your service provider (the company or organization that provides you access to the Internet) at little or no cost. If you're a student, you may be able to have your pages hosted by your school's server. Many online services, such as Compuserve or America Online, also will host Web pages at a reasonable cost. If you want to create a commercial Web site that offers a product or service, or you want to create a more sophisticated Web site that requires more space, higher traffic allowances, more technical support, and a wider range of features, you may need an Internet Presence Provider (IPP) who focuses on or specializes in providing Web space and can provide a fuller menu of services aimed specifically at Web publishers. A presence provider also can register and maintain a domain name for you, usually at a reasonable cost, that lets you appear to the outside world as if you own your own server, acting as a *virtual host*, rather than as a tenant renting space.

So, a Web site is simply a collection of allied Web pages, along with any graphic or other supporting files, similar to the chapters in a book, tied and linked together, usually through a *home page* that serves as the front door to the rest of the Web site (that is, as a directory, table of contents, or menu). The key here is that the different Web pages that compose the site are interlinked and related to each other as parts of a whole. Dissimilar Web pages unlinked, unrelated, to each other, on the other hand, don't form a Web site, even if they should be stored in the same directory on the same server.

What Is a Home Page?

The term home page can have a number of different meanings. When you start your browser, it loads whatever Web page has been designated as its home page, actually any page you want to designate (including a page on your own hard drive). Most browsers have a Home button or command that takes you back to the home page. Usually, this home page is your access provider's home page, or possibly Netscape's, Microsoft's, or NCSA's home page, depending on what browser you use. The home page sometimes is referred to as a *start page*. Figure 1-6 shows a home page designated in Netscape Navigator, an example of a home page of an Internet access provider.

The term home page also serves to designate any Web page that stands on its own (in keeping with the front door comparison, you could think of a stand-alone Web page as a one-room shack). A home page also can serve as an entry point (or front door) to a Web site, or group of linked and related Web pages. The diagram in Figure 1-7 shows the relationship between home and Web pages.

Figure 1-6.

I have designated this page as my default "home page" when using Netscape.

Figure 1-7.

A home page can be either a stand-alone Web page or the entry point, or "front door" to a Web site.

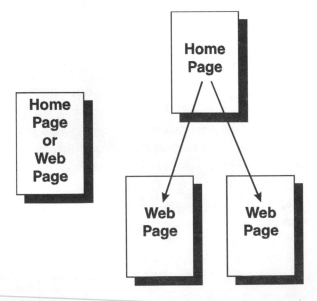

Most servers let you create a default home page, most often "index.html," that loads automatically without having to specify the file name in the URL. This allows you, for instance, to have http://www.myserver.com/mydirectory/ as your URL rather than http://www.myserver.com/mydirectory/index.html.

Home pages used as entryways generally are kept small, often serving simply as menus or directories to the Web pages that comprise the rest of the Web site. The idea here is that a viewer need only display the home page, which is relatively small, and then decide what else to view in the remainder of the Web site.

Having a Web site go deeper than three or four levels is rare, but the number of levels of Web pages you might want to have appended as subpages off of your home, or "main," page, is technically unlimited. The deeper a Web page, though, say a subpage of a subpage of a subpage of a subpage of your home page, the less accessible to visitors to your site. See Figure 1-8 for an illustration of a multi-level Web site.

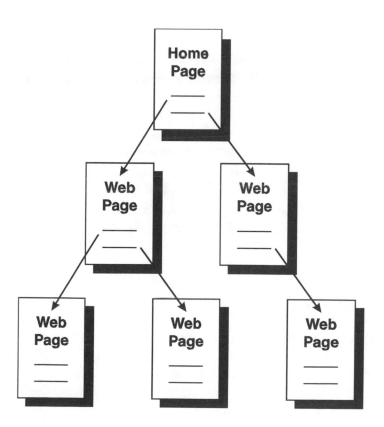

Figure 1-8.
A Web site can have several levels, although it is best to keep it to three or fewer levels.

You also can create a home page that links together multiple home pages. You might, for instance, have a series of Web sites that are relatively autonomous, but that share a common theme, are produced by the same department, or are part of a larger project. Or you may simply want to link pages together to get increased visibility on the Web—as with the various cybermalls increasingly prevalent on the Web.

The Future of HTML (Optional)

This section tries to address the direction HTML may go in the years to come. If you're short on time, please feel free to skip ahead to "Saturday Morning: A Basic HTML Tutorial." You can do the HTML tutorials and plan and create your first Web page without reading this section. Its intention is primarily informational rather than instructional, so don't feel you have to understand how it all works—the main thing is to get a rough idea of where HTML is going.

The Only Constant Is Change

This truism certainly fits the Web—and HTML, too. The Web and HTML form what is a new medium that continues to evolve rapidly. Remember that nearly a decade ago neither the Web nor HTML even existed. In the meantime, HTML 1.0 has come and gone and what was the standard, HTML 2.0, was definitely getting creaky, even though it had been around for only a couple years. HTML 3.0 had been the draft proposal for the next standard for HTML, but was recently abandoned in favor of a more incremental advance, HTML 3.2, the current standard. You now can expect further incremental steps, HTML 3.3, HTML 3.4, and so on, to implement more, if not necessarily all, of what was originally proposed for HTML 3.0. Eventually, HTML 4.0 will show up on the scene (if it doesn't become HMML, Hyper*media* Markup Language, first).

Netscape's Extensions

Several major browser companies, including Netscape Communications, have developed their own special HTML codes, or extensions. These can be used in any Web document, but they translate into special formatting only when a user views the Web page in the particular browser for which they were created, unless the other browser's manufacturer provides support for that extension, too.

Although you don't have to use any of Netscape's extensions to create a wide variety and range of different types of Web pages, you can't surf the Web without running into constant reminders of them. Even if you don't use Netscape Navigator to surf the Web, you can't help but notice the proliferation of "Enhanced for Netscape" icons, indicating the use of one or more of Netscape's extensions on these pages.

Many, if not all, of Netscape's extensions have been widely adopted by other current graphical Web browsers, becoming an ad hoc standard (as opposed to the official standard) for HTML. Before a graphical Web browser qualifies as current, it should support background images and colors (an entirely Netscape innovation). It also should support centering of headings, text, and other elements; flowing of text around images; tables; resizing of the thickness and width of horizontal rules; and specifying of font size and color changes (all of which were Netscape innovations).

Probably the most noteworthy of Netscape's recent innovations is the FRAME tag. Frames now are rapidly proliferating on the Web, compelling other Web browsers to follow suit and incorporate the display of frames into their repertoire. On the other hand, certain other Netscape extensions have not been widely implemented by other Web browsers, such as the BLINK tag.

Most of the Netscape extensions have now been incorporated into HTML 3.2. (Thankfully, however, the BLINK tag has not been included.)

Microsoft's Extensions

Microsoft has introduced a number of extensions to HTML for its Web browser, Internet Explorer. These include, for instance, the capability to display a scrollable text marquee at the bottom of the browser window and to automatically play background sounds. More recently, Microsoft has introduced scrollable background images (when you scroll down through the text, the background image remains fixed). So far, none of these extensions show signs of being widely implemented by other Web browsers, with the exception of scrollable text marquees.

HTML 3.0

HTML 3.0 had been the proposed draft for the next HTML standard. Tables, not part of the HTML 2.0 standard, were proposed as part of HTML 3.0. However, all current major graphical Web browsers have incorporated the HTML 3.0 specification for tables, with some variation (Netscape, for instance, has introduced a number of extensions beyond what was proposed as part of HTML 3.0). Other proposed HTML 3.0 elements that have gained the favor of Web browsers to one degree or another are superscripts and subscripts, font size changing (with the BIG and SMALL tags), and underlining. Those parts of the proposed HTML 3.0 standard that have been most widely implemented in current Web browsers have since been incorporated into HTML 3.2.

HTML 3.2

On May 7th, 1996, the W3 Consortium announced HTML 3.2 as its new specification for HTML. HTML 3.0, which was the previous draft proposal for the next HTML standard, has been abandoned, largely because the differences between HTML 2.0 and HTML 3.0 simply were too large to achieve consensus and agreement. The plan now is to implement new versions of HTML in much more manageable pieces. HTML 3.2 is a much more modest step up from HTML 2.0, which has been developed in cooperation with industry leaders, including IBM, Microsoft, Netscape, Sun Microsystems, and others. Here are some of the primary features now included in the new HTML 3.2 standard:

- Tables
- Applets (for Java and Javascript)
- Background images
- Background, text, and link colors
- Font sizes and colors
- Flowing of text around images
- Image borders
- Height and width attributes for images
- Alignment (left, center, or right) of paragraphs, headings, and horizontal rules, as well as the CENTER tag
- Superscripts and subscripts (the SUP and SUB tags)
- Strikethroughs (the Strike tag)
- Document divisions (the DIV tag)
- Client-side image maps (the MAP tag)
- Provisions for stylesheets (the STYLE tag), but otherwise left undefined

It shouldn't be surprising that a large part of the new HTML 3.2 specification is a rubber stamping of what originally were unofficial and *ad hoc* extensions to HTML by

Netscape. The rest of the HTML 3.2 specification are for those features of HTML 3.0 that already have gained wide acceptance and implementation—tables, for instance. HTML 3.2 really offers little that isn't already widely implemented.

What's Next?

The next version of HTML is code-named "Cougar" (HTML 3.2 was code-named "Wilbur"). As currently planned, it's another incremental step up, and not by any means a leap forward. Probably the two most significant additions to HTML proposed in Cougar are support for stylesheets and incorporation of Microsoft's "face" attribute for the FONT tag.

HTML 3.2 includes a STYLE tag, but otherwise leaves it completely undefined. Stylesheets will allow a great deal more specificity in Web page design—a browser would download both the HTML file and any specified stylesheet. A stylesheet could, for instance, specify the exact fonts to use to display different elements on a page. Any TrueType font, for instance, could be specified and, as long as the user has the font on their system, would be used to display the page. Microsoft has already included support for stylesheets in Internet Explorer 3.0, as so far defined in Cougar. Netscape currently plans to include support for stylesheets in the next version of Netscape Navigator (4.0).

The "face" attribute for the FONT tag will allow the tagging of text to be displayed in a particular type "face," such as a TrueType font. The font has to be installed on your browser. (This might seem a bit redundant, since the STYLE tag can take care of it, but redundancy of this type in HTML isn't exactly uncommon—the real intent here probably is to "rope in" Microsoft's extension and bring it back into the fold, but also to make sure that Web pages already using this attribute are not left out in the cold.)

Probably the major piece of HTML still left hanging in limbo is frames. Frames were introduced in Netscape Navigator, but Internet Explorer now also supports them. Frames, however, were not included in HTML 3.2, nor are they included in Cougar. They probably will be included in the "incremental" specification right after Cougar.

Several widely anticipated features were proposed as part of HTML 3.0 but haven't been included (yet) in HTML 3.2 or Cougar. The scientific community, for instance, anxiously awaits support for equations and math formulas. The academic community expects support for footnotes. The NOTE tag was promised for notes, warnings, and cautions. The INS and DEL tags were promised for marking text insertions and deletions. The BANNER tag was supposed to facilitate the display of company banners or logos. The FIG tag for displaying figures was supposed to replace the IMG tag. A TAB tag was promised for setting and inserting tab stops.

How soon will you see any of these features? Many of these features are of particular interest to the academic and scientific communities, but what really drives the development of HTML today (for now, anyway) is its commercial potential. The emphasis is switching more from distributing ideas to selling products—with visual appeal currently being much more on the front burner than more prosaic "document annotation" features. So cross your fingers, keep your ear to the ground, listen for distant drum beats, and watch for smoke signals. Hopefully, before too long, a clearer idea of what's in store will crystallize.

Running Your Web Browser Offline

As you do the tutorials included in this book, and while you create your first Web page, you'll want to be able to switch back and forth between your text editor and your Web browser, dynamically updating your work as you go. Preferably, however, you'll want to do this while *offline*, so you won't be running up your Internet bill just to edit and preview local HTML files. If you're not paying for your connect time, however, it's not an issue. Most of you probably aren't that lucky, though. The following section shows you how to run Netscape Navigator, Microsoft Explorer, and NCSA Mosaic offline in both Windows 3.1 and Windows 95. You only need to do the section that applies to the Web browser you use.

NOTE

Right about now, you might be wondering whether you should switch browsers if you don't use Netscape Navigator. That depends. Any of the "big three" (Netscape Navigator, Microsoft Internet Explorer, and NCSA Mosaic) are fine for doing the basic HTML tutorial in Chapter 2 and planning and creating a basic Web page in Chapters 4 and 5. For doing the optional Intermediate HTML Tutorial in Chapter 3 and using any of the "extra options" when creating your Web page in Chapter 5, you should use Netscape Navigator 2.0 or higher if you're using Windows 3.1, and Netscape Navigator 2.0 (or higher) or Microsoft Internet Explorer 3.0 if you're using Windows 95. But you don't have to switch now. Which browser you use becomes an issue only if you decide to do the optional intermediate HTML tutorial in Chapter 3 or want to take advantage of many of the "extra options" included in Chapter 5 when you get around to creating your first Web page (unless you're using a real "clunker").

Running Netscape Navigator Offline

Windows 3.1

The following might seem like much to do just to get Netscape Navigator to run offline in Windows 3.1. If you plan to do a fair amount of Web publishing, as opposed to just Web surfing, then the result is worth the effort. And it really isn't all that difficult, as long as you just follow the steps provided here.

The following method for doing this has been tested using Trumpet Winsock 2.0b and Netscape Navigator 2.0 and 2.02. This way isn't necessarily the only way to run Navigator offline in Windows 3.1, but all other methods are variants of this method in one way or another. If you use a winsock program other than Trumpet Winsock, you need to experiment to see whether this method will work (if not, see the "Windows 3.1" section "Running Internet Explorer Offline" later in this session for a workaround that should work for Netscape Navigator as well).

CAUTION

The following directions assume that you have not installed Trumpet Winsock in your Netscape directory. If you aren't sure where Trumpet Winsock is installed, just click once on its icon to highlight it and select File from the Windows menu bar. Next, select Properties to see where your Trumpet Winsock is located. As long as it isn't in your Netscape directory, you can skip the rest of this caution.

On the outside chance that you have installed Trumpet Winsock in your Netscape directory, the easiest solution is simply to copy your Trumpet Winsock files to another directory, such as C:\WINSOCK. The files you need to copy (at least for Version 2.0b) are BYE.CMD, HOSTS, LOGIN.CMD, PROTOCOL, SERVICES, TCPMAN.EXE, and TRUMPWSK.INI. If WINSOCK.DLL is also in your Netscape directory, you should copy it as well. Please, make sure you "copy" rather than "move" these files, just to be safe.

Next, click on your Trumpet Winsock icon to highlight it, then select File from the Windows menu bar, then select Properties. Edit it to point to the new location. Next, run your "new" Trumpet Winsock to connect to the Internet and make sure it's working correctly.

Follow these steps to run Netscape Navigator offline (the following steps assume your Netscape directory is C:\NETSCAPE, so if it's different, be sure to substitute the directory you use):

1. Download MOZOCK.DLL from the Internet.

NOTE

You can download MOZOCK.DLL from the Web site for this book, at http://www.callihan.com/webpage/. You also can find it at TUCOWS, at http://tucows.phx.cox/.

2. Next, use WinZip or PKUnzip to unzip MOZOCK.ZIP. (If you don't have an "unzip" utility, see Appendix A, "A Resource Directory," for where you can download WinZip.)

3. Copy MOZOCK.DLL to C:\NETSCAPE (your Netscape directory). Rename it to WINSOCK.DLL.

4. From your Trumpet Winsock directory, copy TCPMAN.EXE and TRUMPWSK.INI to C:\NETSCAPE (your Netscape directory). (If you don't know where your Trumpet Winsock directory is, see the above Caution.)

CAUTION

Make sure you copy rather than move TCPMAN.EXE and TRUMPWSK.INI. You want to leave the original copies where they are. You still need them for when you want to use Netscape in online *mode.*

5. Run Windows Notepad and load C:\NETSCAPE\TRUMPWSK.INI. Find the dial-option line. To turn off Winsock's automatic login, edit the line so it reads

```
dial-option=0
```

This turns off Winsock's automatic login.

6. Save your new copy of C:\NETSCAPE\TRUMPWSK.INI, then exit Notepad.

Now, to run Navigator offline, just double-click on the Navigator icon, without running Trumpet Winsock first to connect to the Internet. A pop-up window will appear, saying Netscape was unable to create a network socket connection.... No need to worry—just ignore this message and click on the OK button. You're now running Navigator offline. To open and view an HTML file on a local drive, just choose File on Navigator's menu bar, then select Open File.

NOTE

To run Netscape online, first run your Trumpet Winsock software to connect to the Internet, then run Netscape Navigator.

The following section gives instructions on how to set up Netscape Navigator for seamless offline browsing, that is, without the irritating error message each time you try to run it offline. The error message is mostly just a nuisance, and by no means a hindrance to using Navigator for offline browsing. If you don't need to read the "Fill Your Toolbox" section, you can now get a good night's sleep and and start the basic HTML tutorial tomorrow morning.

Getting Rid of the Error Message

When running Netscape Navigator offline in Windows 3.1, you get the error message, Netscape was unable to create a network socket connection..., because Navigator is trying to go up on the Web and download its default home page. You can get rid of this error message by specifying a blank page or a local HTML file as your default home page.

The only problem with this is that you're using the same copy of Netscape Navigator to run both offline and online, so whatever you set here is the default regardless of whether you want to run Navigator offline or online, which may not be what you want. One partial workaround would be to specify your bookmark file as your default home page, then include whatever page you were using as your default home page as a bookmark so you can easily hop up to it when you run Netscape online.

To specify a blank page or a local Web page as your default home page, follow these steps:

1. Run Netscape Navigator and click on the OK button at the error message.

2. In Navigator, click on Options and choose General Preferences, then select the Appearance tab.

3. To specify a blank page in the Startup section, enable the Blank Page radio button on the **S**tart With line. See Figure 1-9.

Figure 1-9.
In Netscape Navigator for Windows 3.1, you can specify a blank page as your default home page.

Blank Page radio button

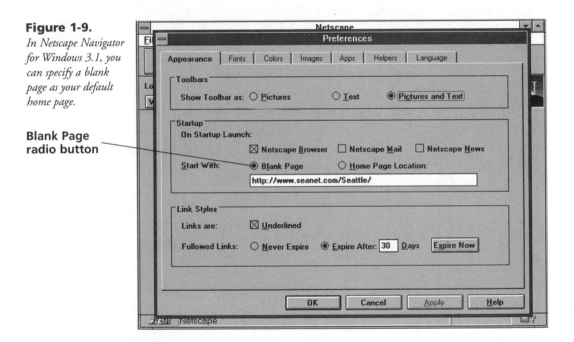

4. To specify a local HTML file, such as your bookmark file, leave the Home Page Location: radio button enabled and type **c:\netscape\bookmark.htm** in the text box below it. See Figure 1-10.

Now, when you click on the Netscape Navigator icon without first running your winsock dialer to connect to the Internet, you won't get that annoying error message telling you it can't connect to the Internet.

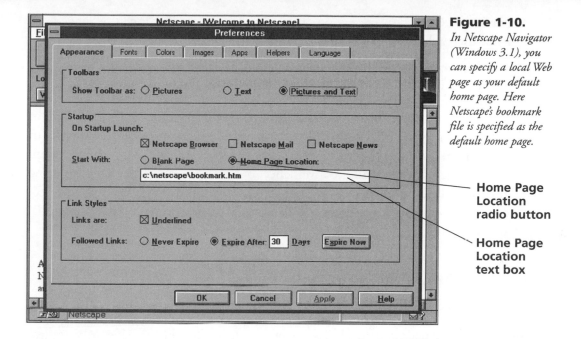

Figure 1-10.
In Netscape Navigator (Windows 3.1), you can specify a local Web page as your default home page. Here Netscape's bookmark file is specified as the default home page.

Home Page Location radio button

Home Page Location text box

Windows 95

You can run Navigator Gold offline in Windows 95 in several ways. This section presents a quick and dirty method, then shows you a bit slicker way to do it.

Quick and Dirty Method

This is the quick and dirty way to run Navigator Gold offline. It's a bit klunky, but it's pretty simple—and it works:

1. Run Navigator Gold.

2. At the Connect To dialog box, which prompts you to make a dial-up connection to the Internet, click on the Cancel button (to not connect to the Internet).

3. You'll get an error message here, Netscape is unable to locate the server.... This is just Navigator trying to tell you it tried to connect to the Internet but couldn't. Just click on the OK button.

4. Navigator Gold displays a copy of its default home page if it can be loaded from the cache. Otherwise, it displays a blank page.

5. To open and display a local Web page (HTML file) from your hard drive, in Navigator Gold choose <u>F</u>ile and Open <u>F</u>ile in Browser.

The following section gives instructions on how to set up Netscape Navigator Gold for seamless offline browsing, that is, without being prompted to log on to the Internet or nagged at with an error message when you press the Cancel button. The log-in prompt and error message are a bit of an inconvenience, but by no means a hindrance to using Navigator for offline browsing. If you don't need to read the "Fill Your Toolbox" section, you can now get a good night's sleep and and start the basic HTML tutorial tomorrow morning.

Loading a Blank or Local Web Page as Your Default Home Page

To specify a blank page or a local Web page as your default home page, follow these steps:

1. Run Navigator Gold and, at the Connect To dialog box, click on the Cancel button to not connect to the Internet.

2. You'll get the error message again. Just click on OK.

3. In Navigator Gold, choose Options and then General Preferences, and then select the Appearance tab.

4. To specify a blank page, enable the Blank Page radio button on the <u>S</u>tart With row. See Figure 1-11.

5. To specify a local Web page such as your bookmark file, leave the Home Page Location: radio button enabled and type **file:///C|/Program Files/Netscape/Navigator/bookmark.htm** in the box below it. See Figure 1-12.

6. Click on the OK button.

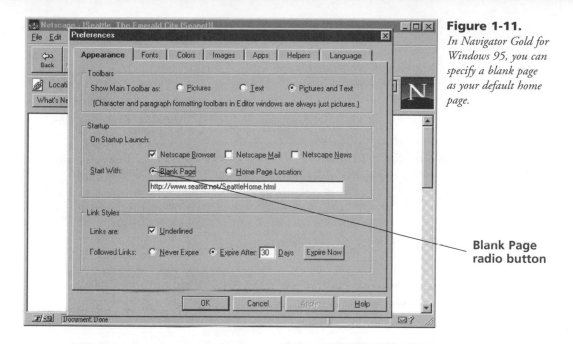

Figure 1-11.
In Navigator Gold for Windows 95, you can specify a blank page as your default home page.

Blank Page
radio button

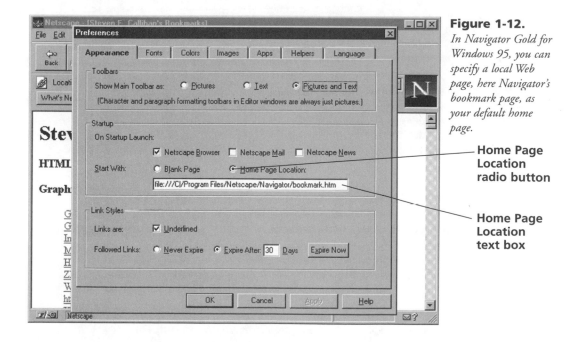

Figure 1-12.
In Navigator Gold for Windows 95, you can specify a local Web page, here Navigator's bookmark page, as your default home page.

Home Page
Location
radio button

Home Page
Location
text box

TIP

Unlike in Netscape Navigator 2.01 for Windows 3.1, in Netscape Navigator Gold 2.02 (and, I presume, above) for Windows 95, you can't type in here the "DOS path" ("c:\...") of a local HTML file, but rather, must insert a genuine URL for a local HTML file ("file:///C\/..."). I don't know about you, but I have a devilishly difficult time remembering all those slashes. A good way to get around having to remember how to spell out a local file URL is to simply 1) load the file into Navigator (File, Open File in Browser), 2) copy the URL from the Location box (at the top of Netscape's main screen) to the Clipboard, and then 3) go back to the Home Page Location box (Options, General Preferences, and Appearance tab) and paste in the URL.

Navigator Gold now loads a blank page or the local Web page you have specified instead of trying to download its default home page down off the Web.

NOTE

The preceding method for seamless offline browsing in Windows 95 works "as is" for Navigator Gold 2.02 (and presumably for earlier versions, as well, but not for the latest version, Navigator Gold 3.0. Even if you select a blank or local Web page as your default home or start page, Navigator Gold 3.0 still prompts you to log on to the Internet. To have Navigator Gold 3.0 not prompt you to log on to the Internet, do the following steps:

1. On the Start Menu, select Settings, then Control Panel.

2. Double-click on the Internet icon.

3. Select the Connection tab.

4. Uncheck the Dial whenever an Internet connection is needed check box. Click on OK.

Now you won't be prompted to log on to the Internet when you run Navigator Gold 3.0 using a blank or local start page. However, clicking on the N icon to go to Netscape's home page or clicking on a hypertext link—on your Bookmark file, for instance—will just get you the error message without a prompt to log on to the Internet. If you want to hop up onto the Web, you must first manually log on to the Internet using My Connection (or whatever connection you have set up).

Microsoft Internet Explorer

Windows 3.1

Internet Explorer Version 2.0 for Windows 3.1 (the version available at the time of this writing) can't be run entirely offline. For that reason, you should avoid using it as your primary Web publishing tool. It's also somewhat quirky and non-standard in how it displays HTML. For offline browsing, both Netscape Navigator and NCSA Mosaic are much better bets, so if you use Internet Explorer Version 2.0, you might want to consider downloading and installing one of those two browsers. If you're determined to run Internet Explorer Version 2.0 offline in Windows 3.1 anyway, however, the following rather kludgy workaround will work (sort of):

1. Run your winsock software to log on to the Internet. After you connect to the Internet, minimize your winsock window (click on the down arrow in the upper right-hand corner of the window) and return to the Program Manager.

2. Run Internet Explorer. Switch back to your winsock window (press Alt+Tab to cycle through open applications or Ctrl+Esc to select from the Task List). Disconnect from the Internet (log off or do a "bye"). Do not exit or close your Winsock window—just minimize it. Switch back to Internet Explorer (Alt+Tab or Ctrl+Esc).

3. You're now running offline and can switch back and forth between your editor and Internet Explorer by pressing Ctrl+Esc or Alt+Tab. This enables you to dynamically see the results of your work in Internet Explorer without going online.

4. To exit Internet Explorer, first switch back to your winsock window and reconnect to the Internet (in Trumpet Winsock, choose Dialer, then Login). After you reconnect to the Internet, switch back to Internet Explorer and close or exit its window.

5. Lastly, switch back to your Winsock window and disconnect from the Internet (log off or do a "bye").

> **CAUTION**
>
> *Do not exit or close the Internet Explorer window without first reconnecting to the Internet. It won't do anything really nasty, but will "hang" Trumpet Winsock, which prevents you from closing it or logging back on to the Internet without having to restart Windows.*

> **TIP**
>
> *When running Microsoft Internet Explorer offline, if you click on any non-local hypertext links, Internet Explorer will* seem *to hang, doing nothing. To unhang it, just click on the Transfer Interrupt button (the button with the red "X" on it).*

Windows 95

Setting up Internet Explorer Version 3.0 for Windows 95 to run offline is a bit simpler. To run this version of Internet Explorer to run offline in Windows 95, you have to set it to load as a local or blank start page. The problem is that Internet Explorer doesn't allow you to simply specify a blank start page, nor does it provide any HTML files that you can select to load as the start page. If you want to load a local HTML file, you have to create one. If you want to load a blank start page, you have to create a blank HTML file. You then have to run Internet Explorer, connect to the Internet, and assign the blank HTML file you've created as the default start page. Just do the following:

1. Run Windows Notepad and save a completely blank file as BLANK.HTM in the directory in which Internet Explorer is installed, or anywhere else (just so you remember where you put it).

2. Run Internet Explorer and connect to the Internet. After its start page loads, select File, Open, and Browse. Go to the directory to which you saved BLANK.HTM and open it in Internet Explorer. You should now have a completely blank page open in Internet Explorer's window.

3. Select View and Options. On the Start and Search Pages tab, click on the Use Current button. See Figure 1-13. Click on the OK button.

Now when you run Internet Explorer, it automatically loads the blank HTML file without trying to connect to the Internet. You can browse offline to your heart's content. If you want to hop up onto the Internet, you must use one of the quick links or the Favorites list, or you just have to type the URL. You are prompted to connect to the Internet, then the requested page loads.

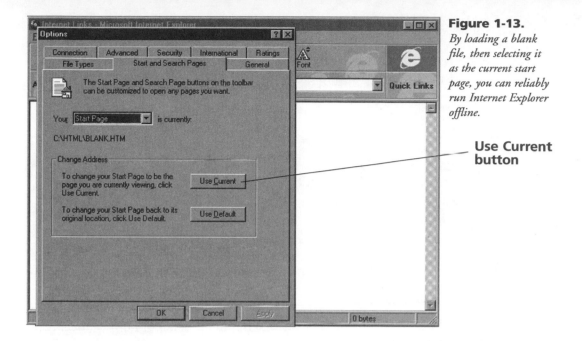

Figure 1-13.
By loading a blank file, then selecting it as the current start page, you can reliably run Internet Explorer offline.

Use Current button

NCSA Mosaic

Windows 3.1

Of the three browsers featured here, NCSA Mosaic for Windows 3.1 is the easiest to set up to run offline. NCSA Mosaic, on the other hand, although a good HTML 2.0 compliant Web browser, doesn't fully support the new HTML 3.2 standard. Therefore, you can use it to do the basic HTML tutorial in Chapter 2, which focuses entirely on HTML 2.0, but you probably wouldn't want to use it to do the optional intermediate HTML tutorial in Chapter 3, which covers much of HTML 3.2.

To run NCSA Mosaic in offline mode in Windows 3.1, you need to make a copy of the NCSA Mosaic icon and then edit the properties for the new icon. To enable NCSA Mosaic to run in offline mode, follow these steps:

1. Locate the NCSA Mosaic program icon. The default installation creates an NCSA Mosaic program group, or you may have copied or moved the NCSA Mosaic icon to another program group. (If the program group window where NCSA Mosaic is located is not currently open, choose Window from the Windows menu bar, then select the program group that contains NCSA Mosaic.)

2. Hold down the Ctrl key and "click and drag" a copy of the NCSA Mosaic icon to another location (this can be in the same program group or any other program group where you might want to put it), then release both the Ctrl key and the mouse button to create the copy.

NOTE

Here, to "click and drag" means to click the left mouse button on the icon, holding it down without lifting it, then dragging the icon to another location. Just clicking and dragging moves the icon. Holding down the Ctrl key while clicking and dragging copies the icon.

3. Highlight the NCSA Mosaic icon you just copied, to highlight it.

4. From the Windows menu bar, select File and Properties.

5. Edit the Description to show it is the stand-alone version. For instance, type **NCSA Mosaic (Stand-Alone)**.

6. At the end of the Command Line, type a space followed by **-s** (the "s" parameter here stands for "stand-alone").

7. Edit the **D**escription box to show that it's the stand-alone version; for example, type **NCSA Mosaic (Stand-Alone)**. See Figure 1-14.

8. Click on the OK button.

Now, to run NCSA Mosaic offline (or in stand-alone mode), just double-click on the NCSA Mosaic (Stand-Alone) icon. To display an HTML file from your hard drive, choose **F**ile, then Open **L**ocal File.

To run NCSA Mosaic online in Windows 3.1, first run your Winsock software to connect to the Internet, then click on the "NCSA Mosaic" icon.

Windows 95

This section presents two ways to run NCSA Mosaic in Windows 95. Note: This isn't a separate version of NCSA Mosaic for Windows 95, but the same version (Version 2.11) of Mosaic referenced in the Windows 3.1 section above—it's just being run in Windows 95 here rather than Windows 3.1 as above.

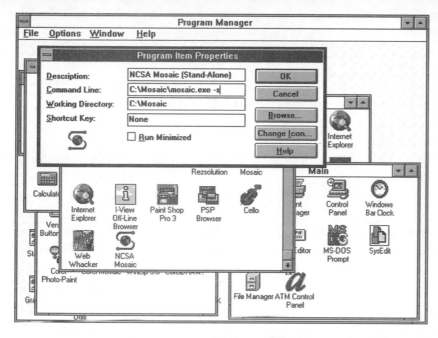

Figure 1-14.
To enable NCSA Mosaic for offline browsing (stand-alone operation) you need to edit its Properties window, adding the "-s" parameter to the command line.

The Quick and Dirty Way

This is the quick and dirty way to run NCSA Mosaic offline in Windows 95. It's a bit klunky, but it works:

1. Run NCSA Mosaic.

2. At the Connect To dialog box, which prompts you to make a dial-up connection to the Internet, click on the Cancel button to not connect to the Internet.

3. You'll get an error message here, `HTAccess: Error accesssing....` That's just Mosaic trying to tell you it tried to connect to the Internet, but couldn't. Just click on the OK button. (Note: You might occasionally get this error message a second time. If you do, just click on the OK button again.)

4. NCSA Mosaic opens a blank page. To open and display a local Web page from your hard drive, choose File and Open Local File.

The following section gives instructions on how to set up NCSA Mosaic for seamless offline browsing, that is, without being prompted to log on to the Internet or nagged at with an error message when you press the Cancel button. The login prompt and error message are a bit of an inconvenience, but by no means a hindrance to using

NCSA Mosaic for offline browsing. If you don't need to read the "Fill Your Toolbox" section, you can now get a good night's sleep and and start the basic HTML tutorial tomorrow morning.

Loading a Blank Page or Local HTML File as Your Default Home Page

To set NCSA Mosaic to load a blank page as its default home page, you must turn off Autoload. Use the following steps:

1. Run NCSA Mosaic.

2. At the Connect To dialog box, click on the Cancel button to not connect to the Internet. (You connected to the Internet when changing the cache setting earlier to make sure you had the most current version of the default home page, NCSA Mosaic's Web page, in the cache. That's not neccesary here, however.)

3. You get the error message, HTAccess: Error accesssing.... Just click on OK.

4. To turn off Autoload, which loads a blank page, choose Options and Preferences. Under Home Page, disable the Autoload check box (click in the check box until it's blank). Doing so turns off Autoload so NCSA Mosaic doesn't automatically try to connect to the Internet to download its default home page. See Figure 1-15.

5. To assign a local Web page as your default home page in NCSA Mosaic, follow these steps:

    A. Choose File and Open Local File. Since you haven't actually created any HTML files of your own yet, just double-click on resource(.htm), which NCSA Mosaic has conveniently created for you. Note: If you want to be able to go online and jump up onto the Web, this file, among other things, provides you links to a number of search engines (EINet, Lycos, WebCrawler, and Yahoo) from which you should be able to jump to just about anywhere you want to go on the Web.

    B. Select **O**ptions and **P**references. On the Document tab, in the Home Page section, click on the Use **C**urrent button. See Figure 1-16.

6. Click on the OK button. Choose **F**ile and **E**xit, then click on **Y**es to save the new setting.

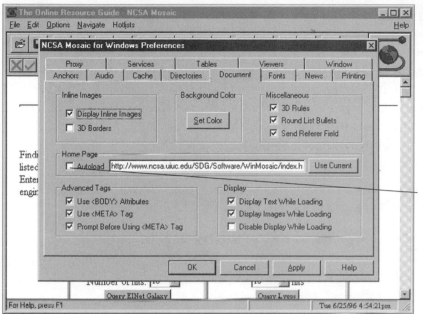

Figure 1-15.
Turn off Autoload in NCSA Mosaic's Preferences menu so that it doesn't try to connect to the Internet and load its default home page off of the Web.

Blank Autoload check box

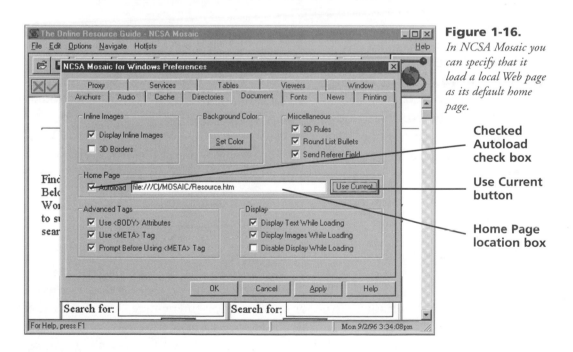

Figure 1-16.
In NCSA Mosaic you can specify that it load a local Web page as its default home page.

Checked Autoload check box

Use Current button

Home Page location box

Running Other Browsers Offline

If you use a browser other than the three already mentioned, you need to check its documentation, help files, or online technical support for the preferred method of running it offline. If you use Windows 3.1, the workaround presented earlier for running Internet Explorer offline should work for most other Web browsers as well. If you use Windows 95, the quick and dirty methods shown for Navigator Gold and NCSA Mosaic should work for most other Web browsers, too.

Using a Dedicated Offline Browser

Another option is to use a dedicated offline Web browser. Two available options are I-View, which is designed specifically for browsing local Web pages, and GNNpress, which works not only as an offline browser, but also as a regular Web browser and an HTML editor.

I-View

I-View, by Talent Communications, Inc., is a browser designed specifically for offline browsing. All you have to do is run the install routine and you're up and running. I-View includes two variants: IVIEW.EXE, primarily intended as a run-time module for distributing HTML files, and IVIEWA.EXE, the "author" version, intended for author developement of HTML files. You will want to use IVIEWA.EXE. I-View is available only in a 16-bit version but can be used in Windows 3.1 or Windows 95. Figure 1-17 shows a local HTML file displayed in the I-View offline browser.

You can download I-View at http://www.talentcom.com/.

GNNpress

GNNpress is a freeware HTML editor provided by GNN Hosting Services to anyone who wants to use it, without restrictions. What is pertinent here, however, is that GNNpress is not just a very good HTML editor, but is also a Web browser, and a pretty good one at that. What's even better is that you can use it as an offline browser straight out of the box—that is, you don't have to take additional installation or setup steps to enable offline browsing. Just run it and start browsing your local files—it's just as simple as that. GNNpress is a 16-bit application that you can use in Windows 3.1

and Windows 95. To browse local Web pages offline, just run GNNpress, then choose <u>F</u>ile and <u>O</u>pen. Figure 1-18 shows a local Web page displayed in GNNpress.

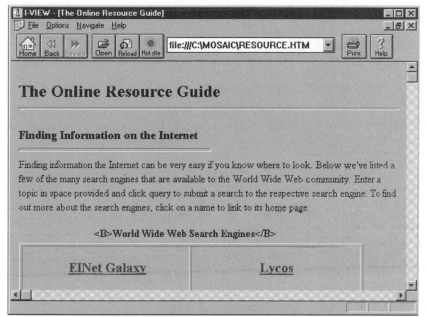

Figure 1-17.
You can use I-View to view HTML files on your local drive without going online.

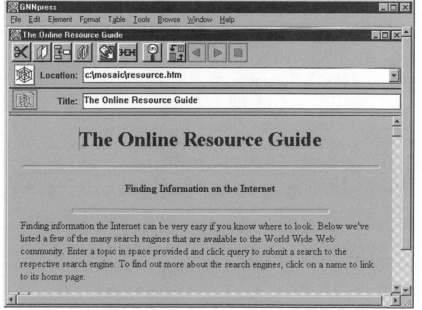

Figure 1-18.
GNNpress is an HTML editor and both an online and offline browser.

GNNpress is available on the CD-ROM, under HTML Tools. You also can download GNNpress at

`http://bin-1.gnn.com/gnn/netizens/gnnpress/`

Filling Your Toolbox (Optional)

You need only the following to create your first Web page:

- A Web browser connected to the Internet
- A text editor for the editing of HTML files
- Graphics software capable of creating, editing, or converting GIF-format graphic files

All current graphical Web browsers should be at least HTML 2.0 compliant. The only fully HTML 3.2 compliant Web browsers as of this writing are Netscape Navigator 2.0 or higher (for Windows 3.1 and 95) and Microsoft Internet Explorer 3.0 or higher (for Windows 95 only).

If you use an HTML 2.0 compliant Web browser, such as NCSA Mosaic, feel free to use it to complete the basic HTML tutorial in Chapter 2. The intermediate HTML tutorial in Chapter 3, however, requires an HTML 3.2 compliant Web browser if you want to preview all the tags featured in your Web browser. You can use NCSA Mosaic, but just realize that it won't support all the tags featured.

The same goes for actually creating your first Web page in Chapter 5. You can use NCSA Mosaic or any other HTML 2.0 compliant Web browser, but just realize that some, many, or all of the "extra options" presented may not be supported.

If you do decide you want to download the latest version of Netscape Navigator (for Windows 3.1 or 95) or Internet Explorer (for Windows 95), see the section "Web Browsers" for where you can download them from the Web.

For a text editor to create your HTML files, Notepad is fine, and in many ways may be preferable to using an HTML editor for someone just starting to learn HTML. Eventually, you probably want to find an HTML editor that can help automate some of the more mundane or arcane, for that matter, HTML coding tasks, but you don't need to do so to use this book to create your first Web page. Feel free, however, to use an HTML editor.

If you want to use an HTML editor, however, you should start out by using it the same way you would use Notepad, that being to type the raw HTML codes rather than select them from pull-down or pop-up menus. Otherwise, if you want to take the time to learn the ins and outs of a particular HTML editing program, feel free to do so, but just realize that you may not be able to do that this weekend. It's up to you, however. So, if you decide you want to use an HTML editor rather than Notepad, see the section "HTML Editing Tools" later in this session for some HTML editors that you can download from the Web.

If you want to graphically "personalize" your Web page, by creating your own personal "logo" or "banner" graphic, for instance, then you need a graphics editor capable of creating or converting GIF. Most current commercial photopaint software, such as Adobe Photoshop or Corel Photopaint, for instance, does quite well for this purpose. Alternatively, some excellent shareware alternatives are available on the Web, such as Paint Shop Pro and LView Pro, to mention two of the best. You can use the sample graphic files provided on the CD-ROM or that you can download from the Web site for this book, which would obviate the need for a GIF-capable graphics editor (for right now anyway). If you don't already have software capable of handling GIF files, you should download Paint Shop Pro or LView Pro from the Web. See the section "Graphics Editing Tools" below for where you can download these programs from the Web. (Don't expect, however, to become a graphics expert in a single weekend!)

So, if, according to the preceding provisos, you feel you're set to go, you can stop reading this chapter now and go get some sleep before your big day tomorrow! If you don't have any of the key components discussed, read the corresponding section in the following pages to get some help choosing and acquiring the component or components you need.

All of the programs and utilities mentioned in the following sections are available on the Web and URLs are provided so you can download them. Many of them also may be included on this book's companion CD-ROM.

NOTE

All comments and descriptions of programs and utilities here apply to versions that were current at the time of this writing. On the Web, however, things change rapidly, with added features, upgraded platform support, changing prices, and so forth, being more the rule than the exception. So, if something sounds interesting, be sure to check the Web sites for version updates.

Web Browsers

The most popular Web browsers right now are Netscape Navigator, Microsoft Internet Explorer, and NCSA Mosaic. Navigator currently dominates the Web browser market with approximately 80 percent of the browser market. The Netscape extensions to HTML should get the bulk of the credit for this development—until fairly recently, you had to have Netscape before you could view a Netscape-enhanced site in all its glory. Now, however, quite a few other current graphical Web browsers have embraced Netscape's extensions to one degree or another. Given the new HTML standard, HTML 3.2, incorporating virtually all of Netscape's extensions, you should expect this trend not only to continue, but to accelerate.

So, you're probably wondering which one would be best. Until recently, the answer would have been simple: Netscape Navigator. Microsoft, however, has chosen with its latest version of Internet Explorer for Windows 95 to embrace, rather than fight against, Netscape's extensions to HTML—so, even a Web page using frames and Java applets should display just fine in Internet Explorer. NCSA Mosaic, partly because it isn't a commercial product, has somewhat lagged behind—but even it can display background images and colors. Commercial offshoots of NCSA Mosaic are available from Quarterdeck, Spry, and Spyglass, for instance, which do provide many more of the cutting edge features of current HTML.

You should use all of them! As a Web publisher, you need to be able to check how your Web pages display in as many Web browsers as possible. The three mentioned above give you a pretty good range—if a Web page displays properly in all three, then it should display properly in most other current graphical Web browsers.

Navigator and Internet Explorer in their current versions are almost indistinguishable when it comes to displaying actual Web pages (Microsoft seems to have made a conscious decision to mimic Navigator as closely as possible here—the "embrace" part of Bill Gates' "embrace and extend" strategy, one would presume), although some fairly minor points of differentiation still exist between them. NCSA Mosaic, on the other hand, can be useful if you want a test-bed that clings more closely to the HTML 2.0 standard, the primary exceptions being its support for background images/colors and tables. Another consideration might be that both Internet Explorer and NCSA Mosaic are free for any and all uses, including commercial or business use, whereas Netscape Navigator is free only for non-commercial use. For references and pointers to even more Web browsers you can use to preview your pages, see Appendix A, "A Resource Directory."

Netscape Navigator

Netscape Navigator from Netscape Communications is available for both Windows 3.1 and Windows 95. (Mac and Unix versions also are available). It is free for individual, educational, or non-profit use. For commercial or business use, the cost is $49. You can download it from at this URL:

```
http://home.netscape.com/comprod/products/navigator/
```

Figure 1-19 shows the Netscape home page as it appears in Netscape Navigator.

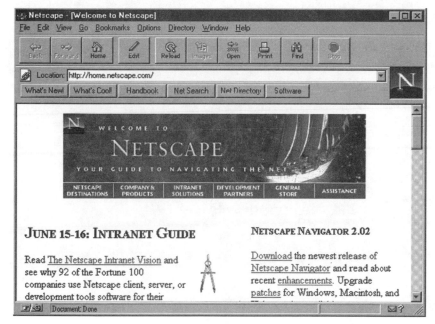

Figure 1-19.
This is how Netscape's home page looks in the Netscape Navigator Web browser.

Navigator is available, as of this writing, in two versions, Netscape Navigator 2.01 for Windows 3.1 and Netscape Navigator Gold 2.02 for Windows 95 or NT. Beta versions of both Navigator and Navigator Gold also are available, if you want to live dangerously. Their features are similar, except that Navigator Gold additionally includes support for Java applets and also has a built-in HTML editor.

NCSA Mosaic

Mosaic, the first graphical Web browser, was created at the National Center for Supercomputing Applications (NCSA) at the University of Illinois at Urbana-Champagne

(UIUC). Mosaic, like Netscape Navigator, is available for Windows, Unix, and Macintosh platforms. You can download NCSA Mosaic at the following URL:

```
http://www.ncsa.uiuc.edu/SDG/Software/WinMosaic/HomePage.html
```

Commercial versions of Mosaic are available from Spry, Spyglass, and Quarterdeck. Figure 1-20 shows the Mosaic home page as it appears in NCSA Mosaic.

Figure 1-20.

This is how NCSA's home page looks in the NCSA Mosaic Web browser.

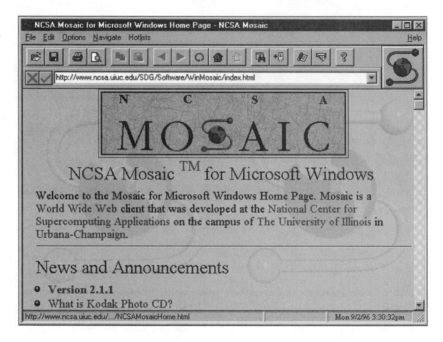

Microsoft Internet Explorer

Microsoft is the new guy on the Web browser block. Originally, Internet Explorer could be used only in conjunction with Microsoft's online service, Microsoft Network. Recognizing, however, the virtually exponential growth of the Web, Microsoft decided to release it as a stand-alone Web browser in direct competition with Netscape and Mosaic. Like Netscape and Mosaic, Internet Explorer is a full-featured, graphical Web browser. It is available currently only for Windows 3.1 and Windows 95. It is free for any and all uses.

Microsoft Internet Explorer 2.0 is available on the CD-ROM under Internet Tools. You can download the Internet Explorer 3.0 at this URL:

```
http://www.microsoft.com/ie/
```

Figure 1-21 shows the Microsoft Network home page as it appears in Internet Explorer.

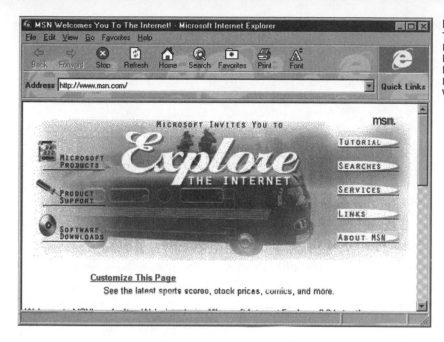

Figure 1-21.
This is how the Microsoft Network home page looks like in the Microsoft Internet Explorer Web browser.

Other Web Browsers

Numerous other Web browsers are available on the Web, including the various commercial off-shoots of Mosaic, as well as Cello, Hot Java, Emissary, NetShark, Oracle PowerBrowser, WebSurfer, and many more. Some of these, such as Cello in particular, lack the more advanced features of today's current browsers, but can be useful if you want to see what a strict HTML 2.0 compliant Web browser is like (in fact, it may be closer to an HTML 1.0 compliant Web browser). Others challenge Netscape Navigator or Internet Explorer for current cutting-edge features. For a more comprehensive listing of available Web browsers and where you can download them, see Appendix A.

Which Browser Should You Use?

If you use Windows 3.1, Netscape Navigator is still by far the best choice. The latest version of Internet Explorer available for Windows 3.1 at the time of this writing (version 2.0) is fatally flawed as a Web publishing tool because you simply cannot run it offline. So, for Windows 3.1, go with Navigator first, NCSA Mosaic second, and Internet Explorer last.

If you use Windows 95, Netscape Navigator Gold or Microsoft Internet Explorer are just about neck and neck as Web browsers. Both do quite well as Web publishing tools for previewing local Web pages. There is, however, no "quick and dirty" method for running Internet Explorer offline. On that account, the edge still has to go to Netscape Navigator Gold—but just barely.

The choice of Netscape Navigator, in either Windows 3.1 or Windows 95, is further reinforced by the fact that more than 80 percent of all Web surfers who are liable to visit any Web page you create will be using it. That's a pretty powerful incentive to use Netscape Navigator as a primary Web publishing tool in creating those pages, that is, if you want to make absolutely sure that your pages are going to display properly for most Web surfers. You should at least use Netscape Navigator to preview how it's going to display your final Web pages before putting them up on the Web.

Actually, when you get the time, you should download and install the latest versions of Netscape Navigator, Internet Explorer, and NCSA Mosaic. As a Web publisher, you should preview your Web pages in at least these three Web browsers, if not in several more. (You don't have to do that *this* weekend, however. But if you decide to get into some serious Web publishing, you should put together a collection of Web browsers that you can use to preview your work.)

For references and pointers to additional information on selecting a Web browser, as well as a much more comprehensive listing of currently available Web browsers (along with their URLs), see Appendix A.

Text-Mode and Shell-Based Web Browsers

To use one of the previously discussed graphical Web browsers, you need a PPP/SLIP account. Many people, however, have nothing more than a "shell account," which enables them to log in to a server and then run Lynx, the Unix text-mode Web browser. Lynx doesn't display graphics, color, or on-screen formatting—it displays only text. A significant number of people still surf the Web in this fashion. Although you can expect it to become less important as time passes, you still need to make sure your pages display properly and are readable in Lynx, or to provide alternative "text-only" pages for Lynx viewers if feasible. Figure 1-22 shows a Web page displayed in the Lynx text-mode Web browser.

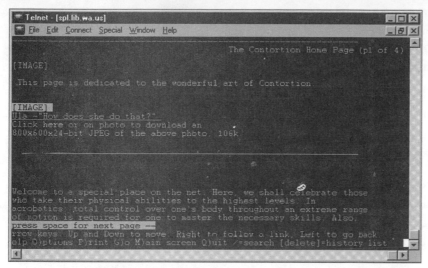

Figure 1-22.
This is the Contortion Home Page displayed in the Lynx Web browser. This page has a great photo of a contortionist, but since Lynx is a text-only browser, sorry, you can't see it.

TIP

So, how do you check out how your Web pages will look in Lynx if you aren't using or don't have a shell-account on a Unix system? Many public libary systems now offer members the capability to log on to their system and surf the Web using Lynx. You may be able to dial in directly using telecommunications software, or you may be able to Telnet to their system using your Web browser or a Telnet software program. If you're interested, check with your local library for details.

HTML Editing Tools

You can use any text editor or word processor to create HTML files, because HTML files are just plain, ordinary text files with the HTML codes, or "tags," added in. You should stick with Windows Notepad (in Windows 3.1 or Windows 95), for reasons detailed in the following section.

Using Windows Notepad

Notepad has a number of advantages, which it's the tool of choice for many professional Web publishers. Its advantages are as follows:

- You already have it.

- It's a small, efficient program, so it can easily remain in memory while your Web browser without hogging precious system resources. Netscape Navigator and other Web browsers, on the other hand, are "resource hogs."

- Because Notepad is a text editor rather than a word processor, you can have an HTML file open in both Notepad and your Web browser at the same time. You can't do that with Write, Word, WordPerfect, and most other word processing programs.

Now, don't get bogged down trying to learn the ins and outs of an HTML editing program when you need to focus on learning HTML (that is, if you want to get your first Web page created in a weekend). Learn HTML first, in other words, then investigate what HTML editing programs can do for you.

You also need to gain a "code-level" familiarity with HTML. Only then can you get a sufficient understanding of how HTML works to be able stick your head under the hood if something doesn't work right. That means typing in your HTML codes the old fashioned way, if you will, not just inserting them from a pull-down menu or toolbar.

Using a Word Processor

You can use any word processor program capable of editing and saving ASCII text files (sometimes called "DOS text files") to produce HTML files. The primary advantage of using a word processor is that you may already know how to use it. The disadvantage (at least in the case of Windows 3.1) is that it may be too large to keep in memory while running your Web browser. Even if you can keep it in memory (and in Windows 95 that isn't a big problem), it probably still won't let you keep the same file open in both it and your Web browser so you can dynamically debug your HTML files.

Another advantage of using a word processor is that you can apply formatting styles that make your page easier to read while you edit it. After you save a file as an ASCII text file, however, all your word processing formatting goes away. If you want to retain that formatting, you need to maintain two versions of the file: the ASCII text version (the HTML file) and the word processing version.

Also, Notepad cannot handle a file that exceeds 32 KB. Many of the more Notepad-like HTML editors also can handle only limited file sizes. Usually, though, you should not have to create a Web page larger than 32 KB, but you may occasionally want to. If so, using a word processor works just fine as long as you're willing to settle for being unable to preview your work on the fly.

Using a Word-Processor Add-On

A number of HTML editor add-ons also are available for specific word processors. Although you still should use Notepad or a Notepad-like HTML editor for the purposes of this book, what you ultimately choose to use depends entirely on your respective needs and preferences. Just don't get bogged down trying to learn how to use a program when you need to focus on learning about HTML. For your information, a brief summary follows of some of the add-on HTML editors that may be available for your favorite word processor.

Microsoft Word

Internet Assistant is available from Microsoft as an add-on HTML editor for Word for Windows. Internet Assistant is available on the CD-ROM under HTML Tools or you can download it:

`http://www.microsoft.com/msoffice/freestuf/msword/download/ia/default.htm`

HTML Author is another add-on HTML editor for Word for Windows. HTML Author is available on the CD-ROM under HTML Tools or you can download it:

`http://www.salford.ac.uk/iti/gsc/htmlauth/summary.html`

WordPerfect for Windows

Internet Publisher for Windows is an add-on HTML editor available from WordPerfect for WordPerfect 6.1 for Windows. Novell, because they sold WordPerfect to Corel, no longer maintains a home page for Internet Explorer. You can download it, however, from any of these addresses:

`http://www.wpmag.com/Windows/1996/apr/WPIPZIP.EXE`

`http://www.schaft.com/ftp/HTML_Stuff/wpipzip.exe`

`ftp://ftp.esva.net/pub/win31/wpipzip.exe`

The latest version of WordPerfect, Corel WordPerfect 7 for Windows, includes a built-in HTML editor.

Using a Stand-Alone HTML Editor

Another alternative is to use a stand-alone HTML editor. Just a year or so ago only a few HTML editors were available. Now you can probably find as many as a couple dozen. Once again, if you use a stand-alone HTML editor, you should start by using one of the Notepad-like HTML editors, such as HTML Notepad or Gomer. A full-featured HTML editor often is extremely useful and valuable for creating and maintaining a Web site—it's just not necessarily the best tool for learning HTML.

> **NOTE**
>
> *The newer, full-featured HTML editors tend to provide WYSIWYG (What You See Is What You Get) editing or a preview mode for seeing what the page will look like on the Web. The point here, however, is that no two Web browsers display the same page exactly alike. The only way to really see what your page will look like is to view it in a Web browser, and even then you only get to see how it's going to look in that one Web browser. You want to make sure your page looks good in all browsers, or at least most browsers, not just great in one browser.*

The following sections review some of the stand-alone HTML editors available on the Web. They range from small Notepad-like HTML editors to full-feature non-WYSIWYG and WYSIWYG HTML editors.

HTML Notepad by Cranial Software

HTML Notepad is a shareware Notepad-like HTML editor. It is an excellent beginner HTML editor, combining small size with a considerable HTML formatting punch. HTML Notepad isn't the prettiest or snazziest-looking, HTML editor—frankly, it has a rather spartan appearance. No button bars, toolbars, tabs, or any of the other whiz-bang interface gew-gaws—just pull-down menus. Remember that old saying, "Appearances can be deceiving." Sometimes simpler is better. It handles background and text colors, forms and tables, extended characters, and most Netscape extensions you might want.

HTML Notepad is available only in a 16-bit version, but that doesn't preclude using it in Windows 95 as well as Windows 3.1. It has an evaluation period of 30 days, after which you're expected to register it. Registration is $30. HTML Notepad is available on the CD-ROM under HTML Tools or you can download it at this URL:

http://www.cranial.com/software/htmlnote/

Figure 1-23 shows an HTML file being edited in HTML Notepad.

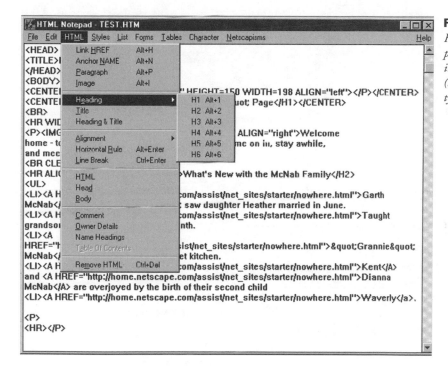

Figure 1-23.
HTML Notepad uses pull-down menus to insert HTML codes (although you can type them too).

Gomer HTML Editor by Stoopid Software

Gomer is another Notepad-like HTML editor, but with a bit snazzier interface than HTML Notepad. In addition to using pull-down menus, it also sports a button bar that you can use to insert HTML tags. It can handle everything HTML Notepad can, as well as frames. It is demoware, however, not true shareware—if you don't register the software before the 30-day trial period, it stops working. Registration, however, isn't expensive—just $15. Gomer is available only in a 16-bit version (but you can use it in both Windows 3.1 and Windows 95). Gomer is available on the CD-ROM under HTML Tools or you can download it at the following URL:

```
http://clever.net/gomer/
```

Figure 1-24 shows an HTML file being edited in Gomer.

Figure 1-24.

Gomer uses a combination of pull-down menus and a button-bar to insert HTML codes.

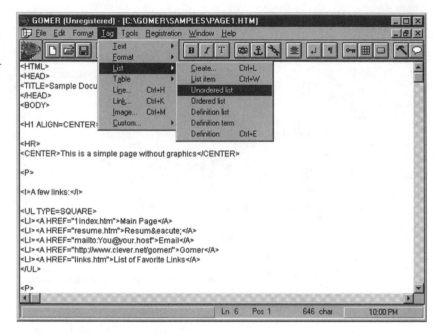

HotDog by Sausage Software

HotDog represents HTML tags in a different color from the text. It's a full-feature HTML editor that's also easy to use. It is available in two versions, HotDog Standard and HotDog Pro, both of which are available in either 16-bit or 32-bit versions. HotDog also is demoware rather than true shareware. Depending on the version, it stops working after 14 or 30 days. You can, however, e-mail to have the evaluation period extended one time. Registration of HotDog Standard is $29.95. HotDog Pro is $99.95. HotDog is available on the CD-ROM under HTML Tools or you can download it at this URL:

```
http://www.sausage.com/
```

Figure 1-25 shows an HTML file being edited in HotDog Standard.

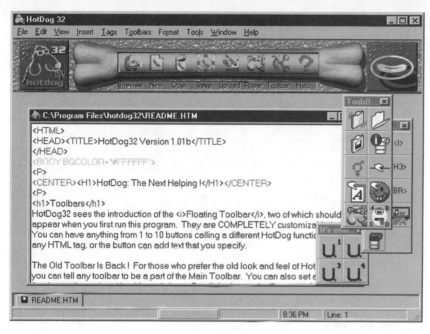

Figure 1-25.
HotDog Standard used both pull-down menus and button bars to insert HTML tags.

HoTMetaL by SoftQuad

HoTMetaL is available in a freeware version, HoTMetaL Free, and a commercial version, HoTMetaL Pro. HoTMetaL is a full-feature HTML editor that uses on-screen icons to represent HTML tags and distinguish them from the text being tagged. HoTMetaL is available only in a 16-bit version (but you can use it in Windows 95 or Windows NT). Registration is $159. You can download HoTMetaL Free and HoTMetal Pro at this URL:

```
http://www.sq.com/
```

Figure 1-26 shows an HTML file being edited in HoTMetaL Free.

Figure 1-26.

HoTMetaL Free uses icons to represent tag elements.

Aardvark Pro by Functional Business Systems

Aardvark Pro has a built-in preview function that lets you see what your page is going to look like without having to launch your Web browser. Aardvark Pro has two versions, a free version and a shareware version. The shareware version has a 30-day trial period, after which you're expected to register. Registration is $59. Aardvark Pro is available on the CD-ROM under HTML Tools or you can download it at this URL:

```
http://www.ozemail.com.au/~kread/aardvark.html
```

Figure 1-27 shows an HTML file being previewed in Aardvark Pro's WYSIWYG previewer.

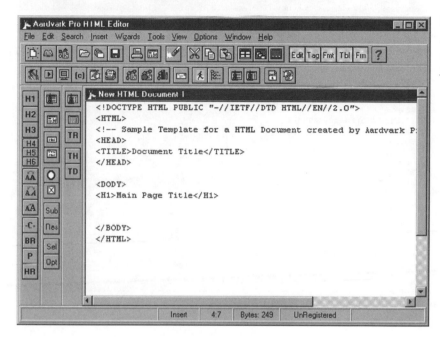

Kenn Nesbit's WebEdit

Kenn Nesbit's WebEdit is a full-feature shareware HTML editor. It has a built-in previewer that displays alongside the edit window, so you can see what your page is going to look like without having to launch your Web browser. It is available in both 16-bit and 32-bit versions. Both have a 30-day evaluation period, after which you're expected to register. Registration is $79.95 for government or commercial users, but only $39.95 for students, educators, home users, and non-profit organizations. Kenn Nesbit's WebEdit is available on the CD-ROM under HTML Tools or you can download it at this URL:

http://www.nesbitt.com/

Figure 1-28 shows an HTML file being edited in WebEdit.

Figure 1-28.

In WebEdit, you can edit an HTML file and see a graphic preview at the same time.

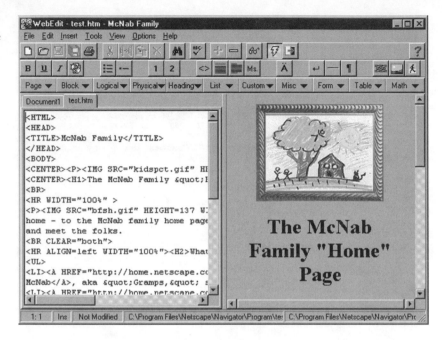

HTMLed by Internet Software Technologies

HTMLed is a shareware HTML editor that has more than the usual complement of features. It has a spell-checker, can import RTF files, and can automate the creation of forms and tables. It also can save text files in Unix as well as DOS format. It also has a Page Builder option that walks you through creating a Web page using easy-to-follow, step-by-step options. And if you have a SLIP/PPP connection active and a Web site on a server, you can directly FTP your edited Web pages up onto the Web. HTMLed is available in both 16-bit and 32-bit versions. The evaluation period is 30 days. Registration is $29 U.S. and $35 Canadian. HTMLed is available on the CD-ROM under HTML Tools or you can download it at this URL:

```
http://www.ist.ca/htmled/
```

Figure 1-29 shows an HTML file being edited in HTMLed.

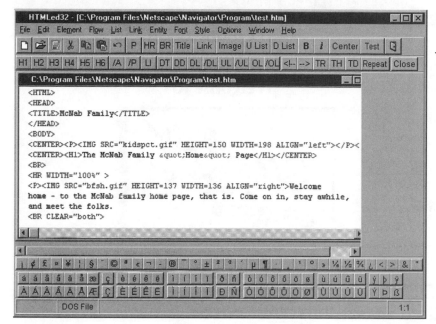

Figure 1-29.
HTMLed uses a different color (blue) to distinguish HTML tags from regular text.

GNNpress by GNN Hosting Service

GNNpress HTML editor provides for the users of the GNN Hosting Service or for anyone else who wants to download it. Not only is it a first-rate HTML editor, and a WYSIWYG one to boot, but a Web browser as well. It also works as an offline Web browser. You can edit HTML files, then save them directly to your Web site, as long as your server supports using the HTTP PUT protocol. Alternatively, GNNpress also can use FTP to place your edited Web pages up on the Web. It's a great deal (hey, it's free!). I don't recommend using it for doing the tutorials and exercises in this book, but after you learn some HTML and put together your first Web page, you definitely might want to download GNNpress to give it a try. GNNpress is available on the CD-ROM under HTML Tools or you can download it at this URL:

```
http://bin-1.gnn.com/gnn/netizens/gnnpress/
```

Figure 1-30 shows a file being edited in GNNpress.

Figure 1-30.

GNNpress not only is a first rate WYSIWYG HTML editor, but a Web browser as well, and it's free for anyone to use.

Navigator Gold's Built-In HTML Editor

Last but not least, the built-in HTML editor that comes with Netscape's Navigator Gold Web browser deserves mention. Currently, it's available only with the 32-bit Navigator Gold Web browser. You have to run Windows 95 or Windows NT to use this editor. It provides a quasi-WYSIWYG HTML editing window, where you can apply different tags and attributes by clicking and dragging. If you want to edit the raw HTML, a copy of Notepad pops up for you. Figure 1-31 shows an HTML file being edited in Navigator Gold's built-in HTML editor, with a Notepad window holding the raw HTML in the background.

For a more comprehensive listing of available HTML editors, see Appendix A.

The third component you need before you can create your first Web page is a graphics editor capable of creating GIF files, or at least a graphics conversion utility capable of converting a graphics file to GIF format.

If you have one of the commercial draw or photopaint programs, such as CorelDRAW! or Adobe PhotoShop, it should be able to create GIF files. Otherwise, you must download a program off the Web that can do it for you. Fortunately, an abundance of graphics software and utilities are available on the Web. They come two flavors: graphics editors and graphics conversion utilities.

Figure 1-31.
*Netscape's Navigator
Gold Web browser
for Windows 95 or
Windows NT has
a built-in HTML
editor.*

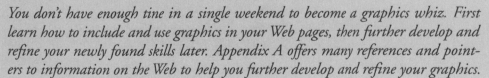

NOTE

*You don't have enough tine in a single weekend to become a graphics whiz. First
learn how to include and use graphics in your Web pages, then further develop and
refine your newly found skills later. Appendix A offers many references and pointers to information on the Web to help you further develop and refine your graphics.*

Graphics Editors

If you want to create your own customized and personalized graphics for your Web
pages, you need a graphics editor capable of creating and editing GIF format graphics

files. If you don't happen to already have one, don't worry—quite a few shareware graphics editors are available for download on the Web. You really should consider downloading at least two programs to start out: LView Pro and Paint Shop Pro.

LView Pro

LView Pro is a shareware graphics viewer and editor. Registration is $30 if you want to continue to legally use it beyond the 30-day evaluation period. You can use it both to view GIFs and JPEGs on the Web and to edit graphics files. It isn't as full-featured as Paint Shop Pro, but it has one trick up its sleeve that Paint Shop Pro doesn't—the capability to create *transparent GIFs*, which are GIFs that have one color defined as transparent so the background color or image shows through. LView Pro is available on the CD-ROM under HTML Tools or you can download it at this URL:

```
http://world.std.com/~mmedia/lviewp.html
```

Figure 1-32 shows a graphic in the LView Pro window.

Figure 1-32.
LView Pro lets you view and retouch graphic files.

Paint Shop Pro

Paint Shop Pro is a full-featured shareware photopaint program. It includes 20 standard image processing filters and 12 deformations and supports Adobe-style image processing plug-in filters. It supports more than 30 file formats, including JPEG, Kodak Photo-CD, PBM, and GIF. Registration is $69 if you want to use it beyond the

30-day trial period. For $99, Kai's Power Tools Special Edition is included. Paint Shop Pro is available on the CD-ROM under HTML Tools or you can download it at this URL:

```
http://www.jasc.com/product.html.
```

Figure 1-33 shows a graphic in the Paint Shop Pro window.

Figure 1-33.
Paint Shop Pro is a full-featured share-ware photopaint program.

Graphic Converters

Quite a few graphics conversion utilities are available. These can be handy if you have a graphics program you like that can't create GIF files, such as the Windows accessory Paint, or if you have graphics you have already created, such as a logo file, that you would like to convert. If you download Paint Shop Pro, however, you shouldn't need anything else to convert any graphics you want to use. For additional references to programs capable of converting graphics to GIF format, see Appendix A.

NOTE

After you create your first Web page, you may want to turn to Appendix A, which lists many references and pointers to information, resources, and tools available on the Web to help you enhance and maximize your use of graphics in your Web pages. The Web site for this book, http://www.callihan.com/webpage/, also maintains a current and updated listing of graphics resources on the Web.

Conclusion

Having finished the first session, you should now have a good grounding in the basics of the Internet and the World Wide Web. You should have a good grasp of URLs, hypertext, HTML, and Web pages. If you read the optional reading section, "Filling Your Toolbox," you also should have a good idea of the tools available on the Web to assist you in creating your Web pages. So, get a good night's sleep, and be ready for the basic HTML tutorial tomorrow morning.

Saturday Morning:
A Basic HTML Tutorial

Last night you read up on the Internet, the Web, hypertext, HTML fundamentals, and Web pages. You're connected to the Internet with a graphical Web browser, you've selected your text-editing tool of choice for creating HTML files, and you have a graphics program that can create or convert GIF files.

This morning, you're going to learn some basic HTML, then this afternoon, if you have the time, you'll learn some intermediate HTML (with a few advanced tidbits thrown in for good measure). Tomorrow, you are going to plan and then create your first Web page. After the weekend is over and you have created your first Web page, you can use the rest of this book to help you decide what more you need to learn to get the most out of HTML, as well as guide you in actually getting your Web page or pages up on the Web.

NOTE

If you don't have a graphics program capable of creating or converting GIF files, you don't need to bother downloading and installing one right now. You won't need it until Sunday (Chapter 4).

The Saturday Morning session is divided into two parts:

- Getting Started
- The Basic HTML Tutorial

The "Getting Started" section introduces you to and prepares you for the "Basic HTML Tutorial" section.

The "Basic HTML Tutorial" section then walks you through a top-down approach to learning HTML, organized according to function. Just start from the beginning and continue to the end, and by then you'll know enough HTML to create several different kinds of Web pages.

Getting Started

Before you actually get started with the HTML tutorial, a few introductory comments are in order.

Go at Your Own Speed

Everyone has his or her own learning style and speed. Although the basic HTML tutorial was designed to be completed in a single morning, you may take more or less time to complete it. The most important thing is to work at your own speed without feeling rushed. Feel free to take extra time if necessary. If you want to take the whole day to do the tutorial, do so.

What You Will Be Learning

HTML contains many more tags for defining document elements than most people could learn in an entire week, let alone in a weekend, let alone on a Saturday morning. But fear not. This book cuts it down to size. This tutorial covers basic HTML, which includes the most useful of the HTML 2.0 tags. All current graphical Web browsers should fully support HTML 2.0, which until just recently was the standard for HTML. The optional intermediate HTML tutorial (Chapter 3), covers many of the HTML 3.2 tags.

HTML is not difficult to learn. It's not rocket science. Most of what really counts in HTML you really can learn in a single morning. So relax, sit back, and have some fun.

A Quick Word about HTML

Before you begin to do the tutorial, a quick reminder about the nature of HTML might save some unnecessary confusion. The philosophy behind HTML is to specify the framework of a page, not its actual appearance or display. Remember: How a Web page appears on-screen is determined by the browser used to view it.

Actually, you do have a good deal of control over how your page appears in most browsers. Today's graphical Web browsers allow you to include not only inline graphics, but interlaced and transparent graphics, background images and colors, image maps, forms, tables, font size changes, animations, as well as streaming audio and animation, and more.

Although the big three in the browser market now support most of these advancements, HTML 2.0 specifies only some of them. Many people still use browsers outside the big three—not to forget those who use text-based browsers such as Lynx because they don't have SLIP/PPP connections to the Internet. You're probably best off trying to design your Web page for the widest possible audience. Visitors are precious; in other words, you don't want to turn anyone away. Not that you shouldn't use many of these features; you just implement them carefully and wisely.

The basic HTML tutorial sticks to standard HTML 2.0. Chapter 3 gets more into many of these features. If you don't have time to get to it today, don't worry—this chapter covers everything you need to know to get started creating your first Web page this weekend. You can always come back and do the intermediate HTML tutorial after you create your first Web page.

The "Scratch Pad" Model

The model that the tutorial employs resembles most a "scratch pad" approach. Think of your text editor as a scratch pad. As you do the basic HTML tutorial (and assuming you have the time or motivation, the intermediate HTML tutorial), just enter the suggested tags and text as though you were jotting them down on a scratch pad; in other words, you don't have to clean the slate each time you move on to a new section. Just move on down the page, leaving everything you have already done in place. Doing so also leaves you with a sample file to which you can return and reference later.

Dynamically Updating Your Work

As you work through the Basic HTML Tutorial this morning, and possibly the intermediate HTML tutorial this afternoon, you will want to be able to dynamically update your work as you go—that is, switch back and forth between your text editor and your Web browser to see the results of your work as you go. Only by being able to make on-the-fly changes to your HTML files can you tell exactly how your page is going to appear in a browser.

NOTE

If you use a word processor, such as Word for Windows, WordPerfect, or Windows Write, to edit your HTML files, you can't dynamically update your HTML files by switching back and forth between your word processor and your browser. If an HTML file is open in your word processor, you can't display it in your browser at the same time. That's why you should use a text editor, such as Windows Notepad (or WordPad in Windows 95), rather than a word processing program. You still can use your word processor to edit HTML files that are too large to fit in Notepad (files larger than 32 KB)— although that shouldn't happen any too often.

Switching between Your Editor and Your Browser

To dynamically update changes to your HTML files, you must switch back and forth between your text editor and your Web browser. (See the "Windows Navigation Tips" sidebar that follows if you don't know how to switch between applications in Windows.) To make this hop, take the following steps:

1. First, run your text editor, then load an HTML file and edit it. Save those changes, but don't exit or clear the window. Hop to the Program Manager in Windows 3.1 (or to the Desktop in Windows 95).

2. Run your browser, preferably in offline mode, then open the HTML file you just edited in your text editor. It will be displayed in your browser, showing the changes you just made. Now switch back to your text editor.

3. In your text editor, make more changes to your HTML file, and save those changes. Switch back to your browser.

4. Click on the Reload button to redisplay your HTML file, showing the changes you just made.

Windows Navigation Tips

In this book, the words "switch" or "hop" refer to switching between open applications.

You can switch among the open applications in several ways, and the best way mainly boils down to individual preference. You can choose the method that works best for you:

- **Alt+Tab.** Hold down the Alt key while tapping the Tab key to cycle through all currently open applications. This works in both Windows 3.1 and Windows 95. When you see the application you want, release the Tab key to bring it to the foreground.

- **Alt+Esc.** This works very similarly to Alt+Tab. It toggles among the open windows, one by one. Hold down the Alt key and tap the Esc key until the window you want comes to the foreground.

- **Ctrl+Esc.** In Windows 3.1, doing this brings up the Task List window, allowing you to select from a list of currently open applications. In Windows 95, Ctrl+Esc displays the taskbar and opens the Start menu.

- **Control Menu.** In Windows 3.1, you can select Switch To from the Control Menu of any windowed application currently in the foreground. Just click on the button in the upper left corner of the window and select Switch To. It's actually the same as simply pressing Ctrl+Esc, so can only be recommended to the dedicated keyboard-a-phobe. In Windows 95, the Switch To option is no longer included in the Control Menu, so it doesn't work.

> **NOTE**
>
> *In Netscape Navigator, the Reload button loads the updated version of your HTML file, and Reload is the term used in this book to describe the reload operation. In Internet Explorer, the Reload button is the one with the little green crosses; in NCSA Mosaic it's the button with the blue circular arrow.*

Repeat these steps as often as necessary. As you work through the tutorial, illustrations show you what each tag looks like in a browser. These illustrations aren't exactly what you would see in your browser, so you can use them as cues to hop over to your browser to have a look.

The Basic HTML Tutorial

Okay, you're ready to go. You've set up your browser to run offline and you know how to hop between your text editor and your Web browser to dynamically update your work.

Run Your Text Editor

Run the text editor you want to use to edit HTML files. As mentioned earlier, consider using Notepad until you master the fundamentals of HTML. In Windows 3.1, you usually can find Notepad in the Accessories window in Program Manager. In Windows 95, you can find it on the Start Menu, under Programs and Accessories.

Before you start, create a new directory for your HTML documents, such as C:\HTML.

NOTE

When you first open Windows Notepad, Word Wrap is not turned on. If you type a line of text without hitting Enter, it will just keep right on going without wrapping. To turn on Word Wrap, just enable the Edit and Word check box. Unfortunately, you must reset this option every time you use Notepad if you want Word Wrap on.

Copy the Sample Graphics

All the sample graphics used in this tutorial, as well as any used in this afternoon's optional intermediate HTML tutorial, are available on the CD-ROM. To have access to these files while doing the tutorials, copy all the files from the tutorial graphics directory on the CD-ROM to your working directory, C:\HTML. If you don't have a CD-ROM drive, you can download these files from this book's Web site:

```
http://www.callihan.com/webpage/
```

Anatomy of a Tag

The words tag or tag element refer to the HTML codes that define the "elements" in an HTML file, such as headings, images, paragraphs, and lists. The two kinds of tags are containers, which bracket or contain text or other tag elements, and empty tags, which stand alone and don't bracket or contain text or other tag elements. A container tag element actually consists of two tags, a start tag and an end tag, which bracket the text they affect. An empty tag functions as a single stand-alone element within an HTML document, and thus doesn't bracket or contain anything else.

HTML tags are inserted into a document within lesser than (<) and greater than (>) symbols (also referred to as left or right angle brackets). For instance, a start tag of a container tag element or an empty tag element looks like this:

```
<tagname>
```

You always precede an end tag of a tag element with a forward slash (/) to distinguish it from a start tag:

```
</tagname>
```

To tag a section of text, you contain it within the start and end tags of a tag element. For instance, text contained in a level-one heading tag would look like this:

```
<H1>This is a Level-One Heading</H1>
```

Whenever you refer to "a level-one heading tag," for example, you're referring to both the start and end tags—that is, to the whole container. When you want to specifically refer to a start tag or an end tag, you say "the start tag" or "the end tag." Note, however, that a few tags look like empty tags, but actually are container tags that have implied end tags.

It is somewhat conventional, although by no means required, to type tag names in ALL CAPS. It helps distinguish and demarcate HTML tags from the remainder of the text being tagged. As a rule, this book presents tag names in ALL CAPS.

Tag Attributes

Attributes allow you to specify how Web browsers should treat a particular tag. An attribute is included within the actual tag (between the left and right angle brackets), either within a start tag or an empty (stand-alone) tag (end tags can't contain attributes). Most of the tags covered in this tutorial don't use attributes. You do use them to include images or hypertext links in a Web page, however, toward the end of this tutorial. Don't feel like you have to fully understand this in detail right now—you get a better feel for attributes after you actually use them.

Most attributes, although not all, are combined with a value to allow you to specify different options for how a Web browser should treat the attribute. Here's the format for including an attribute value in a tag:

```
ATTRIBUTE="value"
```

For instance, to specify that the middle of an image should be aligned with the line of text it is on, you would include the following attribute value inside the IMG tag:

```
ALIGN="middle"
```

Tag attributes are, by convention, usually typed in ALL CAPS. You don't have to do it this way, but it does make it easier to pick them out. You also should place values inside of quotation marks. Sometimes you might have to, such as when spaces are included in a value. Otherwise, you usually can get away with leaving off the quotation marks. Including quotation marks anyway, though, not only plays it safe, but also helps demarcate the value, making it easier to spot.

Nesting HTML Tags

You should always nest HTML tags, and never overlap them. For instance, always do this:

```
<B><I>This is sample text.</I></B>
```

Notice that the <I>/</I> pair is nested within the <B>/<B/> pair. Never overlap tags so that the "outer" one ends before the "inner" one:

```
<B><I>This is sample text.</B></I>
```

HTML operates in an hierarchical, top-down manner. A tag element may contain other tag elements or be contained within other tag elements. If you overlap two tags, a browser can't tell what should fall inside of what. This might not cause a problem; but then again, it might. If you break the rules, you are liable to "break the browser:"

that is, the browser may not be able to display your file at all. Be kind to your browser and those of your potential readers: don't overlap tag elements.

Starting Your Page: Document Tags

All HTML files should include at least these tags:

- The HTML tag
- The HEAD tag
- The TITLE tag
- The BODY Tag

The following sections discuss each tag in turn.

The HTML Tag

Recall that a tag defines a structural element within an HTML document. The HTML tag defines the top-most element, the HTML document itself, identifying it as an HTML document rather than some other kind of document. The HTML tag is a container tag that has a start and end, and all other text and tags are nested within it, like this:

```
<HTML>
Your HTML document's contents and all other tags...
</HTML>
```

In your practice file (in Notepad or another text editor), go ahead and type the start and end HTML tags into your file, putting a single hard return between them, like this:

```
<HTML>
</HTML>
```

> **NOTE**
> *Remember that the HTML start tag (<HTML>) must remain at the very top of your file, while the HTML end tag (</HTML>) must remain at the very bottom of your file. Everything else must fall between these two tags.*

The HEAD Tag

The HEAD tag contains information about your HTML file. It also may contain other tags that help to identify your HTML file to the outside world. The HEAD tag is nested within the HTML tag. In your practice file, type the HEAD tag inside the HTML tag now, as follows:

```
<HTML>
<HEAD>
</HEAD>
</HTML>
```

Usually, the only tag contained within the HEAD tag is the TITLE tag. Other tags also can be contained within the HEAD tag, but for most Web pages the need to use them just doesn't come up.

> **NOTE**
>
> *Of the other tags you might want to include inside the HEAD tag, the most useful, by far, is the META tag. It allows you to include additional "meta-information" about your Web page inside the heading. For instance, you could include the name of the author, the subject matter, a list of keywords, and so on. Web browsers don't actually use this information to do anything—right now it's primarily a way to add further annotations describing your Web page, although some search engines use a description and list of keywords to index your Web page. Chapter 3 covers the META tag in further detail.*
>
> *Among the other tags that you can include in the HEAD tag, only the BASE and LINK tags are particularly useful. The BASE tag allows you to move a "home" page without having to move any of its graphics or subpages, as long its prior address is specified in the BASE tag. The LINK tag allows you to specify how a Web page is related, or "linked," to other Web pages. This book doesn't cover using these tags.*

The TITLE Tag

The TITLE tag is nested inside of the HEAD tag. It identifies your page to the rest of the world. For instance, a search index like Yahoo! or Webcrawler might display the text included in your TITLE tag as a link to your page. The tag also displays on your browser's title bar, but it doesn't appear as part of the page. Keep the title short—no more than 40 or 50 characters if possible—but descriptive. Try to use a short title followed by a brief description. Someone else should be able to tell what your page is about simply by looking at the title. Think of it as your welcome mat. Type the TITLE tag inside the HEAD tag.

> ### NOTE
> *If you want to substitute a title of your choosing for the generic title supplied in the following HTML code, go ahead. Don't, however, bust your noggin right now trying to come up with the perfect title. Sunday morning, when you get around to planning your first Web page, you spend more time figuring out what contributes to a good versus a bad title.*

```
<HTML>
<HEAD>
<TITLE>Your Title: Describe Your Title</TITLE>
</HEAD>
</HTML>
```

Officially, the TITLE tag is a required element that you should include in each and every HTML document. In practice, however, most Web browsers let you get away with not including a TITLE tag. Still, you should include a TITLE tag in your HTML document. If you don't include a title, the title of your page appears in some browsers as "Untitled," while in others just the URL for the page appears on the browser's title bar. If you do want the page to be title-less, however, nothing stops you from including a TITLE tag and leaving it blank—but that sort of defeats the whole purpose of including the tag in the first place.

The BODY Tag

The BODY tag is the complement of the HEAD tag and contains all the tags, or elements, that a browser actually displays as the body of your HTML document. Both the HEAD tag and the BODY tag are nested inside the HTML tag. Note, however, that the BODY tag comes after the HEAD tag; they denote separate parts of the HTML document.

> **NOTE**
>
> *The HEAD and BODY tags are the only tags that are nested directly inside the HTML tag. Other than the TITLE tag, which we inserted within the HEAD tag above, you should nest all text and tags you enter in this tutorial inside the BODY tag. Keep both </BODY> and </HTML> end tags at the bottom of your HTML file.*

Type the BODY tag after the HEAD tag, but inside the HTML tag, as follows:

```
<HTML>
<HEAD>
<TITLE>Your Title: Describe Your Title</TITLE>
</HEAD>
<BODY>
</BODY>
</HTML>
```

You have now started your HTML file. All HTML files begin the same way; only the titles are different. What you have typed so far should look like this:

```
<HTML>
<HEAD>
<TITLE>Your Title: Describe Your Title</TITLE>
</HEAD>
<BODY>
</BODY>
</HTML>
```

Saving a Starting Template

If you want, you can save this as a starting template for creating HTML files. Save it as C:\HTML\START.HTM, for instance.

After you save the file as START.HTM, resave it as C:\HTML\SCRATCH.HTM (or whatever working title you want to give it) so you won't accidentally save over your starting template later. If you were now to hop over to your browser and load this file, it would display nothing but the title in the title bar, as is shown in Figure 2-1.

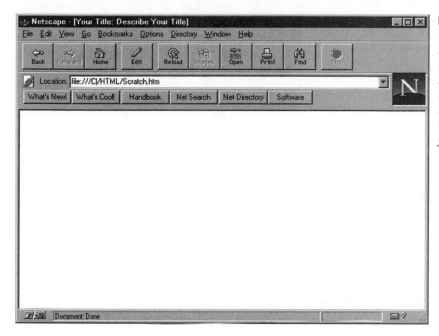

Figure 2-1.
When SCRATCH.HTM is loaded into Netscape Navigator, the Title line appears in Netscape's title bar, but otherwise you get a blank page.

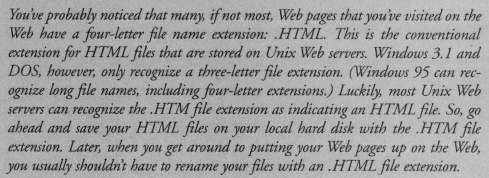

NOTE

You've probably noticed that many, if not most, Web pages that you've visited on the Web have a four-letter file name extension: .HTML. This is the conventional extension for HTML files that are stored on Unix Web servers. Windows 3.1 and DOS, however, only recognize a three-letter file extension. (Windows 95 can recognize long file names, including four-letter extensions.) Luckily, most Unix Web servers can recognize the .HTM file extension as indicating an HTML file. So, go ahead and save your HTML files on your local hard disk with the .HTM file extension. Later, when you get around to putting your Web pages up on the Web, you usually shouldn't have to rename your files with an .HTML file extension.

Structuring Your Web Page with Heading Level Tags

You use headings to organize your Web page into hierarchical levels, in much the same way headings act as separators in a word processing document.

The top-level heading (denoted by the H1 tag or "heading 1" tag) actually is the title for your page; that is, it's the title that appears in a browser window at the top of a Web page. (Don't confuse this with the title that appears in the browser's title bar, which you just set up using the TITLE tag.) Because the H1 tag functions as the title for a Web page, each Web page should have only one H1 tag. (This is the conventional use for this tag—otherwise, nothing positively forbids including multiple H1 tags in a Web page.)

You use a second-level heading (denoted by the H2 tag) to define a major division in your page, and a third-level heading (using the H3 tag) to define a sub-level division within a major division. Most browsers support up to six different heading levels. Within the BODY element that you typed earlier, type six heading level tags, like this:

```
<BODY>
<H1>This is a top-level heading</H1>
<H2>This is a second-level heading</H2>
<H3>This is a third-level heading</H3>
<H4>This is a fourth-level heading</H4>
<H5>This is a fifth-level heading</H5>
<H6>This is a sixth-level heading</H6>
</BODY>
```

As a practical matter, you probably will seldom use more than four heading levels. Displayed in a browser, different level headings appear as different size fonts, from large to small, although each browser decides which fonts to use, as shown in Figures 2-2, 2-3, and 2-4.

NCSA Mosaic doesn't do anything special to display fifth-level or sixth-level headings, displaying them in a normal, non-bolded font. Netscape Navigator displays a sixth-level heading in a small font. You can see why you might want to limit the number of your heading levels to four or five. You never know how the reader's browser is going to deal with the lower-level heading tags.

NOTE

Don't forget to run your Web browser, preferably off-line, and hop back and forth between it and your text editor to check the results of your work. First, save your HTML file in your text editor, then hop out and run your browser and open the same HTML file as you have open in your text editor. Hop back and forth between them as often as you want, saving the HTML file in your text editor and then hitting the Reload button in your Web browser. Remember, you don't really know what you're doing or whether you're doing it right until you can actually see it in a Web browser.

Because the examples switch between different Web browsers in illustrating this chapter, you can't always rely on the illustrations to represent exactly what you might see on your browser. Rather than rely on the illustrations to show you what your work will look like, use them as prompts to hop over to your browser to see for yourself.

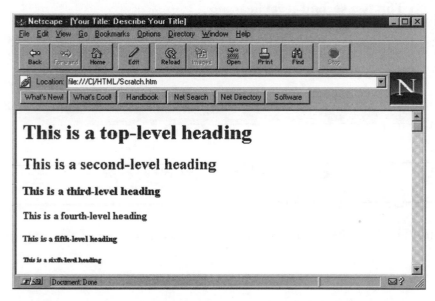

Figure 2-2.
Netscape Navigator displays heading levels one way.

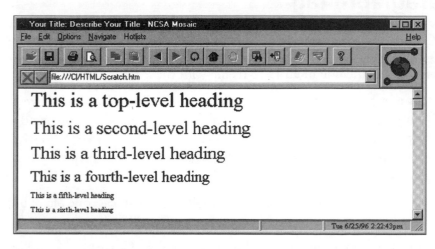

Figure 2-3.
NCSA Mosaic displays the same heading levels another way.

Figure 2-4.
Microsoft Internet Explorer displays those same heading levels in still a different way.

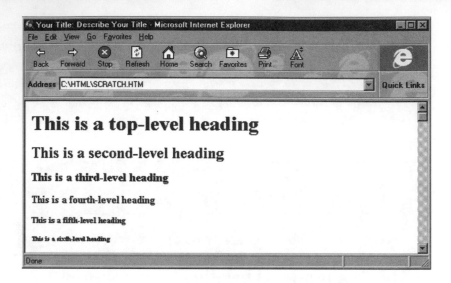

Dividing Your Text with Paragraph and Line Break Tags

The P (Paragraph) and BR (Break) tags let you insert blocks and lines of text on your page.

The P (Paragraph) tag

You can't just type text into an HTML document—all text must be tagged, if not as a paragraph, then as a heading, a list, a block quote, or whatever. Always tag any plain, ordinary text you want to include in an HTML file with the P tag.

The P tag is a container element, but with an implied ending. You don't have to include the </P> end tag. The end of the tag is implied by any following start tag that defines a new block element (a heading, a list, another paragraph, and so on). So when you use the P tag, just insert the <P> start tag at the beginning of a paragraph but leave off the </P> at the end.

Any paragraph that you tag with the P tag should be followed by at least one blank line when it displays in a browser.

Enter the following paragraph, using just the P start tag (<P>) and leave off the implied end tag (</P>):

```
<P>This is paragraph text. This is paragraph text. This is paragraph
text. This is paragraph text. This is paragraph text. This is
paragraph text.
```

The problem is that even though this is spelled out in the HTML 2.0 and 3.2 specifications, some browsers can't interpret a paragraph properly without the </P> at the end. A list following a paragraph, for instance, should be separated by extra space. Microsoft Internet Explorer 2.0 for Windows 3.1, however, doesn't insert the extra space unless you include the </P> end tag at the end of a paragraph preceding a list. Fortunately, Microsoft has fixed this in Version 3.0 for Windows 95, but many people probably still will use 2.0 for quite some time. (Old browsers never go away—they just keep getting used.) Other browsers may have the same problem (but hopefully none with as large a profile as Internet Explorer).

Part of the confusion surrounding how to use this tag element properly goes back to HTML 1.0, where the P tag was defined as a stand-alone element functioning as a separator. HTML 2.0, however, specifically defined this element as a container, but with an implied ending. HTML 3.2 reconfirms the HTML 2.0 definition.

Since it's inarguably non-standard, you should leave off the </P> end tag. Browsers that don't handle this right are clearly misbehaving and, as such, clearly deserve to be spanked.

See Figure 2-5 to see how Navigator Gold, like most other Web browsers, displays a paragraph without the </P> end tag, followed by a list.

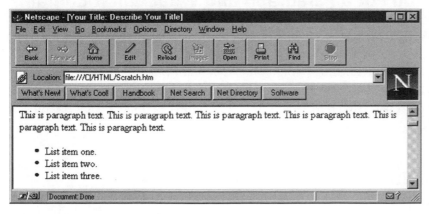

Figure 2-5.
Navigator Gold, as well as most other Web browsers, adds space between a paragraph and a list, even if you don't add the </P> end tag.

NOTE

I went ahead and checked out how leaving off the </P> end tag is treated in three other browsers, in case you're curious. Sun's pre-Beta release of their HotJava Web browser adds the extra space between the end of a paragraph and a following list. I-View and GNNpress, however, do not. However, since leaving off the implied </P> end tag is part of the standard for HTML (both 2.0 and 3.2), I expect these non-conforming browsers to ultimately conform to the standard.

TIP

A Web browser automatically wraps text in an HTML file to fit inside its window. Therefore, you don't have to insert returns at the ends of your lines to get them to fit inside a browser window. It wouldn't work anyway, because Web browsers completely ignore hard returns. So, just let Notepad wrap your text (turn on Word Wrap), but understand that you're doing so purely for the convenience of working in Notepad and are having no effect whatsoever on where the text will break in your Web browser.

Where Can You Put a Paragraph and What Can It Contain?

Generally, your paragraphs simply are nested in the BODY tag. You also can nest paragraphs in block quotes (BLOCKQUOTE), glossary definitions (DD), list items (LI), and address blocks (ADDRESS). A paragraph can contain plain text, highlighting (B, I, EM, STRONG, and so on), special characters (like accented characters or the copyright symbol), line breaks (BR), hypertext links (A), and inline images (IMG). You can learn about these codes later in this chapter.

Don't Use Multiple P Tags To Add Blank Lines

Generally, a P tag that contains no text has no effect. None of the big three browsers let you add blank lines by simply adding P tags, although some browsers might. To illustrate this point, following the text paragraph you typed above, type three <P> tags (leave off the </P> end tags):

```
<P>This is paragraph text. This is paragraph text. This is paragraph
text. This is paragraph text. This is paragraph text. This is para-
graph text.
```

\<P\>
\<P\>
\<P\>

Now, type three more P (Paragraph) tags, but this time include the </P> end tags:

```
<P>
<P>
<P>
```
\<P\>\</P\>
\<P\>\</P\>
\<P\>\</P\>

Go ahead and hop over to your Web browser to see what this looks like. Don't expect to see anything, though—that's the whole point. Multiple P tags, with or without their end tags, in other words, should have no effect whatsoever. Your browser completely ignores them. Even if some browser does display these, you wouldn't want to write exclusively for it anyway.

The BR (Line Break) Tag

The BR (Line Break) tag is an "empty," or stand-alone, tag that simply inserts a line break. Type three text lines separated by BR tags:

```
<P>These lines are separated by BR (Line Break) tags.<BR>
These lines are separated by BR (Line Break) tags.<BR>
These lines are separated by BR (Line Break) tags.
```

As Figure 2-6 shows, only a single line break separates these lines when a browser displays them. (Paragraphs, you may remember, are separated by a line break and an extra blank line.)

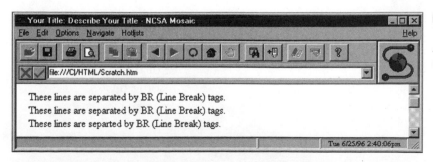

Figure 2-6.
The BR tag inserts a single line break at the end of a line.

> **NOTE**
>
> *You can use the BR tag almost anywhere you have text, not just inside of P (Paragraph) tags—you can put them inside a Heading tag, for instance.*

Don't Use Multiple BR Tags To Add Blank Lines

You might think you could use multiple BR tags to add blank lines to your page. To see what happens when you try this, type a line of text followed by four BR tags:

```
<P>Four BR (Line Break) tags follow this line.<BR>
<BR>
<BR>
<BR>
Four BR (Line Break) tags precede this line.
```

You're not supposed to get away with such a maneuver (according to the official HTML specs, that is). Netscape Navigator, however, has always let you get away with it, as shown in Figure 2-7. NCSA Mosaic, however, doesn't let you get away with it, as shown in Figure 2-8. Internet Explorer didn't used to let you get away with it (Version 2.0), but clearly intent on copying Navigator right down to the BR tags, now does (Version 3.0), as shown in Figure 2-9.

Figure 2-7.

Netscape Navigator lets you get away with using multiple BR tags to add vertical space to a Web page.

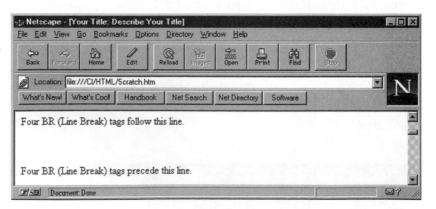

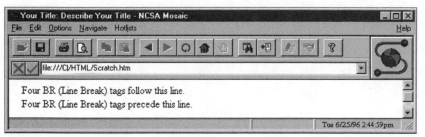

Figure 2-8.
NCSA Mosaic, always the stickler, doesn't let you get away with using multiple BR tags.

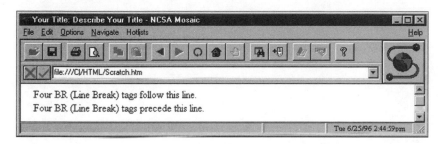

Figure 2-9.
Internet Explorer Version 2.0 used to not display multiple BR tags, but Version 3.0 now does.

NOTE

Go ahead and hop over to your browser to check out how it treats multiple BR tags, especially if you use a browser other than one of big three. Incidentally, I-View and GNNpress do allow you to use multiple BR tags to add vertical space on a Web page, but Sun's HotJava does not (although HotJava is a pre-Beta release).

So, should or shouldn't you use BR tags for blank lines? Good question. The point here is simply that even if Netscape Navigator, Internet Explorer (Version 3.0, that is), and any number of other Web browsers do let you use multiple BR tags, it still doesn't constitute standard HTML. The best bet is to avoid non-standard HTML, even if your favorite Web browser allows you to get away with using it (even if that Web browser is Navigator). Besides, you can get the same result in a perfectly legal way (see the following tip).

Spacing, Tabs, and Returns: For Your Eyes Only

In HTML, the tags themselves do all your page's formatting. A browser ignores more than one space inserted into text (two, five, or ten spaces all appear as though they were a single space), as well as all tabs and hard returns. Any formatting of your HTML file using extra spaces or tabs and returns is "for your eyes only." So feel free to use all the extra spaces, tabs, and returns you want to make your raw HTML files more "readable;" just don't expect a browser to display them.

This works in Navigator, Internet Explorer, and NCSA Mosaic, but might not necessarily work in all Web browsers. In the HTML specs, this character seems to be restricted to only joining together words so they won't be broken by a return, but otherwise must be treated simply as a normal space. This should mean that a Web browser would collapse multiple nonbreakable spaces, like multiple regular spaces, down to a single space. Most Web browsers apparently don't do this, but some do. A couple X-Windows Web browsers don't display nonbreakable spaces at all, displaying them as zero-width characters. Consequently, your wisest course of action probably would be to avoid it altogether. But if you do want to do it, you now know how.

Adding Comments

You also can add comments to annotate your HTML files. The Comment tag is a stand-alone tag that enables you to include messages that will not be displayed in a Web browser in your HTML files, for your own—or anyone else's—future reference. What can be a little confusing about this tag, however, is that no "name" is included in the tag. Instead, a comment always begins with a "<!—" and ends with a "—>". Any text inserted between these two is comment text that a browser completely ignores. Here's an example of the form in which you would enter a comment into an HTML file:

```
<!-Put your comment here->
```

Now, go ahead and type a comment between two lines of text, like this:

```
<P>This line is followed by a comment.
<!-Comments are not displayed by a browser.->
<P>This line follows a comment.
```

The above two paragraph lines appear in a Web browser without any additional vertical space between them. The browser ignores any text inside the Comment tag.

Highlighting Your Text

Just as in a normal book or report, an HTML document can use text highlighting to clarify the text's meaning. You can easily make text in an HTML file bold or italicized, and use other types of highlighting as well.

Using Italic and Bold Highlighting

HTML has two ways to include italic or bold text on your Web page. The first way involves using literal tags: the I (Italic) and B (Bold) tags. The second way is to use "logical" tags: the EM (Emphasis) and STRONG (Strong Emphasis) tags. Most browsers should display the I (Italic) and EM (Emphasis) tags identically, just as they should display the B (Bold) and STRONG (Strong Emphasis) tags identically.

So what's the difference? None really, except perhaps a philosophical one. The basic philosophy behind HTML is to logically represent the elements of a page rather than literally describe them. The browser can freely interpret the logical elements of an HTML page and display them as it sees fit. Thus, the philosophically correct method is to always use logical tags and to avoid using literal tags. So, if you want to be more true to the basic spirit of HTML, then use the EM (Emphasis) tag rather than the I (Italic) tag and the STRONG (Strong Emphasis) tag rather than the B (Bold) tag. Or, if you want to be contrary, do it the other way around—you get the same result either way.

As an example of using the I, B, EM, and STRONG tags for text highlighting, type the following lines of text using these tags, as shown here:

```
<P><I>This is italic text.</I>
<P><B>This is bold text.</B>
<P><EM>This is emphasized text.</EM>
<P><STRONG>This is strongly emphasized text</STRONG>.
```

Figure 2-10 shows how these tags appear in Netscape Navigator.

Figure 2-10.
I and Emphasis are identical, as are B and Strong, in a Web browser.

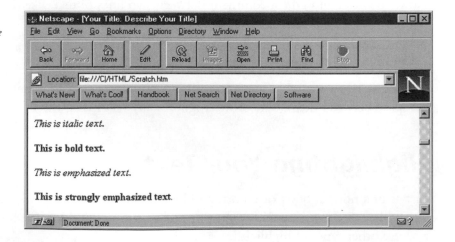

> **TIP**
>
> *You can combine the I and B tags or the EM and STRONG tags to get text that is both italic and bolded. To do this, just combine the tags, like this:*
>
> ```
> <P><I><B>This text is both italicized and bolded. </B></I>
> <P><EM><STRONG>This text is also both italicized (emphasized) and
> bolded (strongly emphasized). </STRONG></EM>
> ```
>
> *Be sure to nest these tags rather than overlapping them.*

You can use two other tags, the CITE (Citation) and VAR (Variable) tags, to highlight text, but neither displays any differently from the I (Italic) or EM (Emphasis) tags in any Web browser.

Embedding Monospace Text

You occasionally you may want to embed monospace text within a paragraph, such as to request keyboard input or to represent screen output. A monospace font, also called a *fixed-pitch font*, is a font in which all the characters occupy the same amount of space on a line (in a "proportional" font, on the other hand, each character occupies a unique amount of space on a line). For example, the following line uses a proportional font:

```
This line uses a monospace font.
```

The most widely used tag for embedding monospace text is the TT (Teletype) tag. It appears more or less the same way, as a monospace font, in all Web browsers. As such, you can think of it as a general-purpose monospace text tag that you can use whenever you want to embed monospace text within a paragraph. Two other tags, the CODE and SAMP tags, generally appear no differently than the TT tag. In other words, just use the TT tag.

The only other possibly useful tag here is the KBD (Keyboard) tag. Unfortunately, however, how any one Web browser might choose to display this tag is rather unpredictable. Navigator displays it the same as the TT tag. Internet Explorer displays it in a monospace font but bolds it as well. NCSA Mosaic, on the other hand, bucks the trend entirely and chooses to display this tag as an italicized proportional font. The tag may "possibly" be useful only because it would allow you to distinguish between screen output (the TT tag) on the one hand and keyboard input (the KBD tag) on the other hand.

> ### NOTE
>
> *NCSA Mosaic 2.11 for some inexplicable reason (surely it's a bug) elevates text enclosed in any of these tags (TT, KBD, CODE, or SAMP) above the baseline of surrounding text, generating a rather ugly effect. To my knowledge, this idiosyncrasy is unique to NCSA Mosaic.*

Type the following as an example of using the TT and KBD tags:

```
<P>This is regular text. <TT>This is an example of the TT (Teletype
or Typewriter Text) tag.</TT> This is regular text. <KBD>This is an
example of the KBD (Keyboard) tag.</KBD>
```

Figures 2-11 and 2-12 show how this text appears in Netscape Navigator and NCSA Mosaic, respectively.

Figure 2-11.

In Netscape Navigator, the TT (Teletype) and KBD (Keyboard) tags both appear in a mono-space, fixed-pitch font.

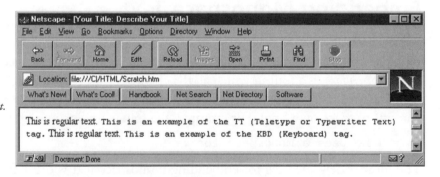

Figure 2-12.

In NCSA Mosaic, the TT (Teletype) tag appears in a mono-space, fixed-pitch font, whereas the KBD (Keyboard) tag appears in a regular (proportional) but italicized font. Notice, also, that NCSA Mosaic elevates text in these tags above the baseline.

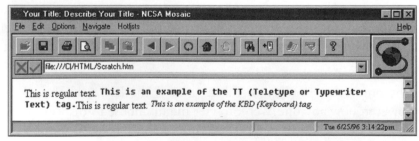

> **NOTE**
>
> *For another way to insert monospace text, but as a separate text block, rather than embedding inside a paragraph, see "The PRE (Preformatted Text) Tag" section, later in this session.*

Inserting Reserved and Special Characters

You may need to enter a special code for a character into your HTML file under two different circumstances: If you want to insert a reserved character that is used to parse (interpret and display) an HTML file, and if you want to enter a special, or extended, character that isn't part of the regular keyboard's character set.

You insert both of these characters into an HTML file in the form of a numerical entity code or a named entity code. Numerical entity codes are inserted in the following form, where number is a three-digit decimal number between 000 and 255:

`&#number;`

Named entity codes are inserted in the following form, where name is the name of a character as listed in the HTML specs:

`&name;`

Reserved Characters

HTML uses the <, >, &, and " characters to parse, or interpret, an HTML document for display. Except for angle brackets, you rarely need to automatically replace these characters with their entity codes:

- **Angle brackets (< and >)** should always be replaced by their corresponding entity codes if you want them to display properly in an HTML file. Use them only to signal the beginning or the end of an HTML tag.

- **Double quotes (")**, on the other hand, only need to be replaced if they're part of an HTML tag that you want to appear as is rather than as interpreted by a browser.

- **Ampersands (&)** signal the beginning of an entity code, but only need to be replaced if they're part of an HTML entity code that you want to appear as is rather than as interpreted by a browser. You never need to replace stand-alone ampersands.

> **!**
>
> ## CAUTION
>
> *If you use a word processor to do this tutorial, be sure to turn off the "smart quotes" feature. When creating HTML files, you always want to use regular "keyboard" quotes. In other words, each quotation mark should be straight up and down, not curled to the left or right.*

One particular situation calls for you to use character entities exclusively to insert any of these characters into an HTML file: when you want an HTML tag to appear on your Web page as is rather than as interpreted by the browser. To have a browser show <EM> on-screen instead of interpreting it as a formatting code, you would have to enter it like this:

<EM>

All Web browsers recognize the named entity codes for these characters, so you don't have to use the numerical entity codes here. For an easy reference, Table 2-1 shows the named entity codes for inserting HTML reserved characters.

Table 2-1 HTML Reserved Character Entity Codes

Character	Entity	Code
Less Than	<	&lt;
Greater Than	>	&gt;
Ampersand	&	&amp;
Double Quote	"	&quot;

Special Characters

Suppose, for instance, you want to post a page devoted to an article you've written, and you want to protect it by showing your copyright. Since the copyright symbol (©) isn't available on the keyboard, you can't just type it into your HTML document as you would a normal keyboard character. Instead, you must use a special code that tells the browser to insert the character where you want it.

In HTML, there are two ways to enter such characters: as numerical entity codes or named entity codes. You can insert the copyright symbol, for example, by using its numerical entity code (©) or its named entity code (©).

HTML uses the ISO 8859-1 character set, which is an 8-bit character set that provides 256 positions (0-255). Of these, however, 000 through 032 and 127 correspond to control characters, while 128 through 159 are designated as undisplayable. Thus, only the last 95 codes (160 through 255) represent all the special characters that you can insert on a Web page. These include many special symbols (cent, copyright, degree, and so on), plus many accented characters (like a capital A with an acute accent).

Numerical character entities use the actual decimal numeration of the character in the ISO-8859-1 character set. For instance, you could insert a copyright symbol into a Web page by using its numerical character entity like this:

```
&#169;"
```

Named entity codes have been designated to correspond to many of these special characters. To insert a copyright symbol using its named character entity, for example, you would type this:

```
&copy;"
```

However, whether a Web browser will display a named character entity is another matter. Other than the upper- and lowercase accented characters (A-grave, a-acute, and so on) that many languages require, only the copyright and registration signs have anything close to universal support. True, certain Web browsers can interpret and display almost all of these named entities, but other than those just mentioned, Netscape Navigator can't—in other words, feel free to use the named entity codes for the copyright or registration symbol, and for any of the accented characters, but otherwise stick to using the numerical character entities.

CAUTION

There is one teensy-weensy problem, however. Although the ISO-8859-1 character set is used to designate special characters to insert in a Web page, it is by no means the universal native character set for all computer operating systems. It is the native character set for both Unix and Windows, but not for the Macintosh or DOS. On a Macintosh, certain characters in the ISO-8859-1 character set aren't available, so if you try to display one of these characters in a Web page on a Macintosh, you see a different character than the one that you intend. The solution is to avoid using these characters on a Web page. Table 2-2 shows these characters and what you want to appear on-screen versus what Macintosh substitutes.

Table 2-2   Characters That Won't Display on a Macintosh

Numerical Entity	Named Entity	Character	Macintosh Displays
&#166;	&brvbar;	¦ (broken bar)	I
&#178;	&sup2;	² (superscript 2)	2
&#179;	&sup3;	³ (superscript 3)	3
&#185;	&sup1;	¹ (superscript 1)	1
&#188;	&frac14;	¼ (one quarter)	_
&#189;	&frac12;	½ (one half)	_
&#190;	&frac34;	¾ (three quarters)	_
&#215;	&times;	× (multiplication)	x
&#221;	&Yacute;	Ý (Y-acute)	Y
&#253;	&yacute;	ý (y-acute)	y

Of these, you might possibly use only the broken bar (¦) and the multiplication sign (×), because Macintosh substitutes a straight vertical bar (I) for the broken bar and a lowercase x for the multiplication sign. For the others, you can see that Macintosh uses entirely different and dissimilar characters.

Table 2-3 shows some of the most commonly used special characters, their numerical and named entity codes, and support by the "big three" browsers (universal support, however, for named entities cannot be guaranteed).

Table 2-3 Special Characters

	Number	*Name*	*Name Support*
Trademark	&#153;	&trade;	Not Netscape
Cent	&#162;	&cent;	NCSA Mosaic only
Copyright	&#169;	&copy;	All three
Registered	&#174;	&reg;	All three
Multiply	&#215;	&times;	NCSA Mosaic only
Divide	&#247;	&divide;	NCSA Mosaic only

Table 2-3 is just a partial list of special characters you can insert into an HTML file.

CAUTION

Named entity codes, such as © or ® above, are case-sensitive. You should type them exactly as they are listed. À and à, for instance, stand for two separate accented characters: an uppercase "A" with a grave and a lowercase "a" with a grave, respectively.

Here is a common example of entering a numerical entity code, in this case that for the Copyright symbol:

```
<P>To notify readers that your material is copyrighted, use the
copyright symbol, like this: &#169; Copyright 1996.
```

This is an example of entering a named entity code, in this case the Registered symbol:

```
<P>If a trademark has been registered, it is best to follow it with
the registered trademark sign, like this: Crumbies&reg;.
```

A good example of the problem with using named character entities appeared, until quite recently anyway, on NCSA Mosaic's home page. NCSA Mosaic supports using the named character entity for the trademark symbol (™), and prominently used it on their home page, as shown here as viewed in their browser in Figure 2-13.

Figure 2-13.

NCSA Mosaic, as shown here on their own home page, used to support displaying the trademark symbol using its named character entity. However, when you viewed the same page in Netscape Navigator, you got the named entity "as is," and not the trademark symbol.

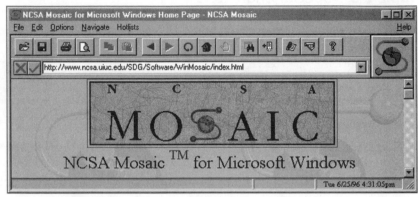

Figure 2-14.

When you viewed NCSA Mosaic's home page, however, with Netscape Navigator, what was displayed was the named character entity itself ("™"), not the trademark symbol.

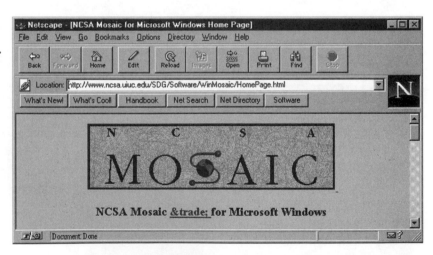

As you can see, when a browser doesn't recognize a named character entity, it doesn't just ignore it (see Figure 2-14). What you get is the code itself, which usually isn't the effect you intend. NCSA Mosaic's home page, of course, was doing this intentionally. It was NCSA's way of thumbing its nose at Netscape Navigator, showing the legions of Navigator users that Mosaic supported something that Navigator didn't. You don't want to follow suit here, however. (NCSA has since mended its ways, or decided that

Navigator users had had enough, and removed the offending named entity code, replacing it with the numerical entity code for the trademark symbol.)

> **NOTE**
>
> *The trademark entity poses one additional problem. It isn't included in the ISO-8859-1 character set. Its numerical code, ™, displays the trademark on both Windows and Macintosh computers, but only because their native character sets include it. You can't rely on its availability on other platforms. A workaround is to insert "(TM)" inside SMALL and SUP (Superscript) tags (Chapter 3 discusses using those tags).*

Using Block Quotes

The BLOCKQUOTE (Block Quote) tag double indents a block of text from both margins. You usually use it to display quotations, as the name of the tag implies. You can use it to double indent any block of text, however; you aren't limited to using it on quotations. According to the specification for the tag, you aren't supposed to put raw text inside a block quote—you are only supposed to put other text elements, such as paragraphs (P tag elements), for instance, inside a block quote, and then put the text in those other elements. In practical terms, however, none of the big three browsers care one way or the other. So, if you want to be kosher, or just play it safe, put the P tags in; otherwise, don't worry about it.

Now, type a paragraph of text, followed by a paragraph of text inside a BLOCK-QUOTE tag:

```
<P>In <EM>Notes From Underground</EM> Dostoevsky plumbs the depths of
human psychology, revealing the complexity and contradictions under-
lying even the most normal and decent of human beings:

<BLOCKQUOTE>

<P>Every man has some reminiscenses which he would not tell to
everyone, but only to his friends. He has others which he would not
reveal even to his friends, but only to himself, and that in secret.
But finally there are still others which a man is even afraid to
tell himself, and every decent man has a considerable number of such
things in his mind.

</BLOCKQUOTE>
```

The various Web browsers display block quotes quite differently. Figures 2-15, 2-16, and 2-17 show how block quotes appear in Netscape Navigator, NCSA Mosaic, and Internet Explorer.

Figure 2-15.
Netscape Navigator double-indents a block quote, but does no other special formatting.

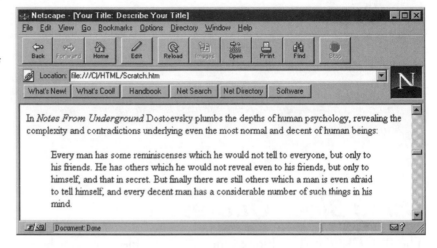

Figure 2-16.
NCSA Mosaic double-indents a block quote, but also bolds it and displays it in a smaller font.

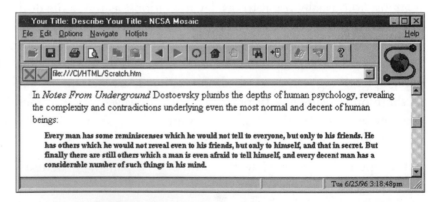

Figure 2-17.
Microsoft Internet Explorer double-indents a block quote, but also displays it in italic.

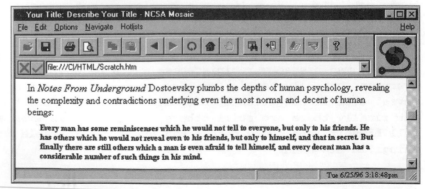

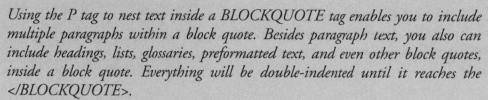

> **TIP**
>
> *Using the P tag to nest text inside a BLOCKQUOTE tag enables you to include multiple paragraphs within a block quote. Besides paragraph text, you also can include headings, lists, glossaries, preformatted text, and even other block quotes, inside a block quote. Everything will be double-indented until it reaches the </BLOCKQUOTE>.*

Using BR (Line Break) Tags in a Block Quote

You can use BR (Line Break) tags in a block quote to display stanzas of poetry, the verses of a song, or other indented text for which you don't want the lines to wrap. Type a paragraph of text, followed by a paragraph of text using BR tags inserted inside a BLOCKQUOTE tag.

```
<P>In <EM>Porgy and Bess</EM>, in the song "Summertime," George
Gershwin evokes the hazy, lazy days of a Southern summer:
<BLOCKQUOTE>
<P>Summertime and the living is easy,<BR>
Fish are jumping and the cotton is high.<BR>
Oh your Daddy's rich and your Ma is good looking,<BR>
So hush little baby, don't you cry.
</BLOCKQUOTE>
```

Figure 2-18 shows how a block quote using BR tags appears in a Web browser.

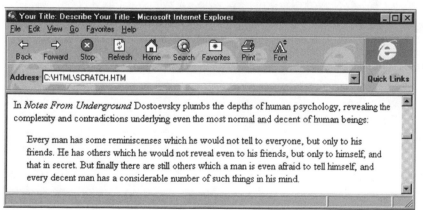

Figure 2-18.
Using the BR tag in a block quote, you can format poetry stanzas or song lyrics.

Using Preformatted Text

You would use the PRE (Preformatted Text) to display "preformatted" text in a mono-space, fixed-pitch font. As its name implies, you use the PRE tag to display text as is, including all spaces and hard returns. You primarily use it to display text in a tabular or columnar format in which you want to make sure that columns are properly aligned.

NOTE

Always use spaces, not tabs, to align columns when using the PRE tag, because different browsers can display tabs in PRE tagged text differently.

Actually, the PRE tag is the original "tables" tag for HTML. Its merit is that, unlike the TABLE tag (part of HTML 3.2, but not HTML 2.0), it is that all Web browsers support it. It can be particularly handy for displaying worksheets or reports. Another common usage is for displaying program code or output.

CAUTION

When typing tabular or columnar text with a PRE tag, make sure that you have a monospace, fixed-pitch font, such as Courier, turned on in your editor or word processor. Windows Notepad automatically displays all text in a monospace font. Word processors, however, normally use a proportional font as the default. Most HTML editors display PRE tagged text in a monospace font, but a prominent exception here is HTML Notepad (Version 1.9, anyway, which displays everything in a proportional font).

For an example of using the PRE tag, type a table using rows and columns:

```
<PRE>
      Sales Figures for First Quarter of 1996

               January        February         March           Totals
Anderson     $ 10,200      $   20,015      $   14,685      $    44,900
Baker          30,500          25,885          50,225          106,610
Peterson       15,900          20,115          18,890           54,905
Wilson         40,100          35,000          29,000          104,100

               _____          _____         _____          _____
Totals       $ 96,700      $ 101,015       $ 112,800       $ 310,515
</PRE>
```

Figure 2-19 shows the above table as it appears in a Web browser.

> ## TIP
>
> *A trick that works in both Netscape Navigator and NCSA Mosaic to double indent preformatted text, rather than display it flush to the left margin, is to put it inside a BLOCKQUOTE tag. Enclose the PRE tag text you just typed inside a BLOCK-QUOTE tag, as follows:*
>
> ```
> <BLOCKQUOTE>
> <PRE>
>       Sales Figures for First Quarter of 1996
>
>                January        February         March           Totals
> Anderson     $ 10,200      $ 20,015        $ 14,685        $ 44,900
> Baker          30,500          25,885          50,225          106,610
> Peterson       15,900          20,115          18,890           54,905
> Wilson         40,100          35,000          29,000          104,100
>
>                _____          _____         _____          _____
> Totals       $ 96,700        $101,015        $112,800        $ 310,515
> </PRE>
> </BLOCKQUOTE>
> ```
>
> *This trick doesn't work in Internet Explorer Version 2.0. However, true to Microsoft's mission to copy and ape ("embrace and extend") Netscape Navigator in every detail, they've fixed this in Version 3.0. (In Version 2.0, preformatted text inside a block quote appears flush left.)*

Figure 2-19.
The PRE tag allows you to preserve text alignment and line breaks in tables or columns.

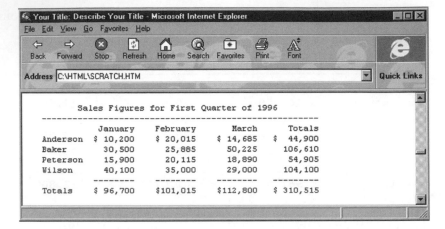

```
                Sales Figures for First Quarter of 1996
          -------------------------------------------------------
                   January     February       March        Totals
          Anderson  $ 10,200   $ 20,015     $ 14,685    $  44,900
          Baker       30,500     25,885       50,225      106,610
          Peterson    15,900     20,115       18,890       54,905
          Wilson      40,100     35,000       29,000      104,100
                    --------   --------     --------    ---------
          Totals    $ 96,700   $101,015     $112,800    $ 310,515
```

Creating Lists

Only headings and paragraph text elements are used more commonly than lists. Many Web pages are nothing but lists of hypertext links. You, like anyone else surfing the Web, have been on that merry-go-round a few times—going from one page of lists to another page of lists to another. If you're going to create Web pages, you need to know how to make lists!

Seriously though, you want to know how to create two kinds of lists: ordered and unordered. An *ordered list* is simply a numbered list and an *unordered list* is a bulleted list.

NOTE

You don't have to physically type the numbers for the items in an ordered list or insert bullet characters for an unordered list. A Web browser automatically sequentially numbers any list items included in an OL tag. When a Web browser encounters the UL tag, it inserts the bullet characters for you.

The OL (Ordered List) Tag

The OL (Ordered List) tag defines a sequentially numbered list of items. Therefore, the OL tag must surround the entire list. The LI (List Item) tag is nested inside the OL tag and defines each individual item within the list.

Go ahead now and create an ordered list to see how these tags work together:

```
<P>When visiting Florence, one should be sure to visit:
<OL>
<LI>The Church of Santa Maria Novella
<LI>The Medici Chapels
<LI>The Church of San Lorenzo
<LI>The Baptistry of St. John
</OL>
```

NOTE

Notice that the LI tags do not have end tags in this example. The reason is that the end tag (</LI>), like the end tag for the P tag, is implied. It's another case of a container tag masquerading as an empty tag. Don't worry, though, there aren't very many of them—just a couple more.

Figure 2-20 shows an ordered list in Netscape Navigator.

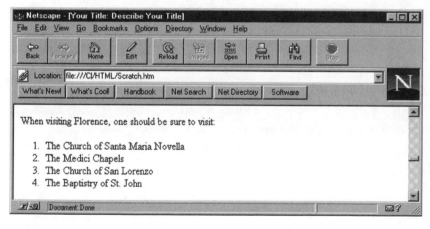

Figure 2-20.
Ordered lists are automatically sequentially numbered in a Web browser.

The UL (Unordered List) Tag

The UL (Unordered List) tag defines a bulleted list of items. Once again, the LI (List Item) tag is nested inside the UL tag and defines each item within the list.

Create a bulleted list now:

```
<P>In this course we will be studying the philosophical thought of
the Milesians:
<UL>
<LI>Thales
<LI>Anaximander
<LI>Anaximenes
</UL>
```

Figure 2-21 shows an unordered, or bulleted, list displayed in NCSA Mosaic.

Figure 2-21.
Unordered lists auto-matically get bullets in a Web browser.

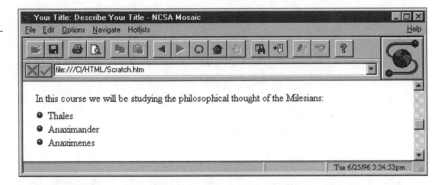

NOTE

So, how do you create all those fancy, colored, 3-D bullets that you see all over the Web? Well, the truth of the matter is that they aren't really lists; that is, they don't use OL or UL tags. Those fancy bullets are actually inline graphic images that the Web author has inserted into the page. The separate lines are simply paragraphs broken up by line breaks (BR tags).

The IMG tag (covered later in this chapter) enables you to display inline graphics on your Web page. Don't worry if you don't know what an "inline graphic" is yet—you get to that in today's afternoon session (in Chapter 3).

Nesting Lists

You can nest a list inside another list. The browser automatically indents nested list lev-els. You can nest the same or different kinds of lists.

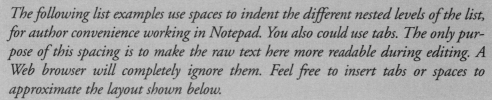

NOTE

The following list examples use spaces to indent the different nested levels of the list, for author convenience working in Notepad. You also could use tabs. The only purpose of this spacing is to make the raw text here more readable during editing. A Web browser will completely ignore them. Feel free to insert tabs or spaces to approximate the layout shown below.

```
<UL>
<LI>Some Pre-Socratic Philosophers
    <UL>
    <LI>The Milesians
      <UL>
      <LI>Thales
      <LI>Anaximander
      <LI>Anaximenes
      </UL>
    <LI>The Eleatics
      <UL>
      <LI>Parmenides
      <LI>Anaxagoras
      </UL>
    </UL>
</UL>
```

Figure 2-22 shows an unordered, or bulleted, list nested three levels deep as it appears in Netscape Navigator.

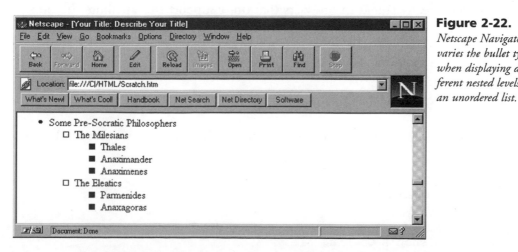

Figure 2-22.
Netscape Navigator varies the bullet type when displaying different nested levels of an unordered list.

Using the TYPE Attribute in Lists

Netscape Navigator will vary the bullet type for different nested levels of an unordered list, but neither Internet Explorer nor NCSA Mosaic will. They both display nested bullet lists using the same bullet type for each nested level. (Actually, this seems to be one of the few instances in which Internet Explorer 3.0 has failed to duplicate Navigator feature-for-feature.

An additional feature, at this time still supported only by Netscape Navigator, is the capability to assign different bullet types using a TYPE attribute in the UL tag. You have three choices here: "disc" (the default), "circle," and "square." The "circle" doesn't actually appear as a circle, at least not in Windows 3.1 or 95, but rather, as a hollow square. The "square" displays as a filled square.

Using these attribute values really does no harm, in that a browser that doesn't support them just displays its default bullet for each level. If you want to use them, go ahead. Examples of using these attributes are presented in greater depth in the intermediate HTML tutorial (in Chapter 3).

You also can nest ordered, or numbered, lists within each other. However, unlike with the unordered, or bulleted, list, none of the big three Web browsers automatically vary the number type. Netscape Navigator, however, allows you to assign a TYPE attribute, similar to the one you would use in an unordered list, with which you can assign the values of "I," "i," "A," "a," and "1," allowing you to display a real outline.

Internet Explorer 3.0 has managed to ape Navigator here. However, neither NCSA Mosaic nor Internet Explorer 2.0 recognizes these attribute values. Consequently, you're probably better off to avoid using these attribute values—unless you want your outlines to look really stupid in browsers that don't support this attribute. If you still want to use these attribute values. The intermediate HTML tutorial addresses them in greater depth.

Mixing Lists

You can nest an ordered list within an unordered list (or the other way around), if you want to:

```
<UL>
<LI>King-Side Openings
   <OL>
   <LI>Ruy Lopez
   <LI>King Bishop's Opening
```

```
    <LI>King's Gambit
    </OL>
<LI>Queen-Side Openings
    <OL>
    <LI>Queen's Gambit Declined
    <LI>Queen's Gambit Accepted
    <LI>English Opening
    </OL>
</UL>
```

Figure 2-23 shows ordered, or numbered, lists nested inside an unordered, or bulleted, list.

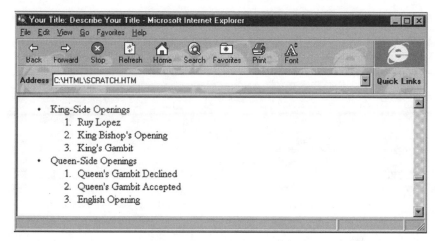

Figure 2-23.
Different list types can be nested inside one another.

Two other list tags, the MENU and DIR (Directory) tags, are available. Both of these tags are perfectly legitimate. At present, however, only NCSA Mosaic bothers to display these tags differently than the UL (Unordered List) tag. So, until wider support among emerges browsers for distinguishing these tags from plain ordinary UL tags, your best bet is to stick with the UL tags and avoid using the MENU and DIR tags.

Creating Glossaries

The DL (Definition List) tag allows you to create glossaries, or lists of terms and definitions. As such, a glossary consists of three tag elements: a tag to define the list (DL), a tag to define the terms (DT), and a tag to define the definitions (DD). Set up a short glossary now:

```
<DL>

<DT>Appeal

<DD>A proceeding by which the decision of a lower court may be
appealed to a higher court.

<DT>Arrest

<DD>The legal apprehension and restraint of someone charged with a
crime so that they might be brought before a court to stand trial.

<DT>Bail

<DD>A security offered to a court in exchange for a person's release
and as assurance of their appearance in court when required.

</DL>
```

Figure 2-24 shows the preceding glossary list code as it appears in Netscape Navigator.

Figure 2-24.

A glossary list (DL) is composed of two parts, a term (DT) and a definition (DD).

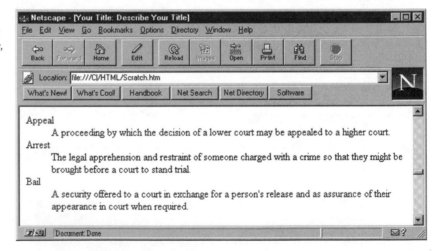

As you probably notice, the end tags for the DT (Define Term) and DD (Define Definition) tags are implied, just like for the LI (List Item) tag in a regular list. The only difference is that a glossary, or definition list, has a two-part item (both a term and a definition), rather than a one-part item. As long as you keep this in mind, you should have no trouble creating glossaries.

You don't have to use these tags just to create glossaries. Anything that fits into the form works. If you have time later in the afternoon, the intermediate HTML tutorial offers some variations on this approach. For now, though, you need to stay right here.

> **TIP**
>
> *By itself, a glossary list is a bit bland. You can dress it up by adding emphasis or tagging the definition terms with a heading tag. For instance, here is an example of adding bold italic emphasis to a definition term:*
>
> ```
> <DT><I><B>Appeal</B></I>
> ```
>
> *Here is an example of tagging a definition term using an H3 heading tag:*
>
> ```
> <DT><H3>Appeal</H3>
> ```

Creating Hypertext Links

One of the main reasons to create a Web page is to create links to other pages, right? To do that, you need the A (Anchor) tag.

If you've surfed the Web at all, you should be quite familiar with hypertext links. You've probably used hypertext links not only to jump to and view another Web page, or jump to a specific place in either the same or another Web page, but to read a Gopher file, display an image, download a program, send an e-mail message, run a script, access a database, telnet to a server, and so on. You can use hypertext links to jump to anything that has an address on the Internet (not just on the Web), as long as you don't need a password. Of course, what happens after you make the jump depends on where you go.

In a sense, the Web is a kind of giant "What's behind door #3?" game, although this perhaps helps explain much of its basic appeal. It's all quite easy and transparent: just click and go. Unfortunately, however, explaining how to make this happen on your Web page isn't nearly as easy or transparent. This section is a valiant effort to make the A (Anchor) tag as possible, or as least confusing or difficult as possible, as the case may be. The three basic kinds of hypertext links are as follows:

- **Links to other HTML documents or data objects.** These are by far the most commonly used links on the Web. They allow you to jump from one Web page to another, as well as to anything else that has an address on the Net (not just the Web), such as Gopher files, FTP archives, and images.

- **Link to other places in the same HTML document.** These links allow you to jump from one place in the same Web page to another point on the same Web page. Many Web pages have directories or "tables of contents" at the beginning of the page, allowing you to decide which part of the page you would like to view and then just click on the link to jump to that section of the page or document.

- **Links to places other HTML documents.** These links are quite similar to links to places in the same document, except you can jump to certain sections on other pages. If you've clicked on a hypertext link and then jumped to some point halfway down another Web page, then you've used this type of link.

You use the A (Anchor) tag to anchor one or both ends of a hypertext link. The first kind of link, where you link to another Web page or data object, requires only one anchor. The second and third kinds of links, where you link to another place in the same or another Web page, however, require both ends of the link—that is, both a "launch pad" and a "landing spot." This "other end" of a hypertext link, where you link a specific place in the same or another Web page often also is called a *target* anchor.

NOTE

You actually can include a "target" anchor inside a Gopher text file, which is just a plain text file, and then have a hypertext link jump to that specific place in that file, even though it isn't an HTML file. You don't see this often, but you can do it.

Anatomy of the A (Anchor) Tag

Think of a hypertext link as being composed of three elements: 1) start and end tags that enclose the whole link, 2) the link target, and 3) the link text. Figure 2-25 illustrates the three parts of a hypertext link.

Figure 2-25.
A hypertext link has three parts: the start and end tags, the link target, and the link text.

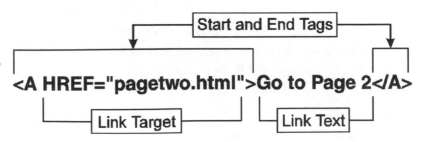

Figure 2-25 uses the HREF (Hypertext Reference) attribute to specify the URL or address of the "object" of the link, which here is simply another Web page. Note that the full address (URL) is not given, just the file name. This means that the Web page being linked to (the "linkee," if you will) is in the same directory as the Web page from which the link is being made (the "linker," if you will). If you want to form a link to a Web page on another server, however, you must include the full URL (not just "webpage.html," but "http://www.somewhere.com/somepage.html," or something like that).

When using the A (Anchor) tag, you must include the HREF attribute or the NAME attribute. You use the NAME attribute, however, only when you want to create a target link. So, linking to another Web page or data object requires only that you use one A (Anchor) tag with the HREF attribute, while linking to another place in the same or another Web page requires that you use two A (Anchor) tags, the first with the HREF attribute and the second with the NAME attribute.

If you find this confusing, don't worry—it is confusing. The next sections engage you with some hands-on examples of creating the three kinds of links and using both the HREF and NAME attributes. Learning by doing should go a long way toward dissipating your confusion.

Rather than get too involved in the differences between the HREF and the NAME attributes, for instance, which you are likely to find confusing, you should jump immediately into some hands-on examples of how to create the different kinds of links. After you actually get your hands dirty, it should all become much clearer.

Linking to a File or Data Object

You can form an HTML link to anything on the Web that has an address, or URL. You can jump to Australia, or simply to a file residing in your own directory on your own server. To create a hypertext link that jumps to a file that isn't in your own directory, include the whole URL of the file to which you want to jump. For instance:

```
<P>Click here to jump to <A
HREF="http://www.some.com/where.html">somewhere else</A>.
```

If a "www.some.com" actually existed somewhere with a file in its root directory called "where.html," you could link to it simply by putting the above A tag in your own HTML file. Substitute an actual URL for the dummy URL here if you want to actually link to somewhere. Do that now by creating a hypertext link that jumps to a real document on an actual Web site:

```
<P>You can find out more about the WWW at the home page of the <A
HREF="http://www.w3.org/pub/WWW/">W3 Consortium</A>.
```

Figure 2-26 shows how this appears in Netscape Navigator.

Figure 2-26.

This is a hypertext link to the home page of the W3 Consortium.

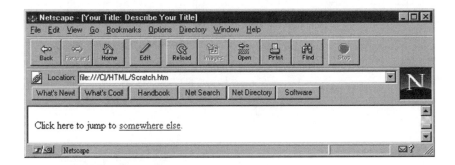

When you click on the hypertext link shown in Figure 2-26, a hypertext "jump" takes you to the target address shown in Figure 2-27. (Note: You must actually go online if you want to check this out on your browser.)

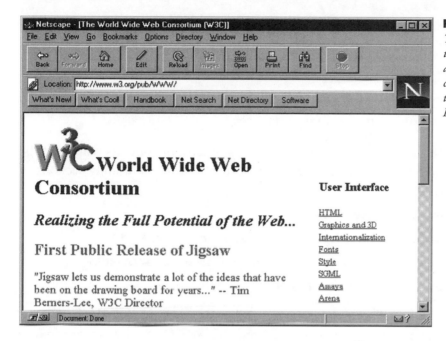

Figure 2-27.

The home page of the W3 Consortium appears when you click on the hyper-text link shown in Figure 2-22.

Linking to Non-WWW Files

You can link to files other than just HTML files. Generally, your browser should be able to directly display any ASCII text file, whether on a Web or a Gopher server, for instance, and should also be able to display GIF or JPEG graphics. Other kinds of files may require viewers or players, such as sound, animation, or video files. One of the newest things, however, is support for streaming audio and animation with RealAudio or Shockwave, which allows audio and animation clips to be *streamed* (played while being downloaded) rather than downloaded first and then played. (For pointers on where to find information on RealAudio and Shockwave, see Appendix A.)

Linking to a Place in the Same HTML File

To link to another place in the same HTML file requires both an HREF anchor and a NAME anchor. An HREF anchor that links to a NAME anchor has a special form:

```
<A HREF="#anchorname">anchortext</A>
```

Notice the # sign. In an HREF anchor, the # sign is the only thing that identifies the HREF attribute as the name of a NAME anchor rather than an address or file name. (The # sign combined with the following anchorname sometimes also is called a *fragment identifier*.)

Some of the more common uses for linking HREF and NAME anchors on the same page might be as

- a directory or table of contents that links to the major headings of a page.

- cross references between different points in the text.

- links to footnotes at the bottom of the page.

The following is an example of creating a directory or table of contents that might be displayed at the top of a Web page and that will then link to subheading sections in the same document:

```
<H2>Using Hypertext Links</H2>

<P><A HREF="#page">Linking to Another Page or File</A><BR>

<A HREF="#locat">Linking to a Place on the Same Page</A><BR>

<A HREF="#locpg">Linking to a Place on Another Page</A>

<H3><A NAME="page">Linking to Another Page or File</A></H2>

<P>You can form a link with anything on the Web that has an address,
or URL...

<H3><A NAME="locat">Linking to a Place on the Same Page</A></H2>

<P>You can form a link with another place on the same page by link-
ing an HREF and a NAME anchor...

<H3><A NAME="locpg">Linking to a Place on Another Page</A></H2>

<P>You can not only link to another HTML file, but to a place in
that file...
```

Figure 2-28 shows how the above HTML looks in Netscape Navigator.

Linking to a Place in Another HTML File

You not only can make a hypertext link with another HTML file, but also with a place in that HTML file, as long as you mark it with a NAME anchor. The form for an HREF anchor that links to a place in another HTML file is:

```
<A HREF="address#anchorname">anchortext</A>
```

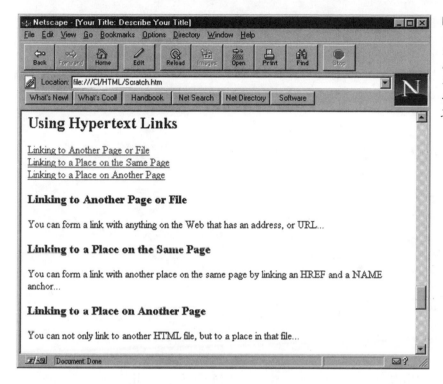

Figure 2-28.

You can create a menu (or directory) of hypertext links that will jump to subheadings within your document.

This actually combines the forms for linking to another page and linking to a place on a page. First, the link is made to the address, which is either a URL or a file name of an HTML file, and then following the # sign, the link is made to the place in that file that is marked by the Name anchor corresponding to the anchorname. So, now go ahead and create a hypertext link that jumps to a place in another (hypothetical) HTML file:

```
<P>Go to <A HREF="links.htm#parttwo">Part Two</A> of the <A
HREF="links.htm">How to Use Links</A> web page.
```

The preceding HTML includes links both to "Part Two" of the "How to Use Links" Web page and to the whole "How to Use Links" Web page. The only difference between linking to a location in a Web page and simply linking directly to that Web page is that you add "#parttwo" to the HREF string value. Figure 2-29 shows how these two links look in a Web browser.

Figure 2-29.

The first link jumps to a place in the "How to Use Links" Web page, while the second link just jumps to the Web page itself.

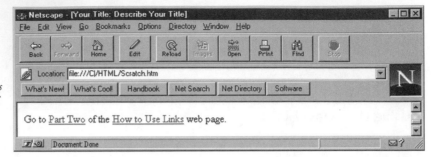

NOTE

As noted earlier, HTML files that you create and save on your own hard drive have an .HTM file extension, whereas other examples that use an .HTML file extension indicate an HTML file that is on the Web or hypothetically might be. (Actually, .HTM pages can be up on the Web too, on a Windows NT server, for instance, or on a Unix server that recognizes the .HTM extension in addition to the .HTML extension.)

To actually use this link, you must create a second HTML file, "links.htm," with the heading for Part Two marked with a NAME anchor, as shown here:

```
<H2><A NAME="parttwo">Part Two</A></H2>
```

When you activate the first link in the other Web page, you jump first to LINKS.HTM and then to the place in that Web page where the preceding target anchor has been placed.

Creating Link Lists

So far, the discussion has focused on creating lists and creating links, but hasn't explained creating link lists. A *link list* is just what it sounds like—a list of hypertext links, usually bulleted but sometimes numbered. Because link lists are so ubiquitous, everybody should know how to create them. To create a simple link list, all you need to do is combine an unordered list and some hypertext links.

Creating a Simple Link List

In the simplest form of a link list, the text of each link comprises the entire list item. Often the link text simply is the title of a Web page being linked, although sometimes a little editing is necessary to make it more informative. No other explanatory or descriptive text is included (outside the link, but on the list item line). The following example sets up a simple list of actual yo-yo links using the titles of the linked Web pages as the link text:

```
<H2>Yo Yo Links</H2>

<UL>

<LI><A HREF="http://www.li.net/%7Eautorent/yo-yo.htm">Jon's Yo-Yo
Kingdom</A>

<LI><A HREF="http://pages.nyu.edu/%7Etqm3413/yoyo/index.htm">

Tomer's Page of Exotic Yo-Yo</A>

<LI><A HREF="http://www.socool.com/socool/yo-yo.html">Just Say YO-
YO</A>

<LI><A HREF="http://www.pd.net/yoyo/">American Yo-Yo Association</A>

<LI><A HREF="http://www.socool.com/socool/yo_hist.html">The History
of the Yo-Yo</A>

</UL>
```

NOTE

When you enter Web addresses (URLs), you should always type them exactly as they appear. Unix commands are case-sensitive and most Web servers run Unix.

Figures 2-30 shows how the preceding link list example appears in Netscape Navigator.

Figure 2-30.

In a simple link list, the link text and the link items are one and the same.

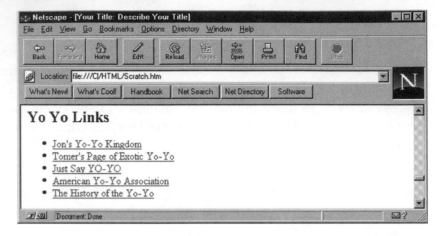

Creating a Link List with Descriptions

A simple list of links can prove somewhat empty. Even if you edit the link text for the links rather than simply use the Web pages' titles as is, the list still may not provide enough information to be truly useful. However, just cramming more information into the link text itself doesn't do either, because you want it to be concise and succinct, so that the reader can scan at a glance. The solution is to add explanatory text outside of the link text. In the list of links you just typed, add some explanatory text for each link:

```
<H2>Yo Yo Links</H2>

<UL>

<LI><A HREF="http://www.li.net/%7Eautorent/yo-yo.htm">Jon's Yo-Yo
Kingdom</A> Claims to have the largest Yo-Yo link list on the Web.

<LI><A HREF="http://pages.nyu.edu/%7Etqm3413/yoyo/index.htm">Tomer's
Page of Exotic Yo-Yo</A> Dedicated to the "little-known, original,
unusual, difficult, or otherwise interesting tricks."

<LI><A HREF="http://www.socool.com/socool/yo-yo.html">Just Say YO-
YO</A> Features the Web's first Yo-Yo animation.

<LI><A HREF="http://www.pd.net/yoyo/">American Yo-Yo Association</A>
Read past issues of the AYYA Newsletter.

<LI><A HREF="http://www.socool.com/socool/yo_hist.html">The History
of the Yo-Yo</A> All you want to know about Yo-Yo history.

</UL>
```

Figure 2-31 shows the newly expanded list.

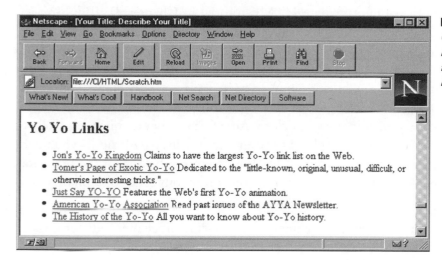

Other Ways To Create Link Lists

The preceding examples illustrate the most simple and direct ways to create link lists. A variation you might want to try on this is to create a glossary link list in which the links are inserted in the DT tags, with the descriptions inserted in the DD tags. You also might want to tag the definition terms with a heading tag to display the links more prominently. Chapter 3 discusses how to create icon link lists using colorful, 3-D graphic bullet images.

Using Inline Images

The IMG (Image) tag allows you to display inline images on your Web page. The term *inline* here simply means that an image is inserted at a particular location, "in a line," if you will, within a Web page.

The most commonly used image format for inline images is the GIF format. All current graphic Web browsers should be able to display GIF images as inline images. On the other hand, not all current graphical Web browsers support the JPEG graphic format, which provides file compression and more colors than GIF (up to 6.2 million possible colors versus 256 possible colors), although Netscape Navigator, which introduced this feature, NCSA Mosaic, and Internet Explorer all do.

More often than not, just sticking with using GIF images is your best option. You also can set up GIFs as interlaced, transparent, or both (these features of GIF images are explored in the optional intermediate HTML tutorial in Chapter 3). JPEG images, however, are gaining wide support from current Web browsers, so the level of available support among Web browsers is becoming less and less of a reason to not use JPEG images. A rule of thumb you should follow is to use JPEG images only when you want to include a photographic image in your Web page. This not only allows you to display many more colors, but to do so while using a much smaller file. When you want to include a non-photographic image, stick to using GIFs—they're much less likely to require more than 256 colors to display effectively and usually, paradoxically you might think, are smaller than a corresponding JPEG file (the reason being that the JPEG format's compression algorithms are effective only on continuous tone color photographic images).

The IMG (Image) tag is an empty, or stand-alone, document element. Its form is:

```
<IMG SRC="imagefile">
```

The SRC (Source) attribute is a required attribute that identifies the full or partial address (URL) or just the name of the file to display. Now, insert an inline graphic into your HTML file:

```
<P>The inline graphic, SAMPLE.GIF, is displayed here:</P>
<IMG SRC="sample.gif">
```

Notice the inclusion of the </P> end tag. The IMG tag doesn't form a new block element here and would appear on the same line as the text that precedes it unless you added it (the </P> end tag) here. Because you want the image to appear beneath the line of text, you use the end tag. You also could produce the same effect by preceding the IMG tag with a <P> start tag.

> **NOTE**
>
> *If the graphics file you want to display as an inline graphic resides in the same directory as its HTML file, you only need to refer to the name of the graphics file, "sample.gif," for instance, rather than its whole address.*
>
> *If you copied the sample graphic files from the CD-ROM to C:\HTML, then you can include them in any local Web pages you create that are stored in the same directory, simply by including their file names.*

Figure 2-32 shows SAMPLE.GIF as an inline image in Netscape Navigator.

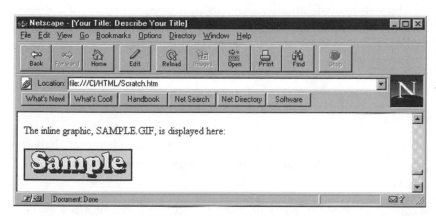

Figure 2-32.
All graphical Web browsers can display GIF format inline graphics files.

CAUTION

You actually can link to a graphic file anywhere on the Web and display it on your own Web page by using the IMG (Image) tag. To do this, for instance, you might do something like this:

```
<IMG SRC="http://www.anywhere.com/some.gif">
```

Doing so, however, generally is frowned upon on the Web. Not only might you be violating somebody's copyright, you most certainly would be generating traffic on their server simply so you can display a particular inline image on your Web page. Also, they can tell you are doing it, and trace it back to you. It may not be against the law, but they could complain to whoever is running your server and maybe get you kicked off your server, or they could at least flame you. Bottom line: it's not the way to make friends on the Web.

It's perfectly okay to link to others' Web pages, though. That's how you make friends on the Web. Just don't claim their Web stuff as your own. And if they give you permission to use any of their graphics, you can download them to your server, then include them on your own Web page. But don't just willy-nilly go around downloading and using other people's graphics—they may be copyrighted. Plenty of repositories of public domain graphics exist on the Web. See Appendix A for references to public domain graphics on the Web.

Using the ALT Attribute

You use the ALT attribute to provide an alternative to an image in the case of someone using a text-only browser such as Lynx or using a graphical browser with images turned off. Most browsers offer the capability of turning off the display of images to help pages load faster.

Here's an example of how to use the ALT attribute with your IMG tags:

```
<IMG SRC="sample.gif" ALT="">
```

The above example viewed in Lynx would show absolutely nothing, rather than the usual [Image]. On a Web browser that has image loading turned off, the ALT="" attribute value has no effect.

To have a message replace [Image] in Lynx or display along with the dummy graphic in a graphical browser with the graphics turned off, enter the following:

```
<IMG SRC="sample.gif" ALT="A sample graphic">
```

The above example viewed in Lynx displays the message, A sample graphic rather than just [Image]. For a graphical Web browser with image loading turned off, the message A sample graphic would appear alongside the dummy image appears in place of the actual one, as shown in Figure 2-33.

NOTE

Some people argue that you should use the ALT attribute, with a text string attribute value (not just blank as with ""), with all inline images. That seems a bit excessive to me. If an image is decorative and serves no informational purpose, then just use the ALT attribute with a blank attribute value (ALT=""). That way, you don't clutter up a Web page in a text-only browser, such as Lynx, with [Images] references.

If your graphic, however, does have informational import (such as a banner graphic that performs the function of a level-one heading, and where the level-one heading is left out, so the "title," if you will, of the page appears only in the graphic), then by all means always include an ALT attribute text string (ALT="Georgy-Porgy's Home Page" or ALT="Diagram of the X-27P Circuit Board," or something like that) so that somebody using a text-only browser or a graphical Web browser with graphics turned off can still know what is going on.

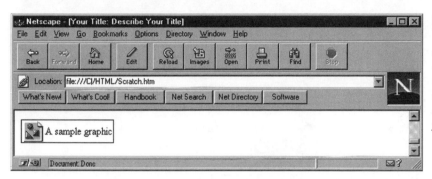

Figure 2-33.
You can use the ALT attribute with an image to include a message that appears even if graphics loading is turned off in your browser.

Using the ALIGN Attribute in Inline Graphics

The ALIGN attribute allows you to position an inline image relative to the line of text that it is on. All current graphical Web browsers should recognize these values: top, middle, and bottom. The following examples use the TOP.GIF, MIDDLE.GIF, and BOTTOM.GIF sample files from \SAMPLE\IMAGES on the CD-ROM disk. Just copy them from the CD-ROM disk to C:\HTML.

Insert an inline graphic using the "top" ALIGN value:

```
<P>The image on this line <IMG ALIGN="top" SRC="top.gif"> is top-
aligned.
```

Here's an example of using the "middle" ALIGN value:

```
<P>The image on this line <IMG ALIGN="middle" SRC="middle.gif"> is
middle-aligned.
```

Insert an inline graphic using the "bottom" ALIGN value:

```
<P>The image on this line <IMG ALIGN="bottom" SRC="bottom.gif"> is
bottom-aligned.
```

Figure 2-34 shows the above examples as they appear in Netscape Navigator.

Figure 2-34.
Inline images can be aligned relative to the baseline of the line they are on.

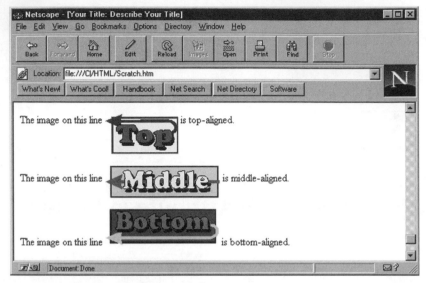

Using Relative or Partial URLs

When creating a hypertext link or inserting an inline image, you don't always need to specify a full, or absolute, URL or Web address. If a Web page or other file to which you are linking or a graphic file you are inserting into your Web page is 1) in the same directory, 2) in the same directory structure, or 3) on the same server (in the same domain), then you can leave off those parts of the URL that are common to both. A URL that provides only those parts of a Web address that are not common to both the linking and the linked file thus often is called a *partial URL.* One of the advantages of using this type of URL, apart from its simply being shorter, is that you can move a Web page and its locally linked files from one directory to another, and even from one server to another, without having to redo the links.

NOTE

Actually, in this tutorial you already have used some partial, or relative, URLs. For instance, <IMG SRC="sample.gif"> uses a partial URL (the full, or absolute URL would be "file:///C\/html/sample.gif," which is what the full URL for a "local" file on your own hard drive looks like. If you used the full URL here, you wouldn't be able to put your Web page, along with any included inline images, up onto the Web *without having to redo all your image links, which you don't want to have to do. What you want to be able to do is create and test out your Web pages on your own computer and then be able to FTP them, along with any locally linked files or images, up to your Web site (when you get one) without having to redo any of the links.*

Linking to a File That Is in a Subdirectory of the Linking Page's Directory

If C:\HTML is the directory where you currently store your HTML files, you might want to store your graphic files in C:\HTML\IMAGES. You could then use a relative or partial URL (rather than an absolute or full URL) to display the graphic, like this:

```
<IMG SRC="images/sample.gif">
```

If you plan to create a Web site that uses multiple subpages, you might want to store your subpages in separate directory from your home page. For example, if your home page is in the \HTML directory, and the subpage (SUBPAGE.HTM) to which you want to link is in the \PAGE\SUBPAGES directory, then a hypertext link between the two might look like this:

```
<A HREF="subpages/subpage.htm">
```

The two examples above might then indicate a directory structure something like this:

```
\HTML-|-\IMAGES
      |
      |-\SUBPAGES
```

Linking to a File in a Subdirectory of a Directory of Which Your HTML File Is a Subdirectory

Suppose your HTML files are stored in /PUB/HTML, but your graphic files are stored in /PUB/IMAGES. To display an inline image, FLOWER.GIF, stored in /PUB/IMAGES, you would use this partial URL in your Web page:

```
<IMG SRC="../images/sample.gif">
```

Or, suppose you want to insert a hypertext link in the same Web page mentioned above, /PUB/HTML, to another Web page, PRICES.HTM, stored in a parallel directory, /PUB/SALES. For this, the hypertext link that would link the two would look like this:

```
<A HREF="../sales/prices.htm">
```

The two examples above might then indicate a directory structure something like this:

```
\PUB-|-\HTML
    |
    |-\IMAGES
    |
    |-\SALES
```

Using Horizontal Rules

The HR (Horizontal Rule) tag is a stand-alone, or empty, document element that allows you to add horizontal rules to your Web pages. Go ahead now and set up a text paragraph followed by an HR tag:

```
<P>A horizontal rule is displayed below this line.
<HR>
```

Netscape Navigator, NCSA Mosaic, and Internet Explorer all display a horizontal rule as a shaded line. (If you set the default background is set to white, however, the shading in NCSA Mosaic and Internet Explorer, which is white, disappears.) Figure 2-35 shows a horizontal rule displayed in Netscape Navigator.

NOTE

You can use certain additional attribute values to alter the appearance of horizontal rules, for instance, to alter the width or height of a rule, its alignment, or whether it's shaded or unshaded.

You probably also have noticed on the Web horizontal rules that are in different colors or multiple colors, have shadows or 3-D effects, and so on. These aren't actually horizontal rules; they're graphic files inserted into a Web page as inline graphics.

The optional intermediate HTML tutorial covers both how to assign attribute values to HR tags and how to include multicolor graphic lines in your Web pages.

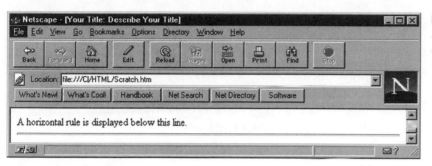

Figure 2-35.
Netscape Navigator displays a horizontal rule as a shaded line.

Signing Your Work

You generally use the ADDRESS tag to define a signature block for your Web page. It might contain your name, title, organizational or business affiliation, as well as information on how to contact you. A horizontal rule usually separates an address from the rest of a Web page.

Following the HR tag you created in the last example, type some address text separated into individual lines by BR tags:

```
<HR>
<ADDRESS>
Ricardo De Caro<BR>
Fantastic Creations, Inc.<BR>
(800) 569-8432<BR>
</ADDRESS>
```

Although Netscape Navigator and NCSA Mosaic both italicize Address text, they don't do anything else to distinguish Address text from any other block of text. Internet Explorer doesn't do anything at all to distinguish Address text from any other block of text. Therefore, feel free to add any additional text formatting codes. For example, you can bracket your address text with an I (Italic) tag, as shown here:

```
<HR>
<ADDRESS>
<I>
Ricardo De Caro<BR>
Fantastic Creations, Inc.<BR>
(800) 569-8432<BR>
</I>
</ADDRESS>
```

> **NOTE**
>
> *Feel free to substitute your own name, company name, phone number, or whatever.*

Although this doesn't have any effect in Navigator or NCSA Mosaic, it does ensure that your Address block is also italicized in Internet Explorer.

Adding a Mailto: Link to Your Address

You also can add a mailto: link, which is a hypertext link to your e-mail address. When a user clicks on a mailto: link, the browser pops up a form that allows the reader to send a message to the e-mail address in the link. See Figure 2-36 for an example of a mailto: pop-up window in Netscape Navigator.

Figure 2-36.
When you click on a mailto: link, you can send an e-mail message to the address included in the link.

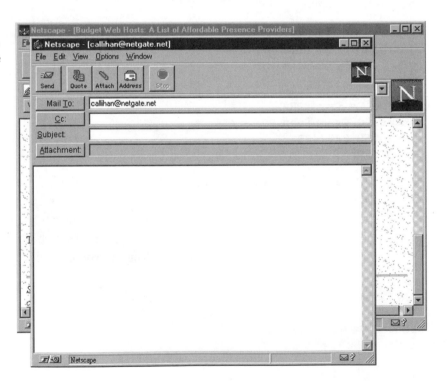

Now, there are some gotchas here. First, not all browsers support mailto: links. Second, even if your browser does support mailto: links, it has to be configured properly. So, no matter which way you cut it, you are going to have viewers who can't use a mailto: link.

Does that mean you should avoid mailto: links? Absolutely not! The solution is simply to make sure that your full e-mail address is the "link text" for your mailto: link. This means you actually enter your e-mail address twice for a mailto: link, as shown in the following example. That way, if someone can't use your mailto: link, they can always click and drag to copy your e-mail address or just write it down, then send you a message using their regular e-mail client.

```
<HR>
<ADDRESS>
<I>
Ricardo De Caro<BR>
Fantastic Creations, Inc.<BR>
(800) 569-8432<BR>
<A HREF="mailto:rdc@fantas.com">rdc@fantas.com</A><BR>
</I>
</ADDRESS>
```

NOTE
Feel free to substitute your own e-mail address below for "rdc@fantas.com."

Adding Your URL to Your Address

If your home page isn't the current page, you also can include a hypertext link to it. Since you haven't yet created any Web pages yet, you don't have a home page yet. After you do create your first Web page, however, you undoubtedly will want to create others. Your home page then might serve as an index to the rest of your pages, for instance, or it might just be your personal page, with biographical data just about you.

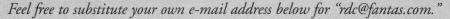

You could then include that URL in the Address block of each of your other Web pages, as follows:

```
<HR>
<ADDRESS>
<I>
Ricardo De Caro<BR>
Fantastic Creations, Inc.<BR>
(800) 569-8432<BR>
E-Mail: <A HREF="mailto:rdc@fantas.com">rdc@fantas.
com</A><BR>
URL: <A HREF="http://www.fantas.com">http://www.fantas.
com</A>
</I>
</ADDRESS>
```

Figure 2-37 shows how the final Address section appears in Internet Explorer.

Figure 2-37.
Internet Explorer italicizes Address text only if you add the I (Italic) tag.

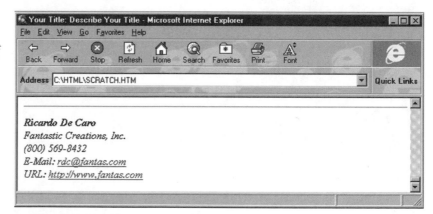

Saving Your Work

Save the HTML file you just created. You can use it later as a reference. If you want, give it a new name, such as SAMPLE.HTM. That way, more than one person can do the tutorial.

Conclusion

You should now have a "working" knowledge of at least basic HTML. Don't worry if you don't remember or fully understand everything that you've done in this tutorial; the best way to learn is simply by doing. The more you do, the more you learn. You've also saved your scratch pad file as SAMPLE.HTM. Feel free to load it into your text editor and view it in your Web browser to refamiliarize yourself with how a particular tag works.

If you've managed to finish the basic HTML tutorial this morning, take a break, have some lunch, then go ahead and do the Intermediate HTML Tutorial scheduled for this afternoon. The intermediate HTML tutorial is optional, however. If doing the basic HTML tutorial has stretched into the afternoon for you, even taken the entire day, or you just feel you have absorbed enough and are starting to suffer from information overload, that's fine. The basic HTML tutorial has covered everything you need to know to be able to plan and create your first Web page. You can always come back later to do the intermediate HTML tutorial after you create your first Web page.

Although the planning session for creating your first Web page is scheduled for tomorrow morning, if you have the time and the energy, feel free to get a head start on it tonight. That will give you more time to actually create your Web page tomorrow. Alternatively, you can just skip the intermediate HTML tutorial for now and go straight to the planning session.

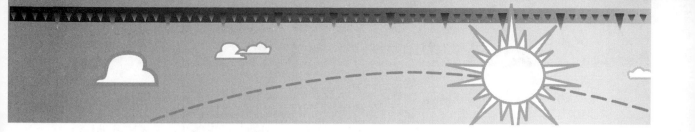

Saturday Afternoon:
An Intermediate HTML Tutorial

By now, you've finished the basic HTML tutorial in the preceding chapter. Although it concentrated on basic HTML, it covered everything you need to know to create a wide range of different types of Web pages. The Saturday session is divided into two parts:

- Getting Started
- The Intermediate HTML Tutorial

The Getting Started section is relatively short, simply guiding you in a few simple things necessary to get you up and running with the tutorial.

The intermediate HTML tutorial covers:

- Some HTML 2.0 features not covered in this morning's tutorial (such as creating banner graphics, image links, and icon bullet lists)
- Many of the newly specified HTML 3.2 tags (formerly "Netscape extensions," by and large), and some Netscape extensions that have not been incorporated into HTML 3.2

This intermediate HTML tutorial is optional. You need not complete this tutorial, nor do any of it, for that matter, to be able to plan and create your first Web page tomorrow. So feel free to do all, part, or none of this tutorial. You don't need to push yourself to get *everything* done. You can always come back and do the intermediate HTML after you plan and create your first Web page.

This chapter covers the Microsoft extensions to HTML, but doesn't deal with them in depth. Appendix A provides pointers to more information on using Microsoft's extensions. Also, this chapter doesn't cover the more advanced features of HTML 3.2, such as using scripts or applets, embedding objects, and using stylesheets. This tutorial also omits treating tables, which is not to say that they're all that advanced, but simply the time space or time here is insufficient to do them justice. Appendix D, however, covers the basics of creating and using tables. This intermediate HTML tutorial also doesn't include any treatment of creating frames, which is a relatively advanced Netscape extension that has not been incorporated into HTML 3.2. (See Chapter 1 if you're wondering about the various versions and extensions of HTML.) This tutorial focuses on intermediate HTML as a whole—on its functional categories—character rendering, document divisions, lists, images, and special effects.

> ## CAUTION
>
> *Since this tutorial focuses on HTML 3.2, you should use an HTML 3.2 compliant Web browser as your off-line browser for checking the results of your work. If you are using Windows 3.1, you should use Netscape Navigator. If you are using Windows 95, use Netscape Navigator or Internet Explorer Version 3.0 (although there are still a couple HTML 3.2 features that Internet Explorer 3.0 doesn't support). Don't use NCSA Mosaic or Internet Explorer 2.0 for this tutorial. NCSA Mosaic supports only a few HTML 3.2 features. Internet Explorer 2.0 for Windows 3.1 supports many more HTML 3.2 features, but doesn't support a number of the tags this tutorial covers.*

Getting Started

> ## NOTE
>
> *For the best results, do this tutorial using Windows set to a screen resolution of 640 × 480 pixels.*

In the following sections, you run your text editor, load the starting template you saved in the last chapter, and then save the "scratch" file you create in this tutorial.

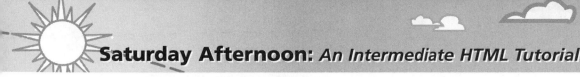
Run Your Text Editor

Run the text editor you use to create your HTML files. As in the basic HTML tutorial, you should consider using Windows Notepad, although a Notepad-like HTML editor such as HTML Notepad or Gomer would also work just fine.

Load the starting template you saved this morning, C:\HTML\START.HTM. It should look like the following listing. (If you didn't save the template, just retype it now.)

```
<HTML>
<HEAD>
<TITLE>Your Title: Describe Your Title</TITLE></HEAD>
<BODY>
</BODY>
</HTML>
```

NOTE

If you substituted a Title element of your own for "Your Title: Describe Your Title," don't worry if your version of START.HTM differs in that regard. Otherwise, however, your START.HTM should look the same.

Save Your Scratch File

Now, resave your "scratch" file as, say, SCRATCH2.HTM (you can name it whatever you want to name it, however). It will serve as your working file for doing the intermediate HTML tutorial. As the file name above suggests, this tutorial adheres to the "scratch pad" paradigm introduced in the basic HTML tutorial. As you do the tutorial, don't erase what you do or open separate files as you cover different areas. Just move down through the file, typing in what you are prompted to enter.

Run Your Browser

As with the basic HTML tutorial, you should run your browser, preferably offline, and then hop back and forth between your text editor and your browser to check your results. The screen illustrations in this tutorial serve as prompts for points at which you might want to hop over and check your results in your browser. This has a two-fold purpose: 1) to check for errors that show up only if you actually check your work in a browser, and 2) to see how something actually displays in the browser you use.

Browser Compatibility

You are informed as you go along of how Netscape Navigator, Microsoft Internet Explorer, and NCSA Mosaic treat different tags, as well as how you can expect most browsers to treat (or not treat) different tags. Remember, even though this tutorial concentrates largely on HTML 3.2 and encourages you to use an HTML 3.2 compliant Web browser, you do want to try to ensure that your use of these tags doesn't unnecessarily "bomb" other less compliant Web browsers. Therefore, despite not advocating that you use NCSA Mosaic, this tutorial still lets you know when any of these features have a particularly deleterious effect on NCSA Mosaic.

The Sample Graphics

If you did the basic HTML tutorial this morning, you should already have copied all the sample graphics that you need for this tutorial from the CD-ROM to your HTML working directory (C:\HTML) or downloaded them from this book's Web site. If you notice when checking your work that the graphics don't display in your browser even with graphics turned on, then you know that the sample graphics haven't been copied to C:\HTML.

The Intermediate HTML Tutorial

This tutorial is organized according in functional categories, as follows:

- Working with text
- Working with images
- Working with lists
- Creating icon link lists
- Creating special effects

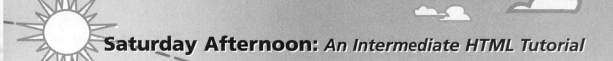

Working with Text

This section covers some additional things that you can do when working with text, including using additional HTML 3.2 text highlighting tags and right- or center-aligning paragraphs, headings, and other document sections.

HTML 3.2 Text Highlighting Tags

HTML 3.2 recognizes a number of additional character rendering tags, including the SUP (Superscript), SUB (Subscript), U (Underline), and STRIKE (Strikethrough) tags.

SUP, SUB, and U were all proposed HTML 3.0 tags that have been implemented widely in current browsers. The STRIKE tag was a proposed HTML 2.0 tag that never made it to the final cut, but nonetheless gained wide acceptance from browsers anyway. An S tag for strikethrough was proposed for HTML 3.0, but evidently has been dropped in favor of STRIKE.

The SUP and SUB tags are highly useful tags that you should use wherever you need superscripts or subscripts. The STRIKE command is more limited to using the Web in workgroup document preparation processes, rather than for displaying final renditions. All three of the major Web browsers support the SUP, SUB, and STRIKE tags.

The U tag, although supported by NCSA Mosaic and Internet Explorer, is not supported by Navigator. Netscape's reasoning is that underlined text too closely resembles the display of hypertext links, which also are underlined in Navigator. Since, in the browser market anyway, Netscape is the 800-pound gorilla, you probably are best off not using the U tag, or at least not until Netscape supports it. But now it's now officially part of HTML 3.2, so that day may not be far off.

If you want to check out how these tags look in your browser, enter the following, and then hop over to your browser and take a look:

```
<P>This is regular text. <SUP>Use SUP for superscripts.</SUP> This is
regular text. <SUB>Use SUB for subscripts.</SUB> This is regular
text. <U>Use U for underlining.</U> This is regular text. <STRIKE>Use
STRIKE for strikethrough.</STRIKE>
```

Figure 3-1 shows how this appears in Internet Explorer.

Figure 3-1.

Internet Explorer, as well as NCSA Mosaic, supports all of the HTML 3.2 character rendering tags. Netscape Navigator, however, does not support the U (Underline) tag.

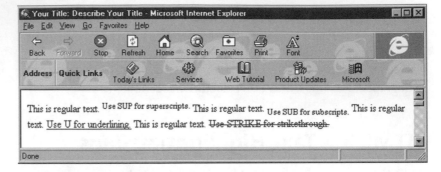

TIP

Many browsers still don't display superscripts or subscripts, such as text-only browsers like Lynx. To account for those browsers but still use superscripts and subscripts, enclose superscripts or subscripts within parentheses to set them apart from preceding or following text in browsers that can't display them. For instance, to include a superscripted trademark symbol, you might type:

```
Xerox<SUP>(TM)</SUP>
```

That way, it appears in Lynx as "Xerox(TM)" rather than as "XeroxTM."

Text Alignment

You can align paragraphs, headings, or other document divisions in a number of ways in HTML 3.2. You can use the ALIGN attribute with paragraphs or headings to center-align, right-align, or left-align these elements. A new HTML 3.2 element, the DIV tag, also can use the ALIGN attribute. Additionally, you can use the CENTER command to center-align any of the above, plus many other document elements. The following sections look at each of these individually.

Using the ALIGN Attribute in Headings and Paragraphs

In HTML 3.2, you can use the ALIGN attribute to center-align or right-align headings and paragraphs by using an attribute value of either "center" or "right" ("left" is the default). For instance, to center-align a level-two heading, you would tag your heading like this:

```
<H2 ALIGN="center">Your Heading Here</H2>
```

You would right-align a level-two heading like this:

```
<H2 ALIGN="right">Your Heading Here</H2>
```

You would center-align or right-align paragraph text in exactly the same way as with headings. For instance, to center-align a text paragraph, you would tag your paragraph like this:

```
<P ALIGN="center">Your paragraph text here.
```

You would right-align a text paragraph like this:

```
<P ALIGN="right">Your paragraph text here.
```

To see what this looks like in your browser, enter the following, save your file and hop over to your browser to check it out:

```
<H3 ALIGN="right">This is a Right-Aligned Level-Three Heading</H3>

<P ALIGN="right">This is a right-aligned text paragraph. This is a
right-aligned text paragraph. This is a right-aligned text paragraph.
This is a right-aligned text paragraph.

<H3 ALIGN="center">This is a Center-Aligned Level-Three Heading.</H3>

<P ALIGN="center">This is a center-aligned text paragraph. This is a
center-aligned text paragraph. This is a center-aligned text para-
graph. This is a center-aligned text paragraph.
```

Figure 3-2 shows how this appears in Netscape Navigator.

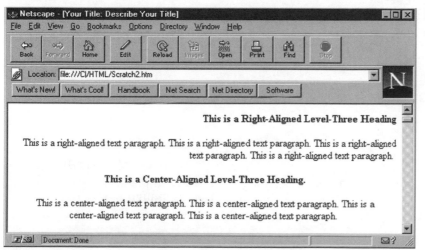

Figure 3-2.

Most current Web browsers can display right-aligned and center-aligned headings and paragraphs.

NOTE

In Figure 3-2, the end of the right-aligned paragraph doesn't quite line up flush with the right margin. Unfortunately, this doesn't happen just in Navigator, but also in Internet Explorer and NCSA Mosaic.

Aligning Document Divisions Using the DIV Tag

The DIV tag defines a "division" within a document. Within it you can nest and align headings, paragraphs, unordered and ordered lists, definition lists, preformatted text, address blocks, tables, and even images. Currently, the only use of the DIV tag is to apply left-, right-, and center-alignment to other elements nested within it. When stylesheets become available, this tag will become even more useful, allowing users to apply different formatting or display characteristics to different sections of a document, such as a table of contents, an index, or a glossary.

The DIV (Division) tag is an HTML 3.2 element that was previously an HTML 3.0 proposed tag. Netscape Navigator and Internet Explorer both support its use, but NCSA Mosaic does not. This tag allows you to "block" tag a whole section (a "division") of a document as center- or right-aligned.

Enter the following for an example of using the DIV tag to apply center-alignment to a document division that includes a level-two heading, a paragraph, and a bullet list:

```
<DIV ALIGN="center">
<H2>Level-Two Heading</H2>
<P>This paragraph, and the level-two heading above it, is centered
using the DIV tag's ALIGN attribute.
<UL>
<LI>First list item.
<LI>Second list item.
</UL>
</DIV>
```

Figure 3-3 shows how this appears in Internet Explorer.

The DIV tag also works well for aligning images. For an example of using the DIV tag to align inline images, see "Working with Images" later in this session.

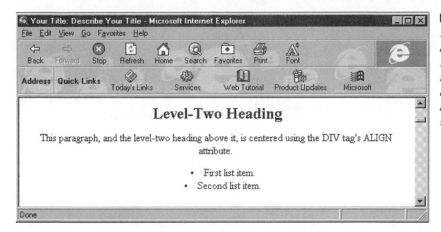

Figure 3-3.
*Internet Explorer,
as well as Netscape
Navigator, allows you
to use the DIV tag to
center-align or right-
align a division
within a document.*

Centering Text and Other Elements Using the CENTER Tag

The CENTER tag is a Netscape extension that has been included in HTML 3.2, where it now represents a shortcut for <DIV ALIGN="center">. Anything that you can nest inside a DIV element you also can nest in a CENTER element. All three major browsers support use of the CENTER tag.

For an example of using the CENTER element to center-align text and other document elements, edit the text you just entered as an example of using the DIV tag, replacing <DIV ALIGN="center"> and </DIV> with <CENTER> and <CENTER>, like this:

```
<CENTER>
<H2>Level-Two Heading</H2>
<P>This paragraph, and the level-two heading above it, is centered-
aligned using the CENTER tag.
<UL>
<LI>First list item.
<LI>Second list item.
</UL>
</CENTER>
```

The <DIV ALIGN="center"> tag and the <CENTER> tag work the same displayed in Netscape Navigator as in Internet Navigator. NCSA Mosaic, however, doesn't recognize use of the DIV tag, but does recognize the CENTER tag. Figure 3-4 shows how the above example appears in NCSA Mosaic.

Figure 3-4.

Although this figure looks quite similar to Figure 3-3, it is the CENTER tag here in NCSA Mosaic that is doing the centering, not the DIV tag. Navigator and Internet Explorer also recognize the CENTER tag.

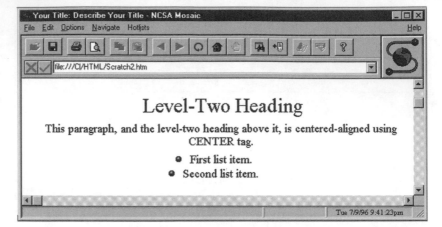

NOTE

Besides NCSA Mosaic, many other non-HTML 3.2 compliant Web browsers aren't likely to support the DIV tag. While NCSA Mosaic, along with Navigator and Internet Explorer, does support using both the ALIGN attribute (in paragraphs and headings) and the CENTER tag, other Web browsers may not support either. Of these methods, center-aligning paragraphs and headings using the ALIGN attribute is probably the most widely supported and so should be the preferred method. Otherwise, using the CENTER tag is preferable to using the DIV tag (that is, until more browsers become HTML 3.2 compliant and support the DIV tag).

TIP

You also could conceivably combine all three of these methods in hopes of catching as many browsers in your net as possible, like this, for instance:

```
<CENTER><DIV ALIGN="center"><P ALIGN="center">The text to be cen-
tered.</DIV></CENTER>
```

For an example of using the CENTER tag to center-align an inline image, see the next section, "Working with Images."

Working with Images

The basic HTML tutorial covered adding inline images to your Web page, as well as top-aligning, middle-aligning, and bottom-aligning an inline image relative to a line of text. It also covered using the ALT attribute with inline images to make life easier for users of text-only browsers or graphical browsers with graphics turned off. This section of the intermediate HTML tutorial covers several additional things you can do with inline images, including using a banner graphic, right-aligning or center-aligning graphics, wrapping text around a graphic, and creating image links.

Adding a Banner Graphic

A *banner* graphic is an inline image that runs along the top of your Web page. It might just be your company name or logo, or a way to add some graphic appeal and pizzazz to your page.

CAUTION

Remember, however, that graphics take much longer to load and display than just text. So, be economical. You don't need a graphic that fills the entire screen, for instance. Just across the top should do.

It's fine if you don't already have a banner graphic created and you don't need to create one now. Don't get bogged down. If you want to become a graphics whiz, you can do that *next* weekend (using some other book). For right now, if you want to create a banner graphic, just create a quick and dirty one that you can plug into your Web page for example purposes.

NOTE

Of course, you can create a banner graphic now if you want. Just use a graphic editor like Paint Shop Pro to create a GIF file. To create a GIF file that fits nicely inside Netscape Navigator's window at a resolution of 640 × 480 pixels, create a graphic that is 595 pixels wide. The height of the graphic depends on what you want to include, but generally it shouldn't have to be more than, say, 150 pixels. (The sample graphic I provide is 595 × 134 pixels.)

If you copied the sample graphics from the CD-ROM to your working directory (C:\HTML), BANNER.GIF should be available, along with all the other sample graphics called for in this section. To add a banner graphic to your Web page, go to the top of your Web page and add the following:

```
<HEAD>
<TITLE>Your Title: Describe Your
Title</TITLE></HEAD>
<BODY>
<IMG SRC="banner.gif">
<H1>The Intermediate HTML Tutorial</H1>
```

As long as you store a graphic file in the same directory as the Web page in which you insert it, you don't need to include anything other than the file name (for example, "banner.gif") as the URL. If you have the graphic stored in another directory, however, you need to insert a full (or absolute) URL, showing the full Web address of the graphic, or a partial (or relative) URL, showing that part of its path that is not held in common with the calling Web page. (For more information on full versus partial URLs, see the section "Using Partial or Relative URLs," in Chapter 2.)

Figure 3-5 shows how your page should look after you add the banner graphic.

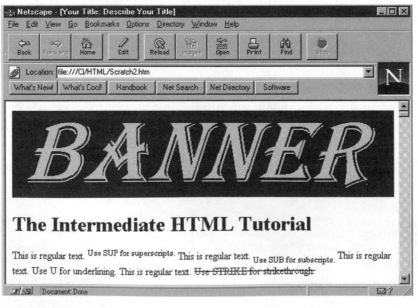

Figure 3-5.
A banner graphic runs across the top of a Web page.

Reducing Image Size

Graphic images take up major disk space and take a long time for the reader to download. For this reason, smart Web publishers do everything they can to reduce the size of the images they use on their Web pages.

One way to manipulate the size of an image is to change its format. Although all the sample graphics used in this book are GIF-format graphics, most current Web browsers now allow you to display both GIF and JPEG images as inline images. GIF graphics are limited to 256 colors, while JPEG graphics can have up to 16.7 million colors. JPEG graphics also use a compression scheme that can make a continuous-tone color photograph actually smaller than a corresponding GIF image. With images other than photos, however, a GIF file is almost always smaller than a JPEG file. So, if you want to include continuous-tone photographic images, JPEG is the best format to use. For other images, stick to GIFs.

Another way to reduce the size of your graphics file is to reduce its color depth. Many graphic editors and photo-paint programs, such as Paint Shop Pro or LView Pro, for instance, allow this.

There are two methods you can use:

1. You can switch the color-palette of the image to one that supports fewer colors (from 256 colors to 16 colors, for instance).

2. You can create an "adaptive palette" that matches the actual number of colors in the graphic. Switching to a color palette that supports fewer colors will definitely shrink the file size, but will also result in a significant loss of image quality. The adaptive palette method isn't as well-known, but it offers higher image quality for your file size savings.

Although a particular palette may support 256 colors, the actual number of colors in the image could be considerably less. By reducing the colors in the palette to the actual colors included in the graphic, you may be able to significantly reduce the size of the file, with no loss in image quality. (For instance, you might have a palette of 16 colors, but an image that actually has only eight colors in it—by creating an adaptive palette that has only those eight colors in it, you can significantly reduce the size of the file with no loss in image quality.)

Appendix A offers some pointers to resources on the Web where you can find more information on optimizing your graphic images.

Setting the Height and Width of a Banner Graphic

HTML 3.2 allows you to specify the height and width of an inline graphic. Normally, a Web browser has to download an image before it can allocate space for it on a Web page. This means that if you have a relatively large graphic, everything else has to wait until the image downloads. A banner graphic, usually the largest graphic on your page, as well as the first thing that displays, can be especially guilty of this.

However, if you set the dimensions of the graphic using the HEIGHT and WIDTH attributes of the IMG tag, Netscape Navigator and Internet Explorer can allocate space for the graphic and then display the remainder of the page without waiting for the banner graphic to download completely. (NCSA Mosaic, however, doesn't recognize these attributes.) So, if you want to use a banner graphic that takes longer to load than it takes ice to melt, then at least be gracious and set the height and width of the image; for instance:

```
<IMG SRC="banner.gif" WIDTH="595" HEIGHT="134">
```

The dimensions set here are the actual dimensions of the graphic. Using dimensions other than the actual ones provides no immediate advantage in this case. True, you could increase the dimensions of a smaller graphic to fit, but image quality likely would suffer. Likewise, you could reduce the dimensions of a larger graphic to fit, but that would be a waste of bandwidth—better that you reduce it to fit in your graphic editor, rather than on your Web page.

You may or may not want to set the WIDTH and HEIGHT dimensions for other inline images you include on your Web page. You should, however, always set these attributes for any banner graphic you insert at the top of your page, so viewers can get a much quicker peek at what your page contains (and decide to stay or go).

Using Width and Height Percentages

You also can use percentages when you use the WIDTH and HEIGHT attributes in the IMG tag. For instance, you could set WIDTH to 100%, like this:

```
<IMG SRC="banner.gif" WIDTH="100%">
```

This will size the banner graphic to fit horizontally within a browser window, regardless of the screen resolution or the width of the browser window. Setting the HEIGHT attribute to a percentage is much less useful and should be avoided. You should still, however, try to create your graphic to match as closely as possible the size at which you

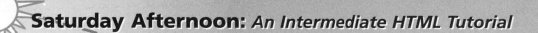

want it to display—that's because not all Web browsers support these attributes, using pixels or percentages.

Using Interlaced and Transparent GIF Graphics

An interlaced GIF will load progressively over several passes, generating what has been called a *venetian blind* effect. It allows the reader to see what the image is going to be long before the whole image has downloaded and displayed.

A *transparent GIF* is a GIF graphic that has one of its colors set to transparent, allowing any background color or background image to show through the graphic. This can be handy, for instance, if you want your graphic to look like it's floating on top of the background.

See Appendix E for information on how to use LView Pro to create these kinds of images. Appendix E also shows you how to do a Navigator-specific trick, the low- to high-resolution flip trick, that you can do using interlaced images.

Images Horizontally

The default alignment of an image is flush with the left margin. You might want, however, to center or right-flush an image, using any of several ways.

Aligning Images Using Paragraph Alignment

You can align an image by placing it in a paragraph that has either right- or center-alignment set. This works in Navigator, Internet Explorer, and NCSA Mosaic, although it won't necessarily work in other Web browsers. For instance, to right-align an image using paragraph alignment, do this:

```
<P ALIGN="right"><IMG SRC="right.gif">
```

Figure 3-6 shows how a right-aligned graphic appears in a Web browser that supports paragraph alignment.

To center-align an image using paragraph alignment, do this:

```
<P ALIGN="center"><IMG SRC="center.gif">
```

Figure 3-7 shows how this appears in a Web browser that supports paragraph alignment.

Figure 3-6.
You can right-align an image in many Web browsers by placing it inside a right-aligned paragraph.

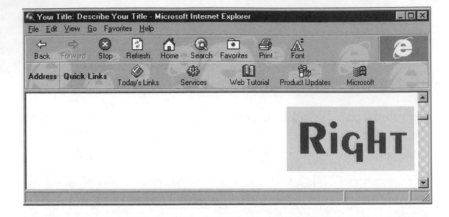

Figure 3-7.
You can center-align an image in many Web browsers by placing it inside a center-aligned paragraph.

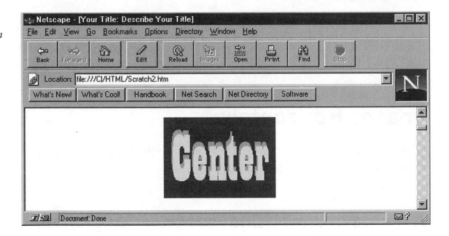

Other Ways To Horizontally Align Images

You also can use the DIV or the CENTER tag to align an image. All three major browsers recognize the CENTER tag, but NCSA Mosaic doesn't recognize the DIV tag. (Other browsers, however, such as the pre-Beta release of HotJava for Windows 95, may recognize the DIV tag but not the CENTER tag.) You're probably best off using paragraph alignment for right-aligning or centering images. (You also can use heading alignment.)

If you should choose to use the DIV tag to right-align an image, however, this is how you would do it:

```
<DIV ALIGN="right"><IMG SRC="right.gif"></DIV>
```

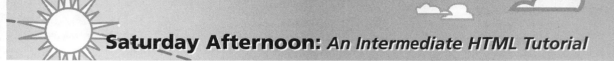

If you should choose to use the DIV tag to center-align an image, this is how you would do it:

```
<DIV ALIGN="center"><IMG SRC="center.gif"></DIV>
```

You also can center-align an image using the CENTER tag. If you should choose to do so, this is how you would do it:

```
<CENTER><IMG SRC="center.gif"></CENTER>
```

TIP

Just as with text elements, as shown in the tip in the "Working with Text" section, nothing says you can't triple up on these tag attributes in hopes that if one of the tag attributes is not supported by a browser, another will be. Just nest the different tags inside each other. For instance, to nest the different center-alignment tags, you might do this:

```
<DIV ALIGN="center"><CENTER><P ALIGN="center"><IMG
SRC="center.gif"></CENTER></DIV>
```

Wrapping Text around Images

In the basic HTML tutorial, you learned how to align an image relative to a line of text using the top, middle, and bottom alignment attributes. In addition to these alignment attributes, HTML 3.2 allows the use of the left and right alignment attributes. You might think that the purpose of these attributes is to align an image at either the left or right margin, but that's not so. Rather, these attributes are used to wrap text around the right-side or left-side of an image.

The methods shown here work with Netscape Navigator and with Internet Explorer 3.0. NCSA Mosaic, however, being more of an HTML 2.0 compliant browser, does not support using left- or right-alignment attributes for wrapping text around images.

CAUTION

Gambling on a browser's capability to support text wrapping can be risky. If a browser doesn't support paragraph alignment of images (or using the DIV or CEN-TER tag), no real harm is done—the image will just be left-aligned. But if a Web browser doesn't support text wrap around images, the results may not exactly be "eye appealing." For that reason, Web pages that you create using text wrap around images you should label "HTML 3.2 only" to give fair warning to users of browsers that aren't HTML 3.2 compliant. You also might create separate HTML 2.0 and HTML 3.2 versions of your pages, although as more browsers become HTML 3.2 compliant, this should become much less necessary.

Wrapping Text around a Left-Aligned Image

Enter the following as an example of wrapping text around a left-aligned image:

```
<P><IMG ALIGN="left" SRC="left.gif">If you set left-alignment in an
inline image, the text will wrap around the right side of the graph-
ic. If you set left-alignment in an inline image, the text will wrap
around the right side of the graphic.
If you set left-alignment in an inline image,

the text will wrap around the right side of the graphic.
```

NOTE

If you're using a screen resolution higher than 640 × 480, you need to add additional example text above to make sure that the image in the following example also doesn't try to wrap here. If you're using a 800 × 600 screen resolution, just add one additional "If you set..." sentence.

Wrapping Text around a Right-Aligned Image

Now, enter the following as an example of wrapping text around a right-aligned image:

```
<P><IMG ALIGN="right" SRC="right.gif">If you set right-alignment in
an inline image, the text will wrap around the left side of the
```

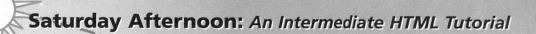

graphic. If you set right-alignment in an inline image, the text
will wrap around the left side of the graphic.
If you set right-alignment in an inline image,
the text will wrap around the left side of the graphic.

> **NOTE**
>
> *As in the previous example, if you're using a 800 × 600 screen resolution, just add one additional "If you set. . ." sentence above to make sure that the text clears the image.*

Figure 3-8 shows text wrapped around both a left-aligned and a right-aligned image in Netscape Navigator.

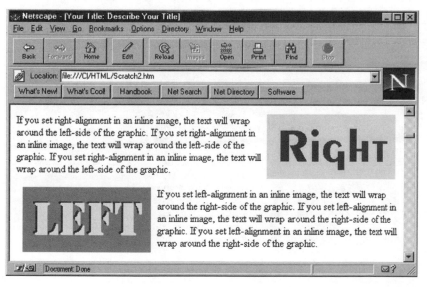

Figure 3-8.
Netscape Navigator, as well as Internet Explorer, can wrap text around left-aligned and right-aligned images.

You aren't limited to just wrapping text around an image. All other elements, including headings, lists, and other images, will wrap around an image with either left- or right-alignment set. (You don't have to actually do anything to make this happen, other than use a left- or right-aligned image. The trick is *stopping* it from happening. For that, see the section "Using the BR Tag's CLEAR Attribute," later in this chapter.)

Adding Space between an Image and Wrapping Text

You may have noticed in the illustrations, or when you hopped over to take a look at the above examples in your browser, that text wrapping around an image, especially around a left-aligned image, is not separated from the image by very much space. In Internet Explorer, text mapping isn't separated by any space at all. To add space between wrapping text and a left- or right-aligned image, you can insert an HSPACE (Horizontal Space) attribute in the IMG tag. Edit the example you created for wrapping text around a left-aligned image and add the following to insert 10 pixels on either side of the image:

```
<P><IMG ALIGN="left" SRC="left.gif" HSPACE="10">If you set left-
alignment in an inline image, the text will wrap around the right
side of the graphic. If you set left-alignment in an inline image,
the text will wrap around the right side of the graphic. If you set
left-alignment in an inline image, the text will wrap around the
right side of the graphic.
```

Figure 3-9 shows what this looks like in Internet Explorer.

Figure 3-9.

In Internet Explorer, as well as in Netscape Navigator, you can control the amount of space between an image and text wrapping around it.

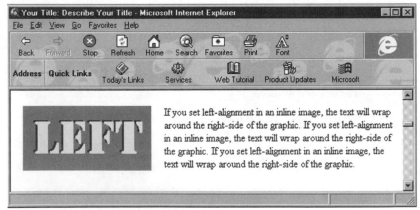

Flowing Text and Other Elements between Images

You not only can wrap text and other elements, even images, around a left- or right-aligned image, but you also can flow text and other elements, even images, *between* left- and right-aligned images.

Flowing Text between Images

For an example of flowing text between a left- and a right-aligned image, enter the following:

```
<P><IMG ALIGN="left" SRC="left.gif"><IMG ALIGN="right"
SRC="right.gif">Text will flow between a left-aligned and a right-
aligned image. Text will flow between a left-aligned and a right-
aligned image.
```

Figure 3-10 shows what this looks like in Netscape Navigator.

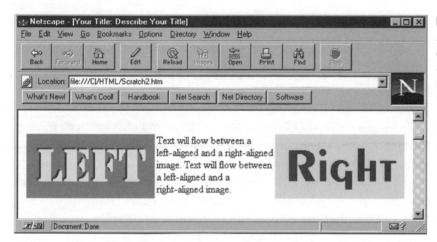

Figure 3-10.

Netscape Navigator, as well as Internet Explorer, allows you to flow text between two images.

Flowing an Image between Two Other Images

Yes, you can even flow a non-aligned image between a left-aligned image and a right-aligned one. To make this even slicker, stick the whole thing in a center-aligned paragraph, so the flowing, non-aligned image is centered between the two aligned images. For an example of how to do this, enter the following:

```
<P><IMG ALIGN="left" SRC="one.gif"><IMG ALIGN="right"
SRC="three.gif"><P ALIGN="center"><IMG SRC="two.gif"><BR CLEAR="all">
```

Notice above that two P (Paragraph) tags are used, the first at the start of the line and the second to center-align the image (TWO.GIF) you want to flow and center between the two other images (ONE.GIF and THREE.GIF).

See Figure 3-11 for what this looks like in Netscape Navigator.

Figure 3-11.
Netscape Navigator, and Internet Explorer both allow you to flow an image between two images.

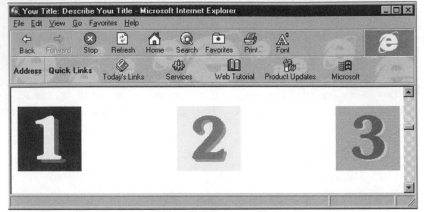

Using the BR Tag's CLEAR Attribute

One thing you have to watch out for when you use left- or right-aligned images is that *everything*, even other images, will wrap around the image as well. Other than putting in lines of blank PRE text or inserting multiple BR tags (which works only in Navigator anyway), the only way to force all following text, elements, and even images to "clear" a left- or right-aligned image is to insert a BR (Break) tag with a CLEAR attribute set to "left," "right," or "all" at the end of any text or other elements that you want to wrap (but before any other text or other elements that you don't want to wrap). You've already learned about the BR tag in the basic HTML tutorial. The following section introduces you to using the BR tag's CLEAR attribute.

In the BR tag, CLEAR="left" will move following text or other elements down until the left margin is clear; CLEAR="right" will move following text or other elements down until the right margin is clear; and CLEAR="all" will move following text or other elements down until *both* the left and right margins are clear.

Clearing a Left-Aligned Image

To see how this works with a left-aligned graphic, insert the following into the example you created above for wrapping text around a left-aligned image (you can copy and move it):

```
<P><IMG ALIGN="left" SRC="left.gif">If you set left-alignment in an
inline image, the text will wrap around the right side of the graph-
ic.<BR CLEAR="left">
```

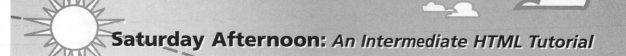

As Figure 3-12 shows, the CLEAR="left" attribute has the effect of moving all follow-ing text past a left-aligned graphic to a position where the left margin is "clear."

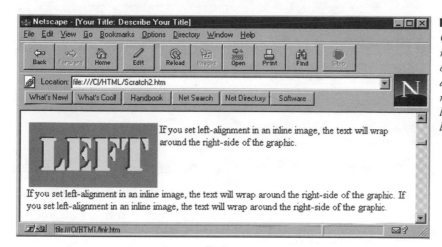

Figure 3-12.
CLEAR="left" will move following text or other elements down until the left margin is clear (is no longer blocked by a left-aligned image).

Clearing a Right-Aligned Image

To see how this works with a right-aligned graphic, insert the following as indicated into the example you created above for wrapping text around a right-aligned image (you can copy and move it if you want):

```
<P><IMG ALIGN="right" SRC="right.gif">If you set right alignment in
an inline image, the text will wrap around the leftside of the
graphic.<BR CLEAR="right">
```

As you can see in Figure 3-13, the CLEAR="right" attribute has the effect of moving all following text past a right-aligned graphic to a position where the right margin is "clear."

Clearing Both Left-Aligned and Right-Aligned Images

Finally, to see how this works when flowing text between both a left-aligned and a right-aligned graphic, insert the following as indicated into the example you created above for flowing text between a left-aligned and a right-aligned image (you can copy and move it if you want):

```
<P><IMG ALIGN="left" SRC="left.gif"><IMG ALIGN="right"
SRC="right.gif">Text will flow between a leftaligned and a rightal-
igned image.<BR CLEAR="all">
```

Figure 3-13.
CLEAR="right" will move following text or other elements down until the right margin is clear (is no longer blocked by a right-aligned image).

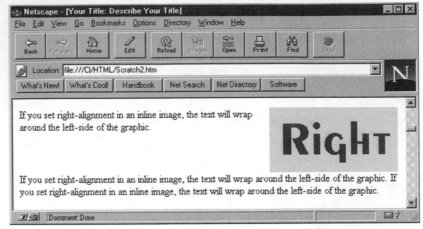

As Figure 3-14 shows, the CLEAR="all" attribute has the effect of moving all following text past a left-aligned or a right-aligned graphic to a position where both margins are "clear."

Figure 3-14.
CLEAR="all" will move following text or other elements down until both the left and right margins are clear (are no longer blocked by a left-aligned or a right-aligned image).

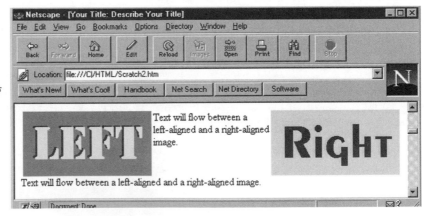

Creating Image Links

If you nest an inline image *inside* a hypertext anchor tag, the image appears with a border (usually blue) around it, allowing you to activate the link by clicking on the image. The following sections examine how to do just that.

Including an Image in a Link

Besides text, you also can include an inline image inside a hypertext link, which causes the image to display a blue border, indicating that it's a hypertext link that you or your users can click on and activate. Enter the following for an example of including both an image and text inside a hypertext link:

```
<P><A HREF="link.htm">
<IMG SRC="link.gif">This image is a link.</A>
```

> **NOTE**
> *The file name for the linked Web page, "link.htm," is a dummy file name. In an actual link, you need to insert the file name (if it's in the same directory) or the URL of an actual Web page.*

Figure 3-15 shows that, when an image is placed inside a hypertext link, the image itself becomes a hot link.

In the above example, you included both an image and text within the same link. The following section discusses using just an image as a link, without any accompanying text.

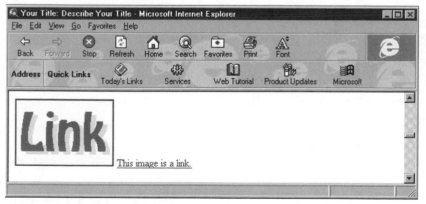

Figure 3-15.
When you insert both an image and text in a hypertext link, the image is displayed with a blue border, allowing you to click on the image to activate the link.

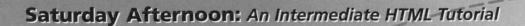
Using an Image Link by Itself

In the above example, the link includes both the image and the text, meaning that clicking on either one will activate the link, and that's how it's usually done on the Web. However, you also can just specify the image as the link, but not the text. To do this in the above example, you would move the </A> end tag so only the image is enclosed within the A (Anchor) start and end tags, like this:

```
<P><A HREF="link.htm">
<IMG SRC="link.gif"></A>This image is a link.
```

Figure 3-16 shows how this appears in Netscape Navigator.

CAUTION

This is a case where someone using a text-only Web browser or a graphical Web browser with graphics turned off might not be able to know what is going on with only an image indicating the link. The way to take care of this is to include an ALT="link description" attribute in the IMG tag, where link description describes the link. The next section gives an example of using the ALT attribute. For a fuller discussion of using the ALT attribute, see the section "Using the ALT Attribute" in Chapter 2.

Using Navigational Icons

The above example at least provides some text to help identify the image link, even if it does fall outside the link. You generally want to include text as part of the link or at least have adjacent text on the same line to help identify the image link.

A common case in which you *don't* want descriptive text next to an image, however, is when you want to use an image link as a navigational icon or button. A *navigational icon* is meant to effectively convey the action that will occur if the link is activated. For instance, a left-hand arrow at the top or bottom of a page indicates returning to the previous page, a right-hand arrow indicates going to the next page, and a house indicates returning to the home page.

One of the problems with using navigational icons or other textless image links is that users of text-only browsers or graphical browsers with graphics turned off might be left

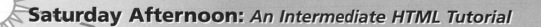

entirely in the dark, without a clue as to the nature of the link. Therefore, whenever you include only an image in a link, you should include ALT text in the IMG tag, indicating that it's a link and describing what it links to. Even if text adjacent to the image link describes it, it's still not a bad idea to add some ALT text in the IMG tag, just to make everything perfectly clear if the text isn't part of the link. Following is an example of using an image link as a navigational icon, with additional descriptive text included in an ALT attribute:

```
<P><A HREF="prevpage.htm">
<IMG SRC="back.gif" ALT="Go to Previous Page"></A>
```

Figure 3-17 shows the navigational icon as it appears in Netscape Navigator with the display of graphics turned on.

Figure 3-18 shows how this looks in Netscape Navigator with the display of graphics turned off.

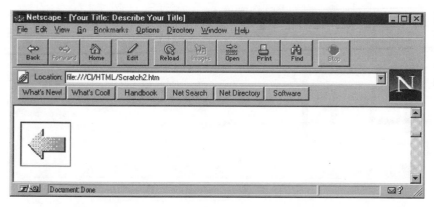

Figure 3-17.
An image link, by itself, is often used to create a navigational icon.

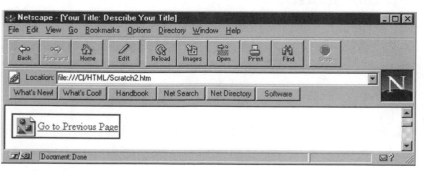

Figure 3-18.
Including ALT text in the IMG tag will clue in users who have turned graphics off or use a text-only browser.

Controlling the Border around an Image Link

The default width of the border around an image link is 2 pixels in Netscape Navigator. The IMG tag's BORDER attribute allows you to specify a custom width for the border. This works in Netscape Navigator and Internet Explorer but not in NCSA Mosaic. For instance, to increase the width of the border around the image link to 10 pixels, you would do the following:

```
<P><A HREF="link.htm">
<IMG SRC="link.gif" BORDER=10>This image is a link.</A>
```

As shown in Figure 3-19, when you increase the border width to 10 pixels, you *really* increase it.

Figure 3-19.
Border width increased to 10 pixels.

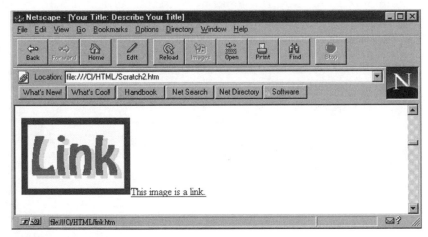

Turning the Image Link Border Off

Navigational icons often are used with their borders turned off. You may want to turn the border of an image link off in other situations. Edit the previous example to turn off the image link border, like this:

```
<P><A HREF="link.htm">
<IMG SRC="link.gif" BORDER="0">This image is a link.</A>
```

Figure 3-20 shows how this should look in Netscape Navigator, Internet Explorer, or NCSA Mosaic.

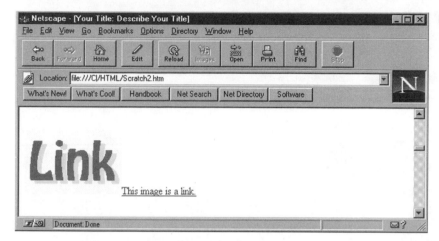

Figure 3-20.
You can turn off the border around an image link.

NOTE

Although NCSA Mosaic doesn't let you set a custom border around an image link, it does inexplicably let you turn it off with a BORDER="0" attribute value.

Positioning Link Text Relative to an Image Link

All of the examples so far have lined the text up at the bottom and to the right of the image link. It might be nice to align the link text with the middle of the image. Just insert an ALIGN="middle" attribute value inside the IMG tag. For the example, copy and paste the first image link example that you used back in the section entitled "Including an Image in a Link" and then insert ALIGN="middle" in the IMG tag (or you can retype the whole example):

```
<P><A HREF="link.htm">
<IMG SRC="link.gif"ALIGN="middle">This image is a link.</A>
```

See Figure 3-21 for how this should look in most Web browsers.

To align the link text with the top of the image link, just insert ALIGN="top" as the attribute value ("bottom" is the default).

Figure 3-21.
Link text can be aligned with the middle of an image link.

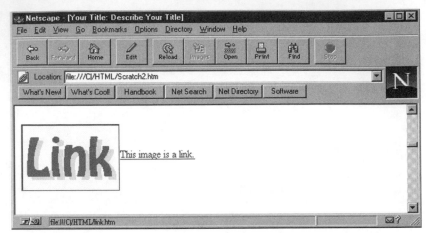

NOTE

You can position only a single line of text relative to an image using ALIGN = "top". Any additional lines will wrap below the image.

Horizontally Aligning an Image Link

You also can align an image link relative to the Web page simply by using an ALIGN attribute in the P (Paragraph) tag that contains the link. For example, to center the link text and image link you just created relative to the page, add the following:

```
<P ALIGN="center"><A HREF="link.htm">
<IMG SRC="link.gif" ALIGN="middle">This image is a link.</A>
```

Figure 3-22 shows the centered image and text.

Using a right-aligned paragraph above, rather than a center-aligned one, would cause the link text and image link to be right-aligned. Left-alignment, on the other hand, is the default.

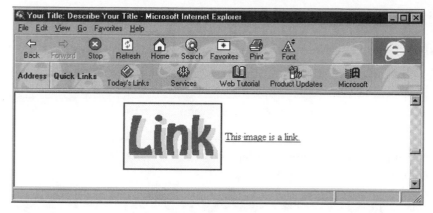

Figure 3-22.
By centering the paragraph that contains them, you also center the image link and the link text.

Displaying the Link Text Underneath the Image Link

This would be even nicer, however, if you could center the link text under the image link. No problem, just insert a BR tag in front of the link text, as shown here:

```
<P ALIGN="center"><A HREF="link.htm">
<IMG SRC="link.gif" ALIGN="middle"><BR>This image is a link.</A>
```

Figure 3-23 shows how this looks in a Web browser.

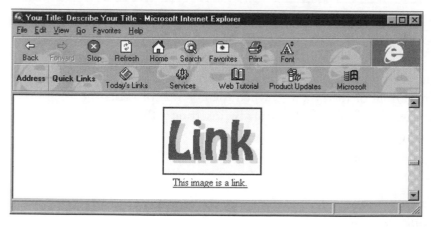

Figure 3-23.
You can center an image link with link text directly beneath it.

Reversing the Position of the Image Link and Link Text

You can reverse the relative position of an image link and its associated link text simply by placing the image link after the link text. As an example, enter the following (paragraph alignment is set to "center"):

```
<P ALIGN="center"><A HREF="link.htm">This image is also a link.
<IMG SRC="link.gif"></A>
```

Figure 3-24 shows the positions of the link image and link text reversed.

Figure 3-24.
You don't have to have your link text follow an image link—you can do it the other way around.

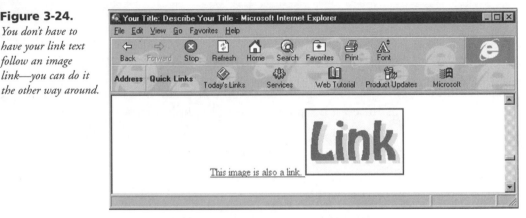

Displaying the Link Text above the Image Link

Just as you previously could display the link text beneath an image link simply by inserting a BR tag in front of the link text, when the link text precedes the image link, you can display it above the image link simply by inserting a BR tag at the end of the link text, as is shown here:

```
<P ALIGN="center"><A HREF="link.htm">This image is also a link.<BR>
<IMG SRC="link.gif"></A>
```

If you view this in your browser, you should see that the link text is centered directly above the image link, as shown in Figure 3-25.

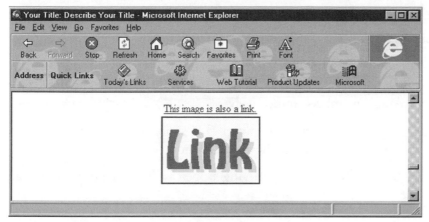

Figure 3-25.
Link text can also be centered above an image link.

More Things You Can Do with Images

The examples above are only some of the things you can do when working with images in HTML. The section "Creating Icon Link Lists" covers how to create icon link lists using colorful icon bullet graphics, instead of the simple black-and-white bullets that you can create using an unordered list. The final section, "Creating Special Effects," covers even more things you can do with images, including using a background images with a Web page.

Working with Lists

The beginning HTML tutorial covered creating unordered (numbered) lists and ordered (bulleted) lists. It also covered nesting lists within each other, and mixing and matching lists. This section of the intermediate HTML tutorial covers some additional ways you can control the display of ordered and unordered lists.

Controlling How Ordered Lists Are Displayed

Netscape provided an extension to HTML 2.0, the TYPE attribute, that allows you to specify the number type for an ordered (OL) list. This attribute value has since been incorporated into HTML 3.2. Besides making it possible for you to specify a number type for a numbered list, this attribute also allows you to create multi-level outlines.

Specifying the Number Type

You can use the TYPE attribute to specify the number type for an ordered (OL) list. The values that you can use with the TYPE attribute are "A," "a," "I," "i," and "1," for specifying uppercase letters, lowercase letters, uppercase roman numerals, lowercase roman numerals, or Arabic numbers, respectively.

Both Netscape Navigator and Internet Explorer 3.0 support using this attribute. Internet Explorer 2.0 and NCSA Mosaic, however, do not.

Enter the following for an example of specifying uppercase roman numerals for an ordered list:

```
<OL TYPE="I">
<LI>This is item one.
<LI>This is item two.
<LI>This is item three.
<LI>This is item four.
</OL>
```

Figure 3-26 shows how an ordered list using a TYPE="I" attribute appears in Netscape Navigator.

Figure 3-26.

Netscape Navigator, as well as Internet Explorer, allows you to change number type for an ordered (numbered) list, here from Arabic to upper-case Roman.

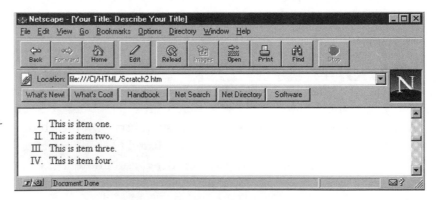

Creating a Multi-Level Outline

By applying different number types to the different levels of a nested ordered list, you can create a multi-level outline. (Neither Netscape Navigator nor Internet Explorer 3.0 automatically varies the number type in nested ordered lists.)

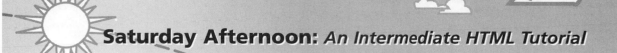

CAUTION

Multi-level outlines displayed in a Web browser that doesn't support the TYPE attribute don't look too good. So, if you want to use this effect in your Web page, label it as an "HTML 3.2 only" page, so that users of browsers that don't support this attribute (NCSA Mosaic or Internet Explorer 2.0, for instance) will understand why they're getting weird results. (Better yet, provide an alternative page for viewers using HTML 2.0 compliant Web browsers.)

NOTE

Tab or space over to create the indents, but realize that this is for your eyes only and will have no effect when displayed in a browser. Also, be careful that you "nest," and don't "overlap," the different nested outline levels.

Enter the following as an example of creating a multi-level outline using TYPE attributes:

```
<OL TYPE="I">
<LI>Level one outline level.
    <OL TYPE="A">
    <LI>Level two outline level.
        <OL TYPE="1">
        <LI>Level three outline level.
            <OL TYPE="a">
            <LI>Level four outline level.
            <LI>Level four outline level.
            </OL>
        <LI>Level three outline level.
        </OL>
    <LI>Level two outline level.
    </OL>
<LI>Level one outline level.
</OL>
```

Figure 3-27 shows how this appears in an HTML 3.2 capable Web browser.

Figure 3-27.

Netscape Navigator, as well as Internet Explorer 3.0, can display multi-level outlines created using the TYPE attribute.

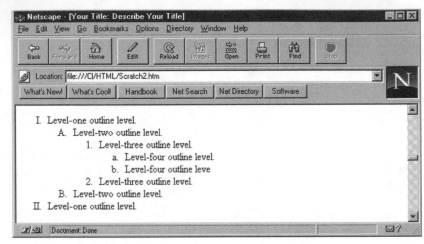

However, if you want to see what this looks like in a non-HTML 3.2 compliant Web browser such as NCSA Mosaic, see Figure 3-28.

Figure 3-28.

In a non-HTML 3.2 compliant Web browser, a multi-level outline will appear with all levels using arabic numbers, as shown here in NCSA Mosaic.

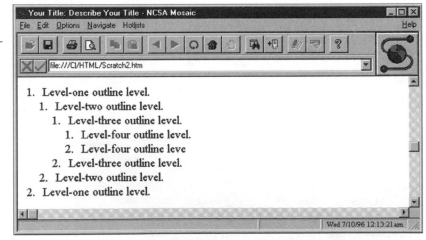

Adding Emphasis to a Multi-Level Outline

The only problem with the outline you created in the last section is that it looks rather bland. It would be nice if you could vary the size of the different outline levels. To do that, tag your different outline levels with heading tags (H2, H3, H4, and so on), as shown here:

```
<OL TYPE="I">
<H2><LI>Level one outline level.</H2>
    <OL TYPE="A">
    <H3><LI>Level two outline level.</H3>
        <OL TYPE="1">
        <H4><LI>Level three outline level.</H4>
            <OL TYPE="a">
            <LI>Level four outline level.
            <LI>Level four outline leve
            </OL>
        <H4><LI>Level three outline level.</H4>
        </OL>
    <H3><LI>Level two outline level.</H3>
    </OL>
<H2><LI>Level one outline level.</H2>
</OL>
```

See Figure 3-29 for how this will appear in a Web browser that supports creating outlines.

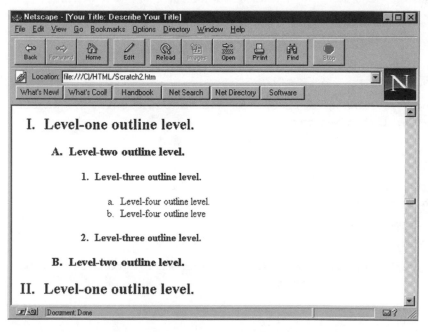

Figure 3-29.
You can add emphasis to an outline by tagging your list items with heading tags.

NOTE

You're not limited to using heading tags to add emphasis to your outlines. You could just add I (Italic) and B (Bold) tags, or EM (Emphasis) and STRONG (Strong Emphasis) tags, as well as combine either of these two to get bold italic. Note, however, that you can't use the FONT tag (see "Creating Special Effects" later) for this.

Including Paragraphs in a Multi-Level Outline

You can insert paragraphs inside of a multi-level outline, as you can inside any list, by inserting a paragraph following a list item. For instance, insert the following in the previous example:

NOTE

Feel free to use tabs or spaces to indent the paragraph text so it's flush with the preceding list item. Remember, however, that this is for your eyes only, to assist you in creating the outline—any tabs and or extra spaces you enter will have no effect in a browser.

```
<OL TYPE="I">
<H2><LI>Levelone outline level.</H2>

<P>Paragraph text following a list item will automatically be indent-
ed flush with the list item text.

    <OL TYPE="A">
    <H3><LI>Leveltwo outline level.</H3>

    <P>Paragraph text following a list item will automatically be
indented flush with the list item text.

        <OL TYPE="1">
        <H4><LI>Levelthree outline level.</H4>

        <P>Paragraph text following a list item will automatically be
indented flush with the list item text.

            <OL TYPE="a">
            <LI>Levelfour outline level.
            <LI>Levelfour outline leve
```

```
        </OL>
      <H4><LI>Levelthree outline level.</H4>
      </OL>
    <H3><LI>Leveltwo outline level.</H3>
    </OL>
<H2><LI>Levelone outline level.</H2>
</OL>
```

Figure 3-30 shows how this looks in a Web browser that supports outlines.

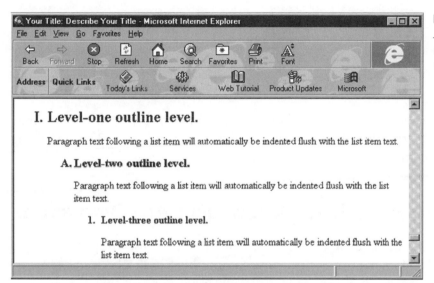

Figure 3-30.
*An outline can con-
tain paragraphs as
well as list items.*

Using START and VALUE Attributes in an Ordered List

The START and VALUE attributes were Netscape extensions that have now been incorporated into HTML 3.2. You can use the START attribute in an OL start tag to start
the numbering sequence at a particular number. You can use the VALUE attribute in
an LI tag to restart the numbering sequence at a particular number. For an example of
first starting the numbering sequence at 3, then restarting it at 8, enter the following:

```
<OL START="3">
<LI>This should be numbered as 3
<LI>This should be numbered as 4.
<LI VALUE="8">This should be numbered as 8.
<LI>This should be numbered as 9.
</OL>
```

Figure 3-31 shows how this appears in an HTML 3.2 compliant Web browser.

Figure 3-31.

In an HTML 3.2 compliant Web browser, you can start and restart the numbering sequence of an ordered list with the START and VALUE attributes.

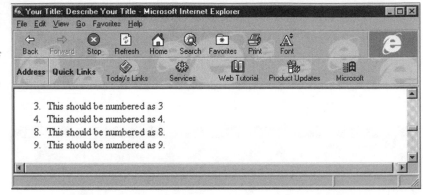

The numbering sequence will be started or restarted using the current TYPE attribute value. For instance, if TYPE="A" is used in the OL tag, then START="3" in an OL tag or VALUE="3" in an LI tag would start or restart the numbering at "C."

Controlling How Unordered Lists Are Displayed

You also can use the TYPE attribute with unordered (bulleted) lists to specify the type of bullet to display. Originally a Netscape extension, this has also been incorporated into HTML 3.2. So far, however, only Netscape Navigator recognizes it. Internet Explorer, even Version 3.0, does not recognize this (nor will it vary the bullet type for different nested bullet levels). NCSA Mosaic, an HTML 2.0 compliant browser, also doesn't recognize this attribute.

Specifying a Bullet Type

You can use the TYPE attribute to specify the bullet type for an unordered (OL) list. The values that you can use with the TYPE attribute are "disc," "circle," and "square." Netscape Navigator by default displays nested bullet lists with the progression of a disc for the first level, a circle for the second level, and a square for the third level.

Enter the following for an example of specifying a bullet-type sequence other than the default for a bullet list three levels deep:

```
<UL TYPE="square">
<LI>Firstlevel bullet.
```

```
<LI>Firstlevel bullet.
   <UL TYPE="disc">
   <LI>Secondlevel bullet.
   <LI>Secondlevel bullet.
      <UL TYPE="circle">
      <LI>Thirdlevel bullet.
      <LI>Thirdlevel bullet.
      </UL>
   </UL>
</UL>
```

Figure 3-32 shows how this looks in Netscape Navigator.

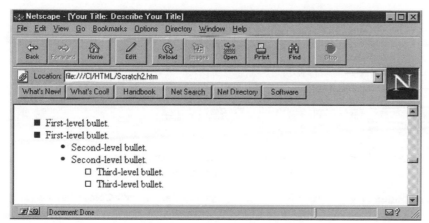

Figure 3-32.
You can vary the bullet types in an unordered list displayed in Netscape Navigator. Neither Internet Explorer (2.0 or 3.0) nor NCSA Mosaic will recognize it, however.

TIP

Just as you could include automatically indented paragraphs in an outline above, you can do the same in a nested bullet list. Just insert paragraphs following a list item, but inside the list, and they automatically are indented to match the list item's indentation.

Creating Icon Link Lists

An "icon link list" is simply a list of hypertext links that uses colorful, 3-D, graphical icon bullets (inline images, actually), other than just plain, ordinary black and white

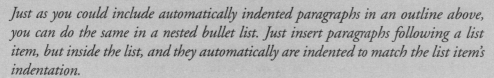

bullets like you get when you create an unordered list by using the UL tag. This is a good way to add some pizzazz to your Web page.

There are a number of ways you can set up an icon link list. The first method doesn't use any list tags at all, just left-aligned bullet icons and BR tags. The second method involves using a "compact" glossary list. The third method uses a regular glossary list, but instead of including the description of the link on the same line, places it below in an indented paragraph.

All the examples use the same list of links. Rather than retype them each time, type the links first and then copy them twice, so that you have a list of links with which to work for each example. First type this:

> ### NOTE
>
> *These are the same links and descriptions that you created in the basic HTML tutorial. If you want, you can cut and paste these links from SCRATCH.HTM and then just edit them to match what is shown below.*

```
<A HREF="http://www.li.net/~Eautorent/yoyo.htm">Jon's YoYo
Kingdom</A> Claims to have the largest YoYo link list on the Web.

<A HREF="http://pages.nyu.edu/~Etqm3413/yoyo/index.htm">Tomer's Page
of Exotic YoYo</A> Dedicated to the "littleknown, original, unusual,
difficult, or otherwise interesting tricks."

<A HREF="http://www.socool.com/socool/yoyo.html">Just Say YOYO</A>
Features the Web's first YoYo animation.

<A HREF="http://www.pd.net/yoyo/">American YoYo Association</A> Read
past issues of the AYYA Newsletter.

<A HREF="http://www.socool.com/socool/yo_hist.html">The History of
the YoYo</A> All you want to know about YoYo history.
```

Make two copies so you have three copies in all, and use one copy for each example of creating an icon link list in the following sections.

First Method: Using Left-Aligned Bullet Icons

This method for creating an icon link list uses left-aligned bullet icons and BR tags to create the list. Edit the first copy of the list of links you typed (or pasted in) above, as shown here:

```
<P><IMG SRC="redball.gif" ALIGN="left" HSPACE=5 VSPACE=5>
```

```
<A HREF="http://www.li.net/~Eautorent/yoyo.htm">Jon's YoYo
Kingdom</A> Claims to have the largest YoYo link list on the Web.<BR
CLEAR="left">
```

```
<IMG SRC="redball.gif" ALIGN="left" HSPACE=5 VSPACE=5>
```

```
<A HREF="http://pages.nyu.edu/~Etqm3413/yoyo/index.htm">Tomer's Page
of Exotic YoYo</A> Dedicated to the "littleknown, original, unusual,
difficult, or otherwise interesting tricks."<BR CLEAR="left">
```

```
<IMG SRC="redball.gif" ALIGN="left" HSPACE=5 VSPACE=5>
```

```
<A HREF="http://www.socool.com/socool/yoyo.html">Just Say YOYO</A>
Features the Web's first YoYo animation.<BR CLEAR="left">
```

```
<IMG SRC="redball.gif" ALIGN="left" HSPACE=5 VSPACE=5>
```

```
<A HREF="http://www.pd.net/yoyo/">American YoYo Association</A> Read
past issues of the AYYA Newsletter.<BR CLEAR="left">
```

```
<IMG SRC="redball.gif" ALIGN="left" HSPACE=5 VSPACE=5>
```

```
<A HREF="http://www.socool.com/socool/yo_hist.html">The History of
the YoYo</A> All you want to know about YoYo history.
```

Figure 3-33 shows what this looks like in a Web browser that supports wrapping text around left-aligned images.

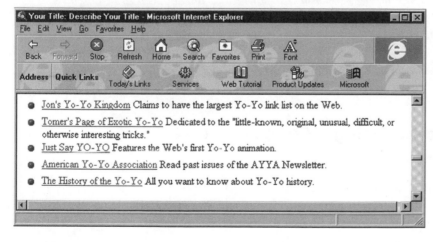

Figure 3-33.
You can use left-aligned icons with BR tags using CLEAR="left" attributes to create an indented icon link list. This works in Internet Explorer and Netscape Navigator.

Notice that this is really all one paragraph, with BR (Break) tags used to break the lines. The CLEAR attribute in the BR tags ensures that each icon bullet is flush to the left margin.

Other than requiring a browser that supports wrapping text around images before the indents will show, this method has one other limitation: it can indent only two lines of text. A third line runs flush to the left margin. The VSPACE amount only allows you two lines of indented text. Any additional lines will wrap to the left margin. And you can't increase the VSPACE amount without also moving the icon bullet down so it is no longer aligned with the text.

TIP

The only problem with an icon list is that someone using a text-only browser or a graphical Web browser with graphics turned off might not realize that the graphics are icon bullets. To clue them in, you might want to edit the IMG tags for the icon bullets above, adding ALT="", so they look like this:*

```
<IMG SRC="redball.gif" ALIGN="top" HSPACE=5 VSPACE=5 ALT="*">
```

NOTE

If you're wondering where you can find more graphic icons to spice up your Web pages, you can find a collection of public domain graphic icons and other Web art on the CD-ROM. Appendix A also lists pointers to tons of Web art that you can download from the Web. The Web site for this book (http://www.callihan.com/web-page/) also offers a list of updated and current resources, including links to graphics and Web art sources.

Second Method: Using a Compact Glossary List

Although the previous method does present the advantage of working in all Web browsers, it has one real disadvantage—a limit of only two lines per list item. This method, on the other hand, allows you as many lines per list item as you want, but works currently only in Netscape Navigator.

This method uses a glossary list, also called a definition list (DL), using the COMPACT attribute. As long as it doesn't take up more room than it is allowed (about five spaces or so), a "compact" glossary list will display the term element (DT) on the same

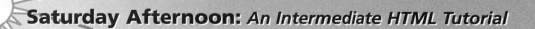

line as the definition element (DD). This allows you to insert an icon bullet as the term while using the definition to display the link and any text used to describe it. As a final refinement, non-breakable spaces ( ) are inserted to nudge the icon bullet closer to the indented definition text.

Use the second copy of the sample links you created to create this example. Add the following to create a compacted icon glossary link list:

> **NOTE**
> *The definition term sections you're going to be adding below are all identical. To save time, just type in the first one and then copy it and paste it into the rest of the locations.*

```
<DL COMPACT>

<DT>    <IMG SRC="redball.gif" ALIGN="top"
VSPACE="5">

<A HREF="http://www.li.net/%7Eautorent/yoyo.htm">Jon's YoYo
Kingdom</A> Claims to have the largest YoYo link list on the Web.

<DT>    <IMG SRC="redball.gif" ALIGN="top"
VSPACE="5"><DD>

<A HREF="http://pages.nyu.edu/%7Etqm3413/yoyo/index.htm">Tomer's Page
of Exotic YoYo</A> Dedicated to the "littleknown, original, unusual,
difficult, or otherwise interesting tricks."

<DT>    <IMG SRC="redball.gif" ALIGN="top"
VSPACE="5"><DD>

<A HREF="http://www.socool.com/socool/yoyo.html">Just Say YOYO</A>
Features the Web's first YoYo animation.

<DT>    <IMG SRC="redball.gif" ALIGN="top"
VSPACE="5"><DD>

<A HREF="http://www.pd.net/yoyo/">American YoYo Association</A> Read
past issues of the AYYA Newsletter.

<DT>    <IMG SRC="redball.gif" ALIGN="top"
VSPACE="5"><DD>

<A HREF="http://www.socool.com/socool/yo_hist.html">The History of
the YoYo</A> All you want to know about YoYo history.

</DL>
```

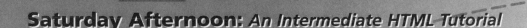

Now, if you save your file and hop over to Netscape Navigator and reload the page, what you see should match what is shown in Figure 3-34.

Figure 3-34.

You can create an indented icon link list by using a "compact" glossary list. This method, however, works only for Netscape Navigator.

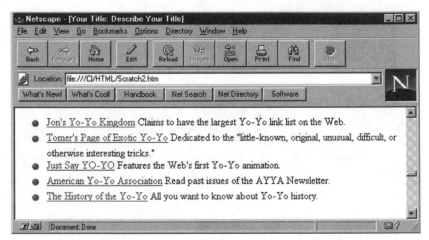

NOTE

The above method of creating an indented icon link list looks really bad in Internet Explorer and NCSA Mosaic because neither recognize the COMPACT attribute in a definition (or glossary) list. For right now, anyway, it's just a "Netscape Only" technique. You should label any Web pages you create using this technique accordingly, as well as provide an alternative page that doesn't use this technique. It constitutes perfectly legal HTML 3.2, however, so Internet Explorer, NCSA Mosaic, and other browsers probably will catch up soon—and when they do, it could be the preferred method of creating an indented icon link list (although it will always break older browsers).

Third Method: Using an Uncompacted Glossary List

This is a variant of an icon link list that you might want to use if you have more than two lines of explanatory text you want to include with each link and don't want to use the "Netscape Only" method just presented. This method works with all HTML 2.0 compliant Web browsers. It uses a regular glossary (or definition) list to display the icon bullet and the link on one line (as the "term"), with the explanatory text indented below the bulleted link (as the "definition").

The only disadvantages of using this method are that 1) it's only really suitable where you want to include a fair amount of comment beneath each link, and 2) it also takes up a good deal more space than the other two methods shown above.

Use the third copy of the sample links you created to create this example. Delete the descriptions and then add the following to create an uncompacted icon glossary link list:

```
<DL>

<DT><H3>

<IMG SRC="redball.gif" ALIGN="middle"> <A
HREF="http://www.li.net/%7Eautorent/yoyo.htm">Jon's YoYo
Kingdom</A></H3>

<DD>This text explains the link above. This text explains the link
above. This link explains the link above. This link explains the
link above.

<DT><H3>

<IMG SRC="redball.gif" ALIGN="middle"> <A
HREF="http://pages.nyu.edu/%7Etqm3413/yoyo/index.htm">Tomer's Page of
Exotic YoYo</A></H3>

<DD>This text explains the link above. This text explains the link
above. This link explains the link above. This link explains the
link above.

</DL>
```

Now, if you save your file and hop over to Netscape Navigator and reload the page, what you see should match what is shown in Figure 3-35.

TIP

You can create an indented icon link list in one other way: formatting it as a table. This would allow you unlimited indents, as well as being displayable in any tables-compatible Web browser (including Navigator, Internet Explorer, and NCSA Mosaic). See Appendix D for a tables tutorial. To create an indented icon link list, you would perform these steps:

1. Create a table of two columns by however many rows as you have icon links.

2. Insert the inline images for the icon bullets in the cells for the first column.

3. Insert the link text and descriptive text in the cells for the second column.

For more detailed information on creating tables, see Appendix D.

Figure 3-35.
All graphical Web browsers can display an "uncompacted" glossary link list.

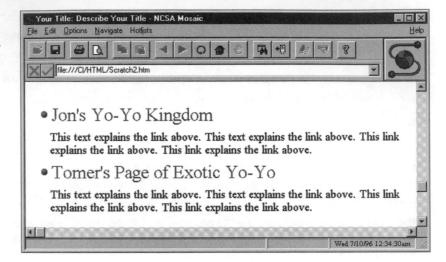

Creating Special Effects

What is a "special effect"? A few features already covered might fall under this heading, such as flowing an image between two other images or creating an indented icon link list. Still, those might qualify more accurately as "neat tricks," while features that can more generally effect the total "look and feel" of your Web page are reserved for "special effects." This section covers how to apply custom rules, background colors and images, and font size and color changes to your Web page.

Creating Custom Rules

The default horizontal rule looks like a rather bland device. True, it does have some shading to give it a bit of a 3-D look—although it is entirely washed out in Internet Explorer if you've set your browser's background to white. So this section covers some things you can do to dress up your horizontal rules, including changing their height and width, as well as their alignment. As a bonus, this section shows you how to use those colorful, 3-D graphic rules you've surely seen on the Web.

The attributes used here in the HR tag were all originally Netscape Navigator extensions. They have since been incorporated into HTML 3.2, so they can now qualify as "official HTML." They are supported not only by Netscape Navigator, but by Internet Explorer and NCSA Mosaic as well.

Changing the Height of a Horizontal Rule

To change the height of a horizontal rule, you set the SIZE attribute value in the HR tag. The value you set is the rule's height, or thickness, in pixels. Enter the following for an example of creating a horizontal rule that is 10 pixels thick and another one that is 15 pixels thick (a regular rule is included for comparison purposes):

```
<P>This is a regular horizontal rule:
<P>This is a 10-pixel thick horizontal rule:
<HR SIZE="10">
<P>This is a 15-pixel thick horizontal rule:
<HR SIZE="15">
```

Figure 3-36 shows how this will look in Netscape Navigator.

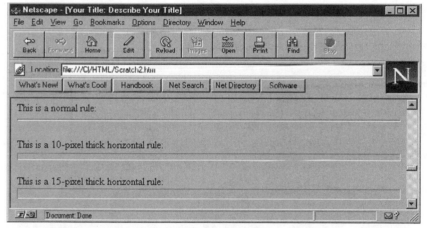

Figure 3-36.
The thickness of a horizontal rule can be adjusted, as displayed here in Netscape Navigator.

NOTE

I changed the background in Navigator above to gray (white is the default) to more clearly show the "shading." The shading is not a fill, as you can see, but a shadow relief. Conversely, as you will see below, an "unshaded" rule does have a fill, but no shadow relief.

Changing between Shaded and Unshaded Horizontal Rules

The default setting for a horizontal rule is "shaded." To set an "unshaded" horizontal rule, just add the NOSHADE attribute to the HR tag, as shown here:

```
<P>This is an unshaded, 15-pixel thick Horizontal Rule:
<HR SIZE="15" NOSHADE>
```

The following three figures, Figure 3-37, Figure 3-38, and Figure 3-39, show how this looks in Netscape Navigator, Internet Explorer, and NCSA Mosaic, all of which display an unshaded horizontal rule somewhat differently from the others.

As you can see, an "unshaded" rule actually is filled with a gray shade in Navigator.

Figure 3-37.

Netscape Navigator displays an unshaded horizontal rule in a gray shade with the corners rounded off.

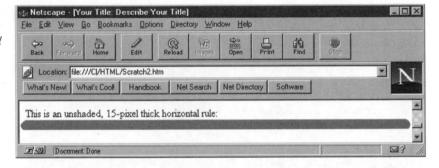

Figure 3-38.

Internet Explorer also displays an unshaded horizontal rule in a gray shade, but without the corners rounded off.

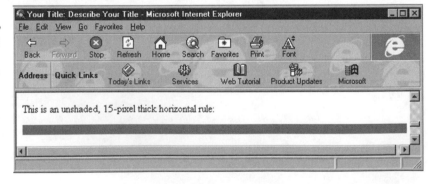

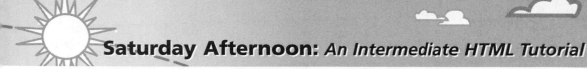

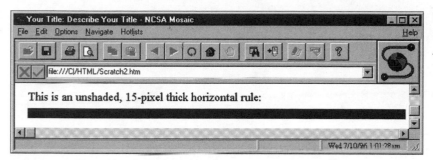

Figure 3-39.
NSCA Mosaic displays an unshaded horizontal rule filled with black, with squared-off corners.

Changing the Width of a Horizontal Rule

You also can change the width of a horizontal rule, either by setting the width in actual pixels or by specifying a percentage of the total width of the browser window. By default, horizontal rules are centered in the browser window. Enter the following for an example of creating a 15-pixel sized horizontal rule with a width that is 75 percent of a browser's window:

```
<P>This is a 75% wide, unshaded, 15-pixel thick horizontal rule:
<HR WIDTH="75%" SIZE="15" NOSHADE>
```

Figure 3-40 shows the resulting rule in Netscape Navigator.

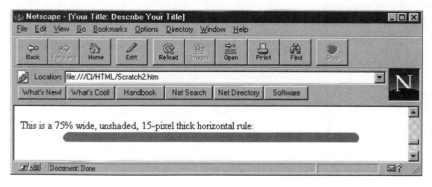

Figure 3-40.
A horizontal rule of a width less than the browser's window is indented and centered on-screen.

> **CAUTION**
>
> *You might be tempted to stack up horizontal rules of different widths, to generate an effect similar to this:*
>
> ――――――――――――――
>
> ――――――――――――
>
> ――――――
>
> *Be advised, however, that in a Web browser that doesn't support setting the WIDTH attribute for the HR tag, your "effect" will, instead, look something like this:*
>
> ――――――――――――――――――――――
>
> ――――――――――――――――――――――
>
> ――――――――――――――――――――――
>
> *This is a good example of a situation in which Netscape Navigator, NSCA Mosaic, and Internet Explorer all support doing something, but you probably still shouldn't do it. The general rule is not to do tricks specific to only a few browsers if they're going to mess up other browsers. One way around this is, of course, to provide alternative pages, or at least label your page as "Netscape Navigator Only," "Microsoft Internet Explorer Only," or "HTML 3.2 Only."*

Setting the Alignment of a Horizontal Rule

HTML 3.2 allows the use of the ALIGN attribute in the HR tag to left-align or right-align a horizontal rule (center-alignment is the default). Enter the following for an example of doing this:

```
<P>This is a left-aligned, 50% wide, 20-pixel thick horizontal rule
(shaded):
```

```
<HR ALIGN="left" WIDTH="50%" SIZE="20">
```

Both Netscape Navigator and Internet Explorer support left- or right-aligning a horizontal rule. Figure 3-41 shows how this looks in Internet Explorer.

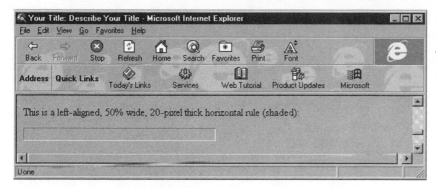

Figure 3-41.
HTML 3.2 allows you to left-align or right-align a horizontal rule.

Setting the background of Internet Explorer above back to its default color of gray shows how Internet Explorer displays rule shading. (With the background set to white, Internet Explorer washes out the shading entirely.)

Using a Graphic Rule Instead of the HR Tag

Instead of the HR tag, you can use a *graphic rule*, which is simply a graphic of a rule that you can insert on your page as an inline image. Enter the following as an example of inserting a graphic rule on your Web page:

```
<P>This is a graphic rule:
<P><IMG SRC="rain_lin.gif">
```

Figure 3-42 shows what this looks like in any graphical Web browser.

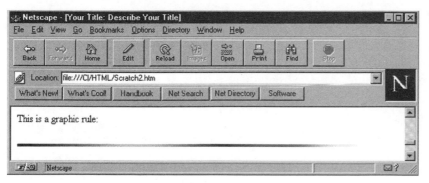

Figure 3-42.
You can use a graphic rule instead of the HR tag.

Notice here that the graphic rule doesn't extend across the whole window. That's because graphic rules, unlike horizontal rules created using the HR tag, are always of a specific width. Two possible solutions consist of centering the graphic rule and resetting the width (and the height) of the graphic rule.

Centering a Graphic Rule

You can center a graphic rule like any inline image simply by placing it in a center-aligned paragraph. Edit the example you just created to center it, like this:

```
<P ALIGN="center"><IMG SRC="rain_lin.gif">
```

Now, as shown in Figure 3-43, the graphic rule appears centered in a browser's window. This works equally well for Netscape Navigator, Internet Explorer, or NCSA Mosaic.

Figure 3-43.

You can center a graphic rule by placing it in a center-aligned paragraph.

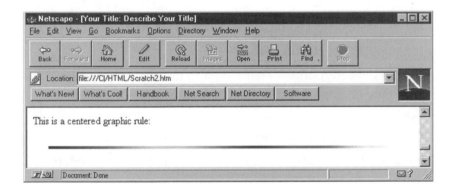

Setting the Width (and Height) of a Graphic Rule

You also can get your graphic rule to extend across more (or less) of the screen by setting the width of the graphic. And, while you're at it, you may as well even further enhance our graphic rule by increasing its height as well. For an example, re-edit the example you created above, like this:

```
<P ALIGN="center"><IMG SRC="rain_lin.gif" HEIGHT="10" WIDTH="595">
```

As Figure 3-44 shows, the graphic rule now extends across more of the screen. The height also has been further enhanced by increasing its height.

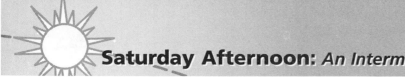

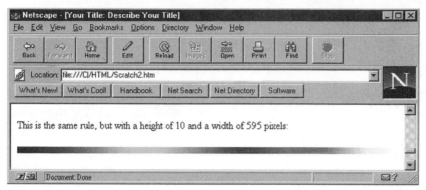

Figure 3-44.
For Netscape Navigator and Internet Explorer, you can control the width and height of a graphic rule.

This works fine in both Netscape Navigator and Internet Explorer. NCSA Mosaic, however, doesn't support using the WIDTH and HEIGHT attributes in the IMG tag (which are HTML 3.2 attributes). It still appears centered in NCSA Mosaic, though— you just can't resize it.

TIP

Actually, the capability to set the width and height of an inline image allows a rather neat trick for creating a graphic rule. It also allows you to create graphic rules that are much smaller, byte-wise, than a normal graphic rule. To do this, in your graphic editor, create a small graphic (say 10 by 10 pixels) using the color of your choice as the background color and save it out to C:\HTML as a GIF file. Next, insert the graphic into your Web page as an inline image and then set the height and width attributes to, say, 10 pixels × 595 pixels. For instance:

```
<P ALIGN="center"><IMG SRC="yourfile.gif" WIDTH="10" HEIGHT="595">
```

If the color of your 10 pixel × 10 pixel graphic was red, for instance, then a red graphic rule, 10 pixels high and 595 pixels wide, would appear on-screen. Also, notice the use of a center-aligned paragraph—those browsers that don't support setting the height and width of an inline image will at least center your 10 × 10 graphic on-screen (if they support paragraph center-alignment, that is).

You also can set the width as a percentage of the total width of the browser window: just insert WIDTH= "75%," or some other percentage, for instance.

Experiment with using different colors, and combinations of colors. Some graphic editors, also, allow you to add textures or patterns to an image with which you can experiment.

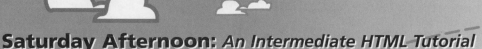

Changing Font Sizes and Colors

The FONT tag allows you to specify the size and color of a section of text. This is an HTML 3.2 element and was originally a Netscape extension. Both Netscape Navigator and Internet Explorer recognize this tag, but NCSA Mosaic does not.

Originally, Netscape's introduction of the FONT tag spawned some controversy, some perceived it as challenging the basic philosophy behind HTML, which is to logically rather than literally describe the elements that compose a document. It has since been incorporated into HTML 3.2, however, and so now qualifies as "standard HTML."

Changing the Font Size

The FONT tag uses the SIZE attribute to change the size of a font. You can set font sizes using absolute or relative size values.

Setting Absolute Font Size Values

There are seven "absolute" (or fixed) sizes, numbered from "1" to "7," that you can set using the SIZE attribute of the FONT tag. The default is "3," which is the same as regular paragraph text. "1" is the smallest and "7" is the largest, which means you can set two absolute font sizes that are smaller than normal paragraph text and four sizes that are larger. Each Web browser determines the actual sizes of these fonts. To see what these different font sizes look like in your Web browser, enter the following and then hop over to your browser:

```
<P><FONT SIZE="1">Font Size 1.</FONT><BR>
<FONT SIZE="2">Font Size 2.</FONT><BR>
<FONT SIZE="3">Font Size 3 (the default).</FONT><BR>
<FONT SIZE="4">Font Size 4.</FONT><BR>
<FONT SIZE="5">Font Size 5.</FONT><BR>
<FONT SIZE="6">Font Size 6.</FONT><BR>
<FONT SIZE="7">Font Size 7.</FONT>
```

As you can see in Figure 3-45 (or in your browser if you're using Netscape Navigator or Internet Explorer), the font sizes you can set range from the very small to the quite large.

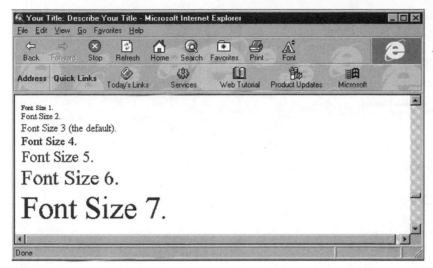

Figure 3-45.
You can set absolute font sizes that Netscape Navigator, Internet Explorer, or any HTML 3.2 compliant Web browser can display. NCSA Mosaic, however, doesn't recognize the FONT tag.

NOTE

You also can nest font tags inside of each other, so conceivably you might do something like this to switch back to the default font size in the middle of a larger set font size:

```
<FONT SIZE="4">This is Font Size 4. <FONT SIZE="3">This is the
default size font.</FONT> This is Font Size 4 again.</FONT>.
```

Setting Relative Font Size Changes

You also can set "relative" font sizes. Relative font size changes are indicated by either a plus (+) or minus ( ) sign preceding the font size number. For instance, FONT SIZE="+1" indicates a font size that is one size larger than the base font. Since the default base font is the same as a Size 3 absolute font size, a Size +1 relative font would be the same as a Size 4 absolute font (3 + 1 = 4). For instance, enter the following for an example of using relative font size changes to indicate the seven possible font sizes:

```
<P><FONT SIZE="-2">Font Size -2.</FONT><BR>
<FONT SIZE="-1">Font Size -1.</FONT><BR>
Default Font Size.<BR>
<FONT SIZE="+1">Font Size +1.</FONT><BR>
<FONT SIZE="+2">Font Size +2.</FONT><BR>
<FONT SIZE="+3">Font Size +3.</FONT><BR>
<FONT SIZE="+4">Font Size +4.</FONT>
```

As you can see in Figure 3-46, "-2" is the same as "1," "-1," the same as "2," "+1," the same as "4," and so on. The default font size, which requires no font size change, is the same as "3."

Figure 3-46.

You can also set font sizes relative to the default font size, "-1" being one size smaller, "+1" being one size larger.

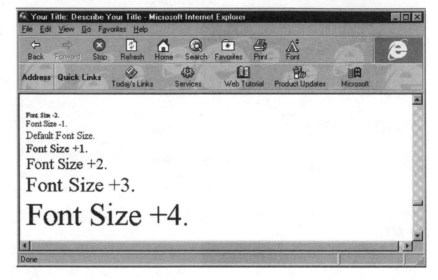

Now, you may be asking, "If relative fonts are just another way to specify the same fonts as absolute fonts, why bother?" The next section, "Setting the Base Font," provides the answer to this question.

Setting the Base Font

The BASEFONT tag allows you to change the size of the "base font" (paragraph text). You can set it to any of the absolute font sizes, 1 through 7 (3 is the default). This is a Netscape extension that by both Netscape Navigator and Internet Explorer recognize, but which hasn't been incorporated into HTML 3.2. It's a stand-alone (or empty) tag. You set the base font size the same way you set an absolute font size. For instance, to set the base font to the same size as an absolute font size of "4," you would enter the following:

```
<BASEFONT SIZE="4">
```

If you change the base font size, then all relative font sizes will change relative to the new base font. For instance, if you change the base font size to "4" as above, then a relative font size of "+1" would then be the same as an absolute font size of "5" (4 + 1 = 5).

You can insert the BASEFONT tag at any point within a Web page to set the base font to any of the absolute font sizes. It takes effect until another BASEFONT tag changes the basefont size. It not only effects relative font sizes and SMALL and BIG font changes (see below), but the size of all paragraph text, character rendering (italic, bold, and so on), list elements, definition lists, block quotes, predefined text, and address blocks that follow it. Headings and text set with absolute font size changes, however, are not effected.

Using the SMALL and BIG Tags

The SMALL and BIG tags also are Netscape extensions that have now been incorporated into HTML 3.2. Besides Netscape Navigator, Internet Explorer Version 3.0 also recognizes these tags (Version 2.0, however, docs not).

The simplest form of using these tags is simply to specify a font that's smaller or larger than the default text font (or base font). Enter the following for an example of using the SMALL and BIG tags:

```
<P><SMALL>This is a small font.</SMALL>.<BR>
This is a normal font.<BR>
<BIG>This is a big font.</BIG>
```

As shown in Figure 3-47, the SMALL font is the same as a font set with the FONT tag's SIZE="2" attribute value, and the BIG font is the same as a font set with the FONT tag's SIZE="4" attribute value. (The default text font is the same as the FONT tag's SIZE="3" attribute value.)

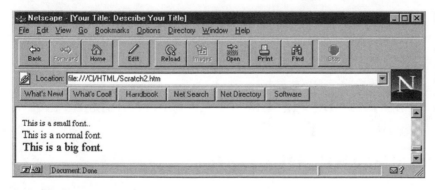

Figure 3-47.
You can use the SMALL and BIG tags to specify a font size that's smaller or larger than the default text font.

You actually can specify all seven of the FONT tag sizes by nesting these tags. For an example of doing this, add the following to the previous example:

```
<P><SMALL><SMALL>Small, small font.</SMALL></SMALL><BR>
<SMALL>Small font.</SMALL><BR>
Normal font.<BR>
<BIG>Big font.</BIG><BR>
<BIG><BIG>Big, big font.</BIB></BIG><BR>
<BIG><BIG><BIG>Big, big, big font.</BIG></BIG></BIG>
```

Notice that the jump between the big, big font and the big, big, big font jumps from the SIZE="5" to the SIZE="7" FONT size. To create a SIZE="6" font using the SMALL and BIG tags, you have to nest a combination of these tags. To see how to do this, add the following to the above example:

```
<BIG><BIG>Big, big font.</BIB></BIG><BR>
```

**<SMALL><SMALL><BIG><BIG><BIG><BIG>This is a big, big, big, big font
nested inside a small, small
font.</SMALL></SMALL></BIG></BIG></BIG></BIG>
**

```
<BIG><BIG><BIG>Big, big, big font.</BIG></BIG></BIG>
```

As shown in Figure 3-48, nesting SMALL and BIG tags in the above manner duplicates the seven possible font sizes set with the FONT tag's SIZE attribute above.

Figure 3-48.

You can also use SMALL and BIG tags to set font sizes.

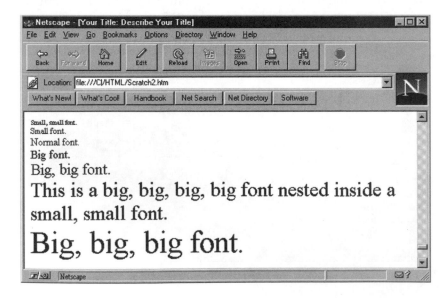

Of course, you might be wondering what the point of this is if the SIZE attribute of the FONT tag already can do the job. The only point here, really, is that in HTML you can do the same thing in more than one way (such as using the CENTER tag and and a center-aligned DIV tag). Here the SMALL tag is the same as setting a relative font size of "-1," while the BIG tag is the same as setting a relative font of "+1." You must decide whether one way or the other has more utility. Nesting SMALL and BIG fonts to get the rest of the possible font sizes—that's just a trick, and of doubtful utility, but worth showing just to show that you can do it.

Changing the Font Color

The FONT tag uses the COLOR attribute to change the color of a font. The two ways to specify a font color are 1) to use one of 16 color names that match Window's 16-color palette, 2) to use RGB hex codes, which is more difficult, but which give you access to a *much, much* wider range of colors.

Setting the Font Color Using Color Names

You can use any one of 16 color names to specify a font color. Besides black and white, you also can specify aqua, blue, fuchsia, gray, green, lime, maroon, navy, olive, purple, red, silver, teal, and yellow.

Enter the following for an example of specifying font colors using color names (this example omits "black" and "white"):

```
<P><FONT SIZE=7><FONT COLOR="aqua">Aqua </FONT><FONT
COLOR="blue">Blue </FONT><FONT COLOR="fuchsia">Fuchsia </FONT><FONT
COLOR="gray">Gray </FONT><FONT COLOR="green">Green </FONT><FONT
COLOR="lime">Lime </FONT><FONT COLOR="maroon">Maroon </FONT><FONT
COLOR="navy">Navy </FONT><FONT COLOR="olive">Olive </FONT><FONT
COLOR="purple">Purple </FONT><FONT COLOR="red">Red </FONT><FONT
COLOR="silver">Silver </FONT><FONT COLOR="teal">Teal </FONT><FONT
COLOR="yellow">Yellow </FONT></FONT>
```

The illustration in Figure 3-49, reproduced here in monochrome, gives only a rough idea of what it would look like in a browser. So, be sure to hop over to your browser, if you have Netscape Navigator or Internet Explorer, to see what it *really* looks like.

Figure 3-49.

In Netscape Navigator and Internet Explorer, as well as in any HTML 3.2 compliant Web browser, you can set the font color to any one of 16 different color names.

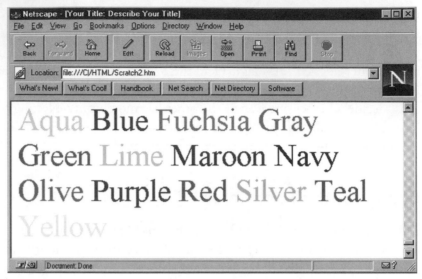

Setting the Font Color Using RGB Hex Codes

This is a much more difficult way to set font colors than using color names, but gives you the choice of a very large range of colors. Essentially, it lets you specify values from 0 to 255 for the Red, Green, and Blue components of a color, providing you with a grand total of no less than 16.7 million different colors from which to choose.

Finding the perfect color when you use this method is somewhat akin to finding a needle in a haystack. Also, many of these possible colors may not display equally well on, say, a monitor that can display only 256 colors. On top of that, you have to specify the RGB values in hexadecimal rather than decimal number format. (Note: One of the reasons hexadecimal is used for this type of thing is that every number between 0 and 255 can be represented with only two characters. For instance, 159 in hex is 9F.)

You set the RGB hex code for a color in the FONT tag in this general form, where *rr* is the hex value for red, *gg* the hex value for green, and *bb* the hex value for blue:

```
<FONT COLOR="#rrggbb">This is the text to be colored.</FONT>
```

For instance, a red color here could be specified as FF0000, a green color as 00FF00, and a blue color as 0000FF. (FF is the highest hexadecimal number, equaling 255, while 00 is the lowest, equaling 0.) Enter the following as an example of assigning font

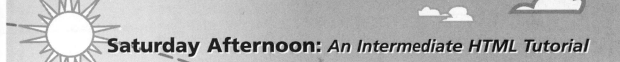

colors using RGB hex codes (the example also sets the font size so it will be more visible in your browser):

```
<FONT SIZE="6"><FONT COLOR="#FF0000">Red (FF0000) </FONT><FONT
COLOR="#00FF00">Green (00FF00) </FONT><FONT COLOR="#0000FF">Blue
(0000FF)</FONT></FONT>
```

Since this is shown in Figure 3-50 only in monochrome, you'll have to hop over to your browser if you want to check what this really looks like.

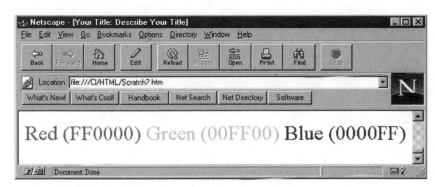

Figure 3-50.
You can also set colors using hexadecimal codes, which is much more difficult, but allows you access up to 16.7 million possible colors, depending on the monitor and graphics card being used.

Showing you how to count in hexadecimal or, for that matter, how an RGB color scheme works goes beyond the scope of this book. Quite frankly, unless you already know hex *and* RGB color theory, the *only* practical way to go is to use some kind of color chart, wheel, or cube that allows you to simply select the color you want and get the corresponding hex code. Many charts, tables, and utilities are available on the Web for getting the hex codes for colors. For a number of pointers to where you can find these on the Web, see Appendix A.

Many HTML editors also have built-in color charts and utilities that let you choose a color and then insert the hex code into your Web page. This is a compartment in which an HTML editor can be far superior to a mere text editor like Notepad. Figure 3-51 shows HTML Notepad's built-in color utility.

Setting the Background, Text, and Links Colors

You can set the colors for the background, text, and links by using these attributes of the BODY tag: BGCOLOR sets the background color, TEXT the text (or foreground) color, LINK the color of hypertext links, VLINK the color of visited links, and ALINK the color of activated links (where you hold down the mouse button on a link, but haven't released it). These were originally Netscape extensions, but have now been incorporated into HTML 3.2. Not only Netscape Navigator and Internet Explorer, but NCSA Mosaic, as well, all recognize these attributes. As with the FONT tag's COLOR attribute that was treated above, you can set these attributes using any of the 16 color names (black, white, aqua, blue, fuchsia, gray, green, lime, maroon, navy, olive, purple, red, silver, teal, and yellow) or by using RGB hexadecimal codes.

Figure 3-51.
Many HTML Editors have built-in color utilities that make inserting hex codes for colors a relative breeze.

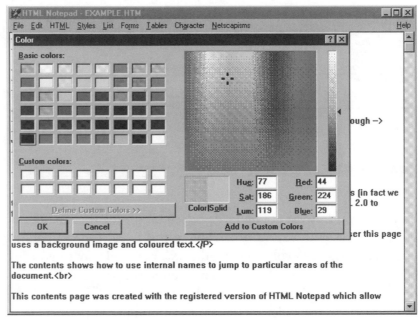

The general form for entering these attributes as color names is shown here where *colorname* is one of the 16 colornames given:

```
<BODY BGCOLOR="colorname" TEXT="colorname" LINK="colorname"
VLINK="colorname" ALINK="colorname"
```

The general form for entering these attributes as RGB hexadecimal codes is shown here, where *rrggbb* is three hexadecimal numbers forming the RGB code for setting the red, green, and blue components of an RGB color:

```
<BODY BGCOLOR="#rrggbb" TEXT="#rrggbb" LINK="#rrggbb" VLINK="#rrggbb"
ALINK="#rrggbb"
```

The following example sets the colors for the background, the text (or foreground), and the three varieties of links—regular links, visited links, and activated links. Go up to the top of the Web page and then add the following to the BODY tag as an example of setting these attributes:

```
<BODY BGCOLOR="#336699" TEXT="#66CC66" LINK="#FFCC00"
VLINK="#ff6666" ALINK="#FF0000"
```

This sets the background color to slate blue, the text to light green, the links to orange gold, visited links to a salmon peach (or something like that), and activated links to bright red.

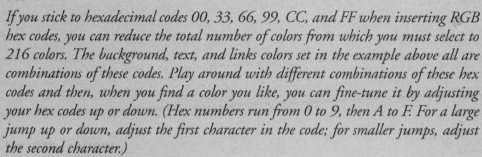

TIP

If you stick to hexadecimal codes 00, 33, 66, 99, CC, and FF when inserting RGB hex codes, you can reduce the total number of colors from which you must select to 216 colors. The background, text, and links colors set in the example above all are combinations of these codes. Play around with different combinations of these hex codes and then, when you find a color you like, you can fine-tune it by adjusting your hex codes up or down. (Hex numbers run from 0 to 9, then A to F. For a large jump up or down, adjust the first character in the code; for smaller jumps, adjust the second character.)

Since the illustrations in this book are not printed in color, Figure 3-52 can only show you the contrast and tone of the colors you set above. You need to hop over to your Web browser to see what this really looks like.

CAUTION

Whatever colors you choose to set for your Web page, if you decide to set colors (and nothing says you have to), you should try to avoid color combinations that render your text font less readable. Some color combinations on the Web render Web pages entirely unreadable. *You see, it doesn't matter how pretty your colors are if they render your page illegible.*

The important thing is to develop and organize your content and then and only then hone the appearance of your Web page. Setting the colors for a badly conceived and poorly organized Web page can only make it worse, not better. Keep the horse in front of the cart, in other words.

Figure 3-52.

You can set the colors of the background, text, and links of a Web page. Netscape Navigator, Internet Explorer, and NCSA Mosaic all recognize these colors.

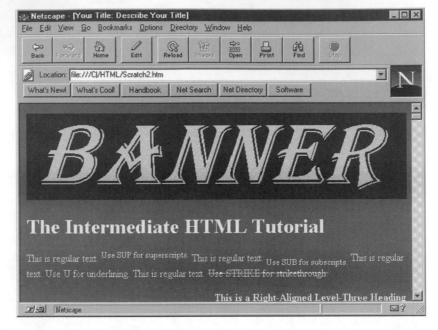

Using a Background Image

The BACKGROUND attribute of the BODY tags allows you to specify a background image. Originally a Netscape extension, it has since been incorporated into HTML 3.2. Netscape Navigator, Internet Explorer, and NCSA Mosaic all support the use of this attribute. The graphic file for the background image can be a GIF or JPEG image. The general format for entering this attribute is shown as follows, where *filename* is a GIF or JPEG file that is in the same directory as the Web page and *URL* is a partial or absolute address of a GIF or JPEG file that is in a directory other than the Web page:

```
<BODY BACKGROUND="filename or URL">
```

A key consideration when using background images is to avoid busy or high-contrast images. If you're going to use a dark background images, you should set the color of your text and links to a lighter color. Go up to the top of the Web page and then add the following to the BODY tag as an example of setting these attributes (note the added comment tags which comment out the old BODY tag with the color attributes you set above):

```
<!--<BODY BGCOLOR="#336699" TEXT="#66CC66" LINK="#FFCC00"
VLINK="#ff6666" ALINK="#FF0000">-->
<BODY BACKGROUND="backgrnd.gif">
```

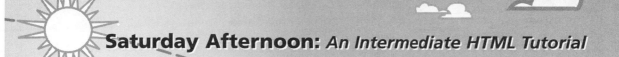

Figure 3-53 shows a Web page that has BACKGRND.GIF tiled in the background. To see what this really looks like, though, you need to hop over to your browser.

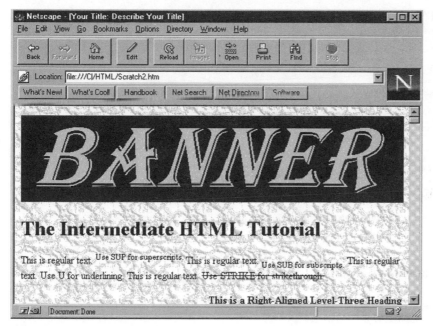

Figure 3-53.
One of the most effective ways to add visual appeal to your Web page is to use a background image.

You should keep your background images small to minimize the time it takes them to load. Background images that are smaller than the window are tiled to fill it. Keep your background images to, say, 100 × 100 pixels. You also can use a photopaint program to reduce the contrast and increase or decrease the brightness of a background image, as well as change the hue or saturation, diffuse the image, and so on. Also, you may have to play around with some images, using the spray paint or the smudger, to prevent the edge of the graphic from showing when you tile it. Many photopaint programs also have patterns you can use to create background images. Use the same background image for all Web pages in a related group of pages—that way the image must load only once.

TIP

If you use a GIF image as a background image, as with any other GIF image you can set one of its colors to transparent. This can allow you to use both a background image and a background color, for instance, at the same time. You might, for instance, create a series of pages using the same background image, but different background colors, or using the same background color but different background images.

Netscape's Dastardly Blink Tag

No tag introduced by Netscape has drawn so much abuse. I'm not sure anyone likes the BLINK tag, but some people use it just the same. I personally find blinking text to just be irritating. If I'm not mistaken, and this may be entirely subjective, Netscape seems to have slowed the blink down, which maybe means that it is only half as irritating as it used to be. So why bring it up? Why, for that matter, show you how to do it? Perhaps for no good reason, except that I don't believe in "don'ts."

If you're going to use this tag, you should *really* use it—blink a big font, not just some puny little scrap of text. Paradoxically, the bigger the blinking text, the less irritating (in my opinion, anyway).

So here's an example of using the BLINK tag, nested inside a big, big font:

```
<P ALIGN="center"><BIG><BIG>Netscape's Dastardly
<BIG><BLINK>Blink</BLINK></BIG> Tag</BIG></BIG></P>
```

Figure 3-54 shows the blink when it is on and Figure 3-55 shows it when it is off.

Microsoft's Extensions

Microsoft has added a number of extensions to HTML, including the capability to specify background sounds, a fixed background image that won't scroll, left and top margins, font faces, horizontal rule colors, and scrolling text marquees. Other than background sounds, which, inexplicably, NCSA Mosaic supports, no other browser supports these extensions. Also, none of these extensions have been included in HTML 3.2. Until they get wider support from other browsers, you should avoid using these extensions in your Web pages.

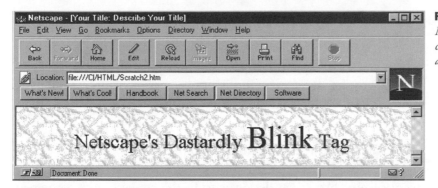

Figure 3-54.
Netscape Navigator can blink a tag on and off—here it is on.

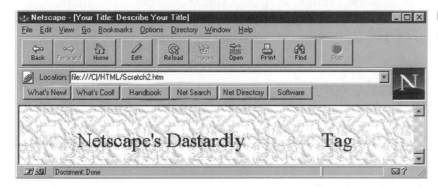

Figure 3-55.
Here it is off.

If you want to play around and experiment with them, however, go ahead. My favorite, personally, is the MARQUEE tag. Microsoft has a full listing and description of all these extensions at

```
http://www.microsoft.com/workshop/author/newhtml/de-fault.htm
```

Save Your File for Future Reference

Go ahead and save your file, using a file name you can remember. You can use it later as a reference sheet for doing any of the things this tutorial covers.

Conclusion

If you've made it this far, you're doing good. If you've skipped ahead to here, that's all right too. The main thing you needed to accomplish today was to complete the basic HTML tutorial. Any parts of the intermediate HTML tutorial you manage to finish are icing on the cake.

You may want to start thinking about what kind of Web page you might want to create tomorrow. To start out, though, think primarily in terms of aims, purposes, and relevant content. Conceptualize it first, then design it to fit the concept. Get some text typed if you want. To start out, though, keep it as simple as you can. A simple structure for a Web page, for instance, might be a banner graphic, a level-one heading, an introductory paragraph, a link list, and an address block. You'd be surprised how many Web pages on the Web fit that profile or a close variant of it. Keep it simple. Stick to basics.

You also might want to experiment tonight with creating a banner graphic you might want to use for your Web page (just save it as a GIF file in the C:\HTML directory). You don't need to get fancy—just create something to personalize your page, about 595 pixels wide.

Get a good night's sleep. See you tomorrow.

Sunday Morning:
Planning Your First Web Page

Before you actually start creating your first Web page, you need to do some planning. This chapter breaks down into the following sections:

1. Getting Started

2. Planning Your First Web Page

3. Examples from the Web

The "Getting Started" section discusses some of the general considerations that you will want to take into account when planning your Web page. The "Planning a Basic Web Page" section covers planning a basic Web page. It provides three generic Web page structures that you can use as guides for planning and organizing your own material. The "Examples from the Web" section presents specific examples of actual Web pages on the Web. They show the wide range of publishing projects you can do using fairly straightforward HTML.

Getting Started

In this chapter, you plan your first Web page, and in the next chapter you create your first Web page. So, this morning, if you're still on schedule, you do some necessary work to prepare for actually creating your first Web page this afternoon.

The Planning Process

This section delineates a process that you may want to follow for planning your Web page, broken down here into four steps:

- Defining your objective
- Doing an outline
- Assembling your materials
- Drawing a map

How you want to execute these steps is up to you. Starting out, use whatever works best for you, which might be Windows Notepad, your word processor, a yellow legal pad, the back of an envelope, a restaurant table cloth, butcher paper taped to the wall; just whatever works for you. If not at the start, at least by the end of this process, you'll be pulling it all together in a text editor, such as Notepad, or in your word processor. The final product will be a text file (exported out as an ASCII text file if you use a word processor to create it) referred to as a *mock-up text file*, which includes everything you want to have in your Web page except for the HTML codes, organized and arranged according to the relative order, precedence, and position in which you want it to appear. Then, this afternoon, you add the HTML to create your first Web page.

Defining Your Objective

You begin by defining your objective. In this case, your objective amounts to what you want to do—in a nutshell, your "idea." If you don't already know what you want to do, or feel you don't have a clear enough idea yet, you might follow one of the suggestions for brainstorming provided in these sections.

Doing Your Outline

You then take your objective and break it down into its main constituent parts, creating an outline, defining the basic structure and order of precedence of your material.

Assembling Your Materials

In assembling your materials, you sketch out what you want to do in more detail. You want to develop and write some text to go with your outline. You also may want to create a customized banner or logo graphic, although you may use the sample banner graphic provided. If you want to include a list of links connecting to other Web pages or sites out on the Web, you need to gather the URLs (Web addresses) you want to use. Additionally, after you become a more sophisticated and experienced Web publisher, you may want to select or create a background image; create and convert some graphs, charts, or diagrams; define a form; design a table; delineate some frames; create an animated GIF; include some streaming audio, animation, or video; and so on.

Don't worry, models are provided for organizing your text and plugging in your banner graphic and hypertext links.

Drawing a Map

The last thing you do is draw a map. Although an outline captures the static structure of a Web page or Web site, a map delineates the dynamic relationships within and between your Web pages. These dynamic relationships are defined by the use of hypertext links that allow you to create alternative paths, rather than just a top-down, linear path along which someone might peruse the information you present. Your first Web page, however, will be quite simple. After you get around to creating more complex and sophisticated multipage Web sites, however, the mapping of the dynamic relationships within and between your Web pages becomes much more important. Some approaches you might want to take in drawing a map when you do reach this stage are suggested.

The End Product

The end product of your planning process is a text file, called a *mock-up text file*. It includes the text you want to include in your Web page, as well as references in your text to any images you want to include (probably just your banner graphic), as well as any URLs you want to use as hypertext links.

This chapter breaks down the planning process into a series of tasks that you can perform. Now, you don't have all day for this (rather, just this morning), so don't get bogged down in any one task. Do your best, but don't take more than 30 to 45 minutes on any one of them. The main point here is not to plan a Web page in depth, but to get a taste of what a real planning process might be like.

Run your text editor or word processor, or get out your yellow legal pad. Or head out to your favorite restaurant or coffee shop if you do your best thinking on napkins.

Planning Your First Web Page

This section walks you through the different steps of the planning process. You need to perform certain tasks at each stage.

Defining Your Objective

First, you must define what you want to do. One way is to try to boil it down to an "objective"—the purpose of your undertaking. (This sometimes is called a mission statement, but that just seems a bit too formal for this activity.) Don't assume that you already know your objective. Even worse than thinking you know all the answers is thinking you know all the questions. The first order of business here, in other words, is to identify the questions.

The Four Questions: Why?, Who?, What?, and How?

Your first question should simply be, "Why do I want to create a Web page?" Try to think of all the reasons you might want to create a Web page. Write them down in a list. Don't just stop at the first answer. For instance, you might find that you not only want to sell a product, but you also want to communicate with clients, provide information, educate and inform, get customer feedback, entertain, and quite possibly more. All of these can lead to further questions, with further lists of answers.

Your second question should be, "Who am I trying to reach?" The Web is all about connecting, but nobody is compelled to connect with anyone else. If people choose to connect with you, they generally do so of their own accord. Push strategies simply don't work well on the Web. Pull strategies *do* work. Offer information, resources, even entertainment. What pulls people to your site or page and keeps them coming back generally isn't that you happen to be selling a product or offering a service, but that you offer "value-added" resources. Think of what you can offer, what you have to give. Target that relative to the audience you would like to attract. Then provide links to descriptions of your company, products, and services. That's what works.

The third question should be, "What kind of page do I need?" you should ask this question only after you've answered the first two. Answer the first two questions, "why?" and "who?" and the following question, "what?" should almost answer itself.

The fourth question should then be something like, "How do I want my page to implement my why, who, and what?" In other words, correlate the "why?" and the "who?" to come up with your "what?" and then let that "what?" determine your "how?" Put it all together and you have your objective.

Stay flexible and open! You can spend so much time and effort creating an objective that you can end up being hesitant to change or alter it in response to changing realities and understandings. So don't get too hung up on your objective. Try to make it an aiming point, a working hypothesis, not a stone around your neck.

Remember right now you're only creating an objective for one page. You probably would come up with a different objective if it were for an entire Web publishing enterprise or undertaking. Tie that into the mission statement of your company, organization, or agency, and you probably can come up with yet another objective.

TASK #1: Define Your Objective

Ask yourself the four one-word key questions and then combine your answers to form a single statement. This statement then becomes your objective.

Develop this statement in a medium with which you're comfortable. You might want to start out working in your text editor or word processor, or you might want to start out working on a pad of paper—whatever gets your creative juices flowing.

Doing Your Outline

Whereas an objective expresses the intentions, purposes, and goals of your project as a whole, an outline organizes it into divisions and subdivisions, establishing the hierarchy and sequence of the material you want to present.

Your outline doesn't have to be complicated or even terribly complete, but it should at least break your objective down into its basic components, even if only just A, B, and C. As with your objective, your initial outline should not be set in slate. It may not take full form, for instance, until you are well into the next phase, assembling your materials. Some people prefer to create an outline right off the bat. Others need to sketch out their ideas first, from which they can then distill their outline.

TASK #2: Do Your Outline

For now, use your objective as the top level of your outline, then break out beneath it the different parts or components that you see as composing it. These components define and order how you want to execute your objective, providing a structure for the information you're going to want to present to a viewer of your Web page. If you want, write a brief description of each component.

Assembling Your Materials

In this stage, you need to flesh out and write the text you want to include in your Web page, create any graphics you want to include, and gather any URLs you want to use as hypertext links.

Gather the information you want to use and then start plugging it into the basic structure delineated by your outline. Realize that, as you gather your data, you may find that your outline, or even your objective, changes. What you should end up with here is a somewhat fleshed-out draft that at least has everything put roughly into place, even if it's in the form of a "To be determined," "Need to create a graphic," "Get photo," "Write product description," "Create chart of sales figures," or other sort of statement.

Whereas your outline provides a skeleton for your idea, the material assembly phase gives it "body." In the material assembly phase, you get into the more concrete process of actually developing your material, thinking of a provisional title (level-one heading), sketching an introductory paragraph, developing some graphics if you want to include them, scanning a photo, and so on.

Using the Example Web Pages

To help cut down the number of choices you have to make, you can use two generic Web page examples to create the text for your Web page. Additionally, a third generic Web page example suitable for creating a multipage Web site is presented, although you should try one of the other two models first. These Web page models are

- A basic Web page with a list. Can be a list of particulars or a list of links to other Web pages.

- A basic Web page with a list of internal links to subsections.

- A basic Web site composed of a main Web page with a list of external links to a series of subpages.

NOTE

Content, content, content. All the whiz-bang graphics aside, what still matters more than anything else is simply content—straightforward, honest information. What the Web doesn't need more of, but which it's getting anyway, are loads of narcissistic, self-congratulatory, bandwidth hogging, but otherwise empty Web pages.

Don't join the parade. Be informative instead. Provide content. Do something that hasn't already been done thousands of times over. Before doing a Web page on a certain subject, do a few searches on the Web using Open Text, Webcrawler, Yahoo!, or some search engine to find out whether someone else has already done what you want to do. If so, just create a link to it rather than cover the same ground.

Task #3: Select a Web Page Example

Choose one of the following example Web pages to use as a model in assembling the materials for your Web page. If you're planning your first Web page, use one of the first two examples. Use the third example Web page only if you have already created your first Web page using one of the first two examples.

Example #1: A Basic Web Page with a List

This very basic Web page example includes a banner graphic, a level-one heading, an introductory paragraph, a list, and an address block.

The list can be either a "list of particulars," if you will, or a link list that links to other Web pages on the Web. An example of using this example with a plain list (no links) would be to create a "business card" where you describe your business in the introductory paragraph, then follow that with a list of products, services, or qualifications. A different kind of example of a page using a link list linking to other Web pages on the Web would be a page that describes a hobby, professional expertise, or area of interest, followed by a list of links to other pages on the Web that share the same interest. See Figure 4-1.

Figure 4-1.

This is a basic Web page example that uses a heading, an introductory paragraph, and a list of links to other Web pages on the Web. An even simpler version of this would use a plain list without the links.

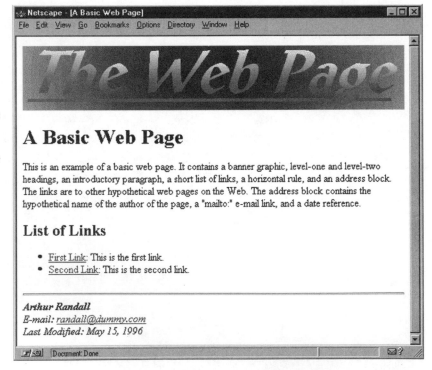

Example #2: A Basic Web Page with Subsections

This is a more complex Web page example, but it's still just a single page. You probably would want to use this example if the idea for your Web page involves more than an introductory paragraph and a list, but includes, for instance, subheadings and sub-sections. The link list here functions as a menu or directory to the subsections of the document, using internal links rather than external ones. See Figure 4-2.

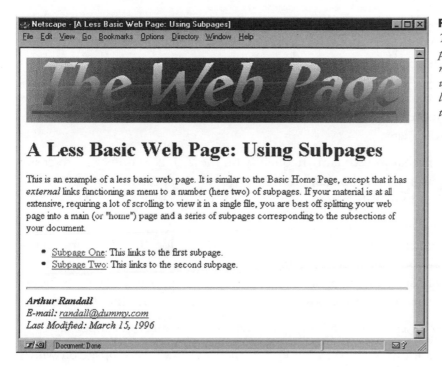

Figure 4-2.
This is a basic Web page that is a little more complicated, using a menu list that links to subsections in the same Web page.

Example #3: A Basic Web Page Linking to Subpages

If the material you want to present is at all extensive, you should consider breaking out the page's subsections into separate subpages. Any time a page extends beyond three or four screens, you probably should break it into more than one page.

NOTE

I don't recommend that you start out using this example. Start first with one of the two single-page examples, then after you create your first Web page, feel free to come back and use this example as a model for creating a multipage Web site using a main (or home) page and several subpages.

One of the advantages of breaking up a long Web page into a main page and subpages is that visitors to your Web site need only load the home page and the particular subpage in which they're interested in seeing rather than wait for the whole document along with any inline images to load before they can read the part they want to read.

On the other hand, breaking up the document into pieces can penalize visitors who want to view the whole document, forcing them to reconnect to the server to retrieve each subpage. Another disadvantage is that a Web document that's broken up into a main page and subpages can't be printed in a single operation, but rather, must be printed in separate pages—and the longer a Web document, especially if it contains mostly text, the more likely that a viewer will want to print it out to read more comfortably or save it for later.

A compromise here that you see fairly frequently on the Web is to do both—to create one version broken up into subpages, but that includes a link to another version that is all in one page and uses subsections.

Another situation in which you might want to create a home page linked to subpages might be one in which you've created a number of different loosely related or unrelated Web pages that you want to link together through an "index" page. It's fairly common on the Web to see personal pages done this way, linking to and serving as indexes for other more specialized pages possibly created for business or other purposes.

See Figure 4-3 for an example of a home page linked to a number of subpages.

A subpage is just another Web page. Figure 4-4 shows an example subpage on which nothing all that special has been done. It doesn't even have a banner graphic. If you use a subpage rather than add subsections to your home page, then what would have been the level-two subheadings are now the level-one headings at the top of your subpages.

There is only one example subpage shown here, but you probably would want to use several subpages. Use this one as a model for any other subpages you need to create.

TIP

I haven't included a banner graphic in the sample subpage. Coordinating your graphics, however, between your main page and your subpages is a good way to give a group of related Web pages, a Web site, a common look and feel. One trick is simply to use a smaller version of the banner graphic that heads your main page.

Figure 4-3.
This is an example of a basic Web page that used subpages rather than subsections.

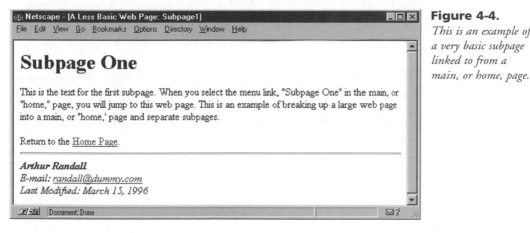

Figure 4-4.
This is an example of a very basic subpage linked to from a main, or home, page.

Notice that the subpage example includes a "loop-back" link at the bottom of the page that returns viewers to the home page. When you use subpages, always include a loop-back link to your home page. A visitor doesn't necessarily have to come through your home page to get to a subpage. If they have the URL on their hotlist or bookmark list or have gotten it from a search engine, they can go directly to your subpage. Without a loop-back link they would have no way to get back to your home page—hitting the Back button doesn't work.

Creating a Mock-Up Text File

The next thing you need to do is create a mock-up of your Web page—a text file that contains everything you want to have in your Web page except the HTML codes. Starting out, you should try to organize this as closely as possible to one of the Web page examples shown here.

TASK #4: Create a Mock-Up Text File

Using the Web page example you've selected as a model, create a mock-up text file of your Web page.

If you selected the first Web page example as your model, create a text tile containing a title, an introductory paragraph, a subheading (optional) for your list, and a list. The list can be simply a list of particulars, or a list of links to other places on the Web. (You learn a bit later in this section how to easily gather URLs that you can use in link lists. For right now, just describe or name the links you want to use, without actually putting in the URLs.)

> **NOTE**
>
> *You also can use the dummy hypertext links provided this afternoon when you get around to using the Web page example file you've selected as a template or guide for creating your first Web page. So right now, you can just put in "First dummy link," "Second dummy link," and so on. Later you can gather some real URLs that you want to use.*

If you selected the second Web page example as your model, create a text file that contains a title, an introductory paragraph, and a list of the subheadings of your Web page, followed by the subsections.

If you selected the third Web page example (you already used one of the first two examples to create your first Web page, and have now chosen to use the third Web page example to create a multipage Web site), create a text file for your main page that contains a title, an introductory paragraph, and a list describing your subpages. You also need to create a text file for each subpage you want to create (the subpages here correspond to the subsections in the second Web page example).

Whichever of the Web page examples you are using, at the bottom of your mock-up text file, insert the information you want to include in the address block at the bottom of your Web page. Include your name, your e-mail address, and the date. Or you could include your mail address, phone number, fax number, and so on, in whichever order you want them to appear.

After you create your mock-up text file, save it in C:\HTML as an ASCII text file (a "text only" file if you're using Word for Windows), giving it a TXT extension. Otherwise, give it a file name that indicates the nature of the Web page you're creating. If you use the third Web page example to plan a multipage Web site, you will need to save ASCII text files for your main Web page and each of your subpages.

Creating Your Graphics

Part of assembling your materials is to create any graphics you want to use. The most complicated effort you should attempt today probably would be to create a personalized banner graphic. For instance you might want to scan in your company logo or a photograph of yourself. Or your might want to design something in a draw or paint program. Just don't spend a whole lot of time right now doing that—you want to try to get this all done today, after all. You can use the sample banner graphic, WEB-PAGE.GIF, which all three basic Web page examples use. Feel free to use it as a placeholder until you can come up with your own graphic.

TASK #5: Create a Banner Graphic (Optional)

Use a graphics editor to create a personalized banner graphic in GIF format. If you don't have a commercial drawing and painting program that you can use to create GIF files (Windows Paintbrush can't create GIF files), you should use Paint Shop Pro, an excellent shareware paint program available on the Web.

Create a graphic that is no more than 595 pixels wide and not more than about 150 pixels high. You might want to create a graphic version of the title for your Web page, for instance, using a fancy font, adding a shadow, or whatever. The details are up to you. Just don't spend a whole lot of time doing this. You can further refine and enhance your banner graphic later, after you create your first Web page.

You may also already have your company logo or some other graphic image you want to use. You may need to scan it in with a scanner, then pull it into your paint or draw program and save it back out as a GIF file. You also may want to resize it, depending on its size and whether you want to use it as a banner graphic.

Gathering Your URLs (Optional)

If you want to include a list of links to other Web pages on the Web, go ahead and gather the URLs you want to use.

NOTE

You need to gather URLs only if you're using the first Web page example with a list that includes links to other Web pages on the Web. Optionally, the actual Web page example file that you use this afternoon as a guide or template includes dummy URLs that you can use. You should still read this section, however, even if you choose not to gather any URLs for now—eventually, and probably sooner than later, you'll want to know how to do this.

Netscape Navigator provides an easy way to gather URLs as you surf. You can highlight the URL of a Web page in the Location box just by clicking on it. You can then press Ctrl+C to copy it to the Clipboard, then paste it (press Ctrl+V) into your mockup text file in Notepad. In Netscape Navigator, you also can copy the URL of any hypertext link simply by clicking on it with the right mouse button, then selecting "Copy This Link Location," to copy its URL to the Clipboard.

TIP

You don't have to remember or write down URLs to include them in a link list, nor do you have to go out on the Web to get them. If you have added URLs to a Bookmark list in Netscape Navigator, a Hotlist in NCSA Mosaic, or a Favorites list in Internet Explorer, you can export any of these lists to a file. You can then edit the file or extract its URLs. (With Netscape Navigator, just copying BOOK-MARK.HTM to another file name accomplishes the same thing as saving it to another file name.) Just load the file into your text editor, copy the URLs to the Clipboard, then paste them into your mock-up text file or your HTML file where you want to use them.

TASK #6: Gather Your URLs (Optional)

If you're going to include URLs in your Web page, go up on the Web and use one of the techniques discussed to copy the URLs you want to use to the Clipboard, then paste them into your mock-up text file at the start of the list items where you want them to appear.

Optionally, see the preceding tip for how to copy URLs from your Bookmark list in Netscape Navigator. You also can export a Hotlist from NCSA Mosaic or a Favorites list from Internet Explorer to a text file, then copy URLs from that text file to where you want them to appear in your mock-up text file.

Skip Ahead?

The following two sections are optional sections. The "Drawing a Map" section is relevant only if you're creating a multipage Web site rather than simply your first Web page. Feel free to come back and read it when you get around to creating your first multipage Web site. You need to read the "Examples from the Web" section only if you're having trouble coming up with an idea for your Web page. If that's the case, the examples shown should stimulate some good ideas. They also illustrate how you can use the basic to intermediate understanding of HTML covered herein to achieve a wide variety of different effects. After you create your first Web page, feel free to look at the examples shown at the end of this chapter for techniques that you too might want to incorporate into your Web pages.

If you're happy with what you've done so far and feel ready to move on, go ahead and save your mock-up text file. Take a break. Have some lunch. See you back this afternoon, in Chapter 5, where you create the Web page that you just planned out.

Drawing a Map (Optional)

You only need to read this chapter if you're creating a multipage Web site. You can create maps for a single Web page, but in most cases it won't be very complex, and can quite easily be skipped. So, if you are not creating a multipage Web site and are running short on time, feel free to skip this section entirely. Before trying to create your first multipage Web site, however, you should read the following section.

An outline defines the static structure of your document but does little to highlight and define the dynamic interrelations within your document. The point and advantage of a hypertext document is that it is dynamic, allowing many different ways to approach and peruse the information you provide. Your "map" may closely mirror your outline, or it may sharply diverge from it, opening uplinks between sections that might otherwise remain estranged and separate from each other.

This map can take many different forms. It can be a simple chart, like an organizational chart, using boxes and lines. It can be a flow chart or a storyboard. Whatever approach you choose to take, it's important that you capture in it the dynamic relationships within and between different parts of your document.

The map of a multipage site can vary considerably. The important thing is to be able to visualize the layout and relationships in your site. In the following figures, the structural relations from the outline are shown in black lines, while the major dynamic relationships (links) are shown in gray lines.

As the first example, you might map your site in the form of an organization chart, as shown in Figure 4-5.

Figure 4-5.
A Web site plan can look like an organization chart.

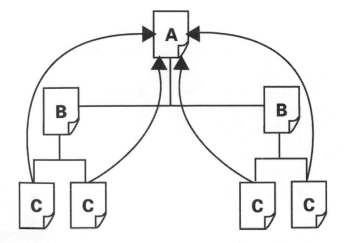

Or, if you're a technical type, you might want to do a flow chart. Another kind of map can be described metaphorically as a "train." A train map might be a good approach for something that uses sequential chapters. In this type of map, your Web pages are like a string of box cars, as shown in Figure 4-6.

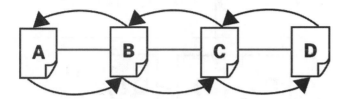

Figure 4-6.
A Web site plan can be organized like a train.

Another approach is to have your home page be the hub of a "wheel," with the sub-pages being the rim, as shown in Figure 4-7.

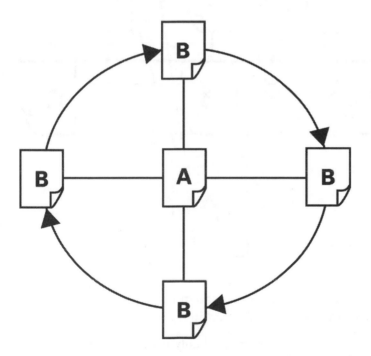

Figure 4-7.
A Web site plan can take the form of a wheel.

And, if you want to create a more complex site, you might want to create a more elaborate map, such as a map that might be pictured as a "tree," which has a trunk, branches, and sub-branches, like what is pictured in Figure 4-8.

Figure 4-8.
A more complex Web site plan might be laid out in the form of a tree.

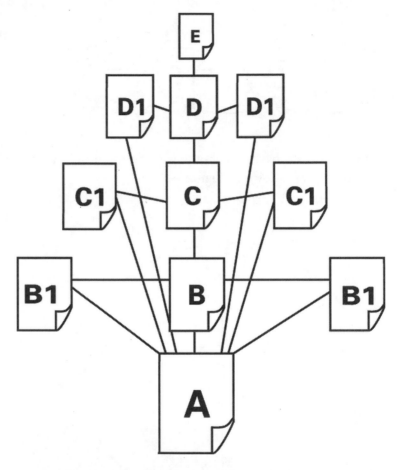

You could conceivably visualize your Web site map in many other ways. The above figures represent only a few of the possibilities, and in quite broad terms.

In planning your very first Web page, there probably is no need to try to draw up a map. Maps are useful only for creating more elaborate, multipage Web sites. Still, even if you're only creating a single page, you might want to try to visualize the kinds of dynamic interrelationships you can activate through links. For instance, if you're creating a Web page using subsections (one of the three generic Web page examples I'll be showing you), in addition to a menu that links to the subheadings of each subsection, you can include at the end of each subsection a "loop-back" link that will return the reader back to the menu. Additionally, at the bottom of the page you might provide a link back to the top of the page.

Examples from the Web (Optional)

If you're just starting out, you should use one of the generic basic Web page examples presented earlier in this chapter for planning and creating the material for your Web page. Don't worry about the fancy stuff yet!

The examples of actual Web pages from the Web are included in this section for two reasons:

- To give you some ideas for different kinds of Web pages you might want to create. If you're having a hard time coming up with an idea for a Web page, check out these pages for examples of different types of pages you might want to create.

- To provide real-world examples of how you can use different tags and techniques to achieve particular effects.

NOTE

You need to read this section first time through only if you're having trouble coming up with a good idea for your Web page. Otherwise, feel free to skip ahead to Chapter 5 at this point. After you create your first Web page, you can come back and review and experiment with some of these techniques and effects.

The Web addresses (URLs) for these pages are included in Appendix A. Feel free to go up on the Web and check these pages out. Most Web browsers let you view the source code for a page being displayed—go ahead and "look under the hood" if you see a page that does something you like. Usually it's nothing too difficult, something you can do easily.

CAUTION

It's perfectly okay to download someone else's Web page, even the associated graphics, if all you want to do is experiment and see "how it's done." It's even okay to use someone else's Web page as a starting template, as long as you replace all the text and graphics with your own.

Whether it's acceptable to copy someone else's "look and feel," even if you do replace all their text and graphics, is a little more of a gray area. I would advise against just slavishly copying someone else's scheme, even if you do replace all the text and graphics.

What definitely isn't appropriate (or even legal) is to download someone else's Web page or Web site, including all the graphics, then just put it up on the Web as your own creation. It's not only unethical—it's patently illegal. Web pages, including all text and graphics, are copyrighted (regardless of whether they display a copyright notice).

If a Web page uses its own original graphics, you also are violating copyright laws if you use them. Many graphics, particularly icons such as for bullets, button, lines, and so on, belong to the public domain. To be safe, unless you know that a graphic is in the public domain, if you want to use it, you should first request permission from the author of the page where you find it.

NOTE

The screen grabs of the example Web pages that follow are intended to illustrate specific types of Web pages, not to serve as examples of good or bad design or the right or wrong way to create Web pages. They also illustrate how you can use different tags to create different effects, and a section that identifies which tags are being used to create which effects follows each example. Copyright for each Web page shown is the property of the author or owner of the page.

A Personal Page

The *personal page* is one of the most common types of Web pages. They abound on the Web, most of them are hardly worth viewing. Don't assume that the topic of the greatest import to you (especially when that subject is yourself) is of any interest to anyone else. Unless you're a celebrity or public figure, why should anyone care about what high school you attended or your dog's name?

Now if your dog has done something really funny, or stupid, or even better, if you have done something really funny or stupid, that's another matter. You should, however, avoid being stupid, as well as infantile, crude, or just generally boorish. In other words, if you're tempted to try to sink to a new low, its already been done. If you want to say something about yourself, say something that says something, not just "I like chocolate." Or, "Party down dudes!" If you say, "I like the classics," explain why, in other words. For an interesting and fun example of a personal Web page, see Figure 4-9.

You'll notice that Charles includes both internal and external links. More to the point, though, is that what he has to offer is actually interesting—and fun! Ultimately, it isn't the design, tasteful or otherwise, that makes or breaks a personal Web page—it's the content. The more "personal," close to the bone, true to life, the better. Show your imperfections in all their glory. Don't embarrass your grandmother, however. Keep it clean.

Including a picture of yourself on a personal Web page seems more common than not, probably because many of these pages are created by "nerds" who have easy access to a scanner, rather than common ordinary "folk." That situation is on the fast mend, however. If you don't have a scanner, never mind—you can leave out the picture. But if you just must have your picture on your page, the local copy shop should be able to scan it for you. They'll probably give you a file in the TIF format, so you'll have to convert it to GIF format.

TECH TIP

The link lists on the page shown in Figure 4-9 are formed using an ordered (numbered) list (OL) interrupted by level-three (H3) headings. The top-level heading (H1) is centered using the CENTER tag, and its size and color is set using the FONT tag. The background, text, and links colors are set in the BODY tag.

Chapter 2 covers these techniques under "Creating Lists" and "Creating Link Lists," and Chapter 3 covers them under "Text Alignment," "Changing Font Sizes and Colors," and "Setting the Background, Text, and Links Colors."

Figure 4-9.

Charles Stuart's Hairy Human's Homepage is a good example of a personal page that is both interesting and fun.

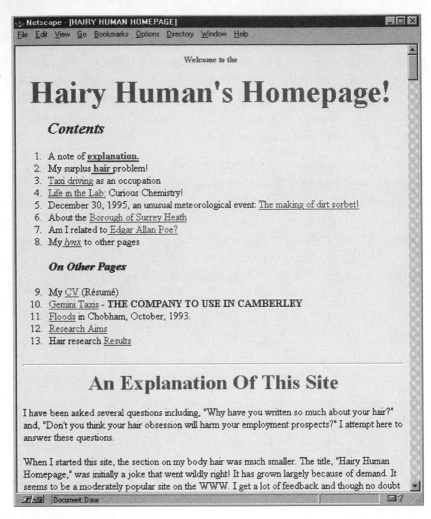

An Online Resume
An Online Resume

An online resume is somewhat like a personal page, except more serious. The main point is to get a job, to make some money, and only secondarily to make some friends. Resumes tend to be rather dull affairs—not exactly interesting or fun. But then, they're not supposed to be. You shouldn't get as personal in a resume as you would in a personal page, right? Right. See Figure 4-10 for a good example of an online resume on the Web.

Send Us
YOUR COMMENTS

Dear Reader:

Thank you for buying this book. In order to offer you more quality books on the topics *you* would like to see, we need your input. At Prima Publishing, we pride ourselves on timely responsiveness to our readers' needs. If you complete and return this brief questionnaire, *we will listen!*

Name (First) _____ (M.I.) _____ (Last) _____

Company _____ Type of business _____

Address _____ City _____ State _____ ZIP _____

Phone _____ Fax _____ E-mail address: _____

May we contact you for research purposes? ❏ Yes   ❏ No

(If you participate in a research project, we will supply you with the Prima computer book of your choice.)

❶ How would you rate this book, overall?

❏ Excellent   ❏ Fair
❏ Very good   ❏ Below average
❏ Good   ❏ Poor

❷ Why did you buy this book?

❏ Price of book   ❏ Content
❏ Author's reputation   ❏ Prima's reputation
❏ CD-ROM/disk included with book
❏ Information highlighted on cover
❏ Other (please specify):_____

❸ How did you discover this book?

❏ Found it on bookstore shelf
❏ Saw it in Prima Publishing catalog
❏ Recommended by store personnel
❏ Recommended by friend or colleague
❏ Saw an advertisement in:_____
❏ Read book review in:_____
❏ Saw it on Web site:_____
❏ Other (please specify):_____

❹ Where did you buy this book?

❏ Bookstore (name):_____
❏ Computer store (name):_____
❏ Electronics store (name):_____
❏ Wholesale club (name):_____
❏ Mail order (name):_____
❏ Direct from Prima Publishing
❏ Other (please specify):_____

❺ Which computer periodicals do you read regularly?_____
_____
_____
_____

❻ Would you like to see your name in print?

May we use your name and quote you in future Prima Publishing books or promotional materials?

❏ Yes   ❏ No

❼ Comments & suggestions: _____
_____
_____

8 I am interested in seeing more computer books on these topics

- ❏ Word processing
- ❏ Desktop publishing
- ❏ Databases/spreadsheets
- ❏ Web site development
- ❏ Networking
- ❏ Internetworking
- ❏ Programming
- ❏ Intranetworking

9 How do you rate your level of computer skills?

- ❏ Beginner
- ❏ Intermediate
- ❏ Advanced

10 What is your age?

- ❏ Under 18
- ❏ 18–29
- ❏ 30–39
- ❏ 40–49
- ❏ 50–59
- ❏ 60–over

SAVE A STAMP

Visit our Web site at **http://www.primapublishing.com**

and simply fill out one of our online response forms.

PRIMA PUBLISHING
Computer Products Division
701 Congressional Blvd., Suite 350
Carmel, IN 46032

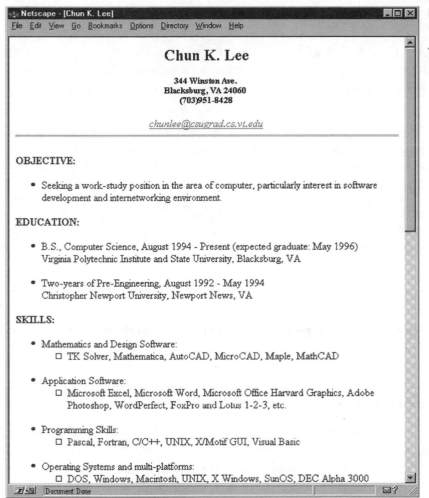

Figure 4-10.
Chun K. Lee's Web page is a good example of an online resume.

Notice that absence of a picture on this resume. I don't know about you, but the idea of someone actually putting their picture on their resume strikes me as weird. Would you hand in a paper resume with your picture on it? I wouldn't. And yet, resumes with the applicants' mugs stuck right on them abound on the Web. I can't help but feel they are trying to be judged on the basis of their looks rather than their talent.

TECH TIP

The bullet list items in Figure 4-10 are separated (spaced out) using separate UL start and end tags for each list item. The Skills section uses nested bullet list items. Rather than head the page with a level-one heading (H1), a level-two heading (H2) is used, while the subheadings are level-four heading tags (H4), befitting the visual understatement that should perhaps be the intention in creating a resume. A horizontal rule is used to separate the heading of the resume from its body. The snail-mail and e-mail addresses are centered using the CENTER tag, and the color of the e-mail link is set in the BODY tag.

Chapter 2 covers these techniques under "Creating Lists" and "The HR (Horizontal Rule) Tag," and Chapter 3 covers them under "Text Alignment" and "Setting the Background, Text, and Links Colors."

The Ubiquitous List of Links Page

Another type of Web page is one that has nothing but links. These pages are everywhere. Much surfing, it seems, comes down to simply hopping from one page of links to another page of links to another page of links.

Why create a list for a subject area that's already well-represented on the Web? Links to other lists are just plain frustrating. However, a good link list in an under-represented area or field of interest is always welcome, such as the one in Figure 4-11. If you were someone interested in dance, for example, this page could be a gold mine.

TECH TIP

The lists in Figure 4-11 are plain unordered link lists without descriptions or explanatory material. Horizontal rules are used to separate the different lists. The level-one heading is centered using the CENTER tag. The background color (#FCF9F6) has been set in the BODY tag.

Chapter 2 covers these techniques under "Creating Lists," "Creating Link Lists," and "The HR (Horizontal Rule) Tag," and Chapter 3 covers them under "Text Alignment" and "Setting the Background, Text, and Links Colors."

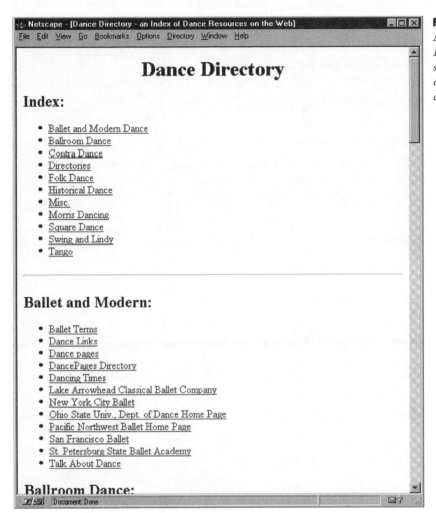

Figure 4-11.
*Marv Vendehey's
Dance Directory
shows that a Web page
of nothing but links
can still be effective.*

A List of Links Page—with Descriptions

Links pages with descriptions can be handy and informative guides to links that might actually amount to something. You avoid the "what's behind door #1?" syndrome that sends your readers off on pointless journeys to pages in which they have no interest. Figure 4-12 shows an effective use of links and descriptions

Figure 4-12.

Mike Bray's Internet Stats and History Web page effectively uses links and descriptions.

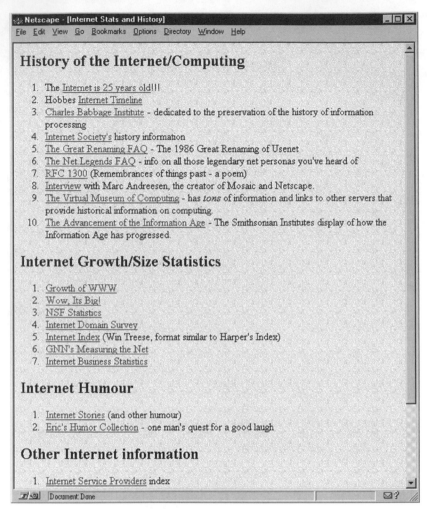

History of the Internet/Computing

1. The Internet is 25 years old!!!
2. Hobbes Internet Timeline
3. Charles Babbage Institute - dedicated to the preservation of the history of information processing
4. Internet Society's history information
5. The Great Renaming FAQ - The 1986 Great Renaming of Usenet
6. The Net Legends FAQ - info on all those legendary net personas you've heard of
7. RFC 1300 (Remembrances of things past - a poem)
8. Interview with Marc Andreesen, the creator of Mosaic and Netscape.
9. The Virtual Museum of Computing - has *tons* of information and links to other servers that provide historical information on computing.
10. The Advancement of the Information Age - The Smithsonian Institutes display of how the Information Age has progressed.

Internet Growth/Size Statistics

1. Growth of WWW
2. Wow, Its Big!
3. NSF Statistics
4. Internet Domain Survey
5. Internet Index (Win Treese, format similar to Harper's Index)
6. GNN's Measuring the Net
7. Internet Business Statistics

Internet Humour

1. Internet Stories (and other humour)
2. Eric's Humor Collection - one man's quest for a good laugh

Other Internet information

1. Internet Service Providers index

TECH TIP

Ordered (numbered) lists (OL) are used in Figure 4-12 to form the link lists. A background image is set in the BODY tag. Notice the absence of a level-one heading here—just a title on the menu bar is used, showing that every rule is meant to be broken (especially when there are no rules).

Chapter 2 covers these techniques under "Creating Lists," and "Creating Link Lists," and Chapter 3 covers them under "Using a Background Image."

Using "In-Context" Links

You don't have to provide links as part of a list. A common way to provide hypertext links is to insert them in context with the material you discuss, as shown in Figure 4-13.

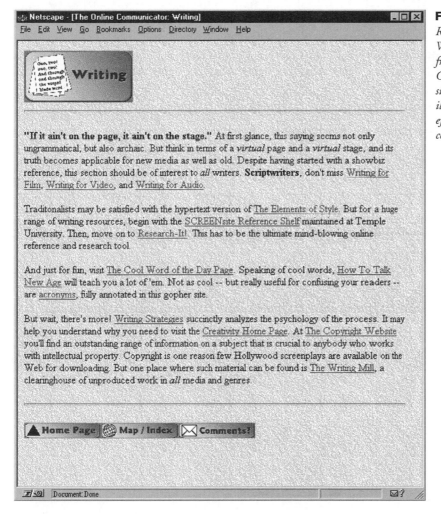

Figure 4-13.
Rich Wilson's Writing Web page from The Online Communicator Web site is an excellent illustration of the effective use of in-context links.

It is important to incorporate this kind of link into the "flow" of what you're presenting or discussing. Don't, for instance, say "For further information on HTML standards, click here." Say something like "Further information on HTML standards can be found at the home page of the W3 Consortium." The idea is to accurately represent what a link is and where it goes so viewers can discern whether they've already been to it or whether they want to go to it again—or at all, for that matter—without breaking the flow and continuity of the material you present. Figure 4-13, Rich Wilson's "Writing" page, shows an excellent example of using in-context links and integrating them into the overall flow of a document. This page is part of Rich Wilson's Web site, "The Online Communicator."

Apart from being a good example of a Web page that uses in-context hypertext links, this is also a good example of a subpage that is part of a larger, multipage Web site. A subpage, for instance, doesn't need a large banner graphic—a small "corner" graphic usually suffices. Also notice the use of navigational buttons at the bottom of the page to link this subpage to the other pages of the site.

TECH TIP

In-context links in Figure 4-13 are simply hypertext links embedded in the flow of a document. A background image is used to create the texture. The BGCOLOR command is also used to set the color of the links. The navigational buttons at the bottom of the page are "image links" all set on the same paragraph with their borders set to zero.

Chapter 2 covers these techniques under "Creating Hypertext Links," and Chapter 3 covers them under "Using a Background Image," "Setting the Background, Text, and Links Colors," and "Creating Image Links."

An Informational Page

An *informational page* is a Web page whose sole purpose is to provide information on a particular subject. This could be anything, and I do mean *anything*, from Spam to Bubble Wrap.

Polly Esther Fabrique's Spam Facts Web page in Figure 4-14 shows that an informational page can be both an informative and fun.

Don't worry about trying to duplicate the graphics here. What matters is that this is probably information you can find nowhere else.

Figure 4-14.

Polly Esther Fabrique's Spam Facts Web page shows that a Web page can be both informative and fun.

TECH TIP

The lists in Figure 4-14 are created by nesting an unordered list (UL) inside an ordered list (OL). A background color and a transparent background image are used together. The size of the text font is reset up one size with the BASEFONT tag.

Chapter 2 covers these techniques under "Creating Lists" and "Nesting Lists" and Chapter 3 covers them under "Changing Font Sizes and Colors," "Setting the Background, Text, and Links Colors," and "Using a Background Image."

The World's Best Bubble Wrap Homepage by Opal Cat in Figure 4-15 is another example of an informational Web page with high entertainment value.

Figure 4-15.

The World's Best Bubble Wrap Homepage by Opal Cat is another fun, informative, and unique Web page.

In Figure 4-15, it isn't graphics special effects that make this page, but simply the content. It really is a lot of fun. And who does not want to know about Bubble Wrap? I wouldn't be surprised if we don't have a Bubble Wrap gene that just lay dormant, passed from generation to generation, until someone finally invented the stuff. It's hard to believe we don't have built-in receptors that respond on a very, very deep level to popping those darn bubbles.

There's nothing terribly complicated about how this page is laid out. In fact, it's somewhat similar to the second Web page example, the one with the internal links to subsections, presented earlier in this chapter. This page does pretty much the same thing—it creates a directory at the top that then links to the different section headings.

TECH TIP

The lists on the page shown in Figure 4-15 are just plain ordinary unordered lists (UL). At the top of the page, the first two heading lines are set using level-one (H1) and level-two (H2) heading tags, which are centered using the ALIGN attribute inside the heading tag. The graphic itself is centered by placing it on a center-aligned paragraph. Chapter 2 covers these techniques under "Creating Lists" and Chapter 3 covers them under "Text Alignment" and "Aligning Images Using Paragraph Alignment."

The two techniques of note are flowing text around a right-aligned image and using a graphic rule rather than a horizontal rule (HR) tag to separate document sections. Chapter 3 covers these techniques under "Wrapping Text Around Images" and "Using a Graphic Rule Instead of the HR Tag."

The Camping in Hawaii Web page shown in Figure 4-16 is an example of getting more out of less. There is nothing fancy here, but it somehow seems clean, clear, and fresh. It makes me want to go to Hawaii, which I guess is the point, after all.

Basically, the only thing this page does differently is use a right-aligned graphic at the top so the first-level heading (H1) wraps down the left side of the image and a few BR (Line Break) tags to move the heading down to the center of the image. It also uses a GIF file of a multicolored bar rather than a horizontal rule. That's it. The multicolored bar is a public domain GIF file available on the Web (it's also included on the CD-ROM).

Figure 4-16.

The Hawaii Visitor's Bureau's Camping in Hawaii Web page is a good example of using graphics to complement the content of a Web page.

> **Netscape - [Camping]**
>
> File   Edit   View   Go   Bookmarks   Options   Directory   Window   Help
>
> # Camping in Hawaii
>
> ## Climate & Weather
>
> With its year-round balmy climate, remote spots and gorgeous scenery, Hawaii is an ideal place to pitch a tent and enjoy the outdoor life of the camper. For those who cherish the feeling of rolling out of a tent to see the first rays of the sun lighting a patch of ocean, there may be no better place.
>
> There are numerous places to camp out on all of the major islands in the state, as well as cabins and hostels for those who seek some shelter. Many beach parks allow oceanfront camping, but spaces may be limited to just a few tents. Visitors may be surprised to see that many local campsites are reserved long in advance by local residents, particularly on weekends and holidays. Hawaiians love the outdoors, and frequently spend their holidays camping out with the whole extended family on a remote beach.
>
> ## Safety First
>
> Campers and hikers are advised to plan ahead and come well prepared. In many of Hawaii's remote areas, such as the Big Island's state and national parks, powerful geologic forces are still quite active, and straying from established trails and campsites can be extremely dangerous.
>
> Weather conditions also change quickly in the islands, and campers should be prepared for sudden showers that can quickly dampen spirits as well as clothing and sleeping bags.
>
> Streams and water taken from catchment systems may not always be potable, and in some places, brackish water may be used for toilets and showers. Campers should check ahead of time with
>
> Document: Done

TECH TIP

The two techniques of note used here are flowing text around a right-aligned image and using a graphic rule rather than a horizontal rule (HR) tag to separate document sections.

Chapter 3 covers these techniques under "Wrapping Text around Images" and "Using a Graphic Rule Instead of the HR Tag."

A Glossary Page

One thing you see on many Web sites are glossaries. Every field or area of interest seems to have its own jargon. A well-done glossary site can be a valuable resource. Many glossaries on the Web are highly technical, focusing on computer-related subjects or on the Web itself. But just to show that a glossary can be put together on just about any subject, Figure 4-17 shows a glossary of poker terms.

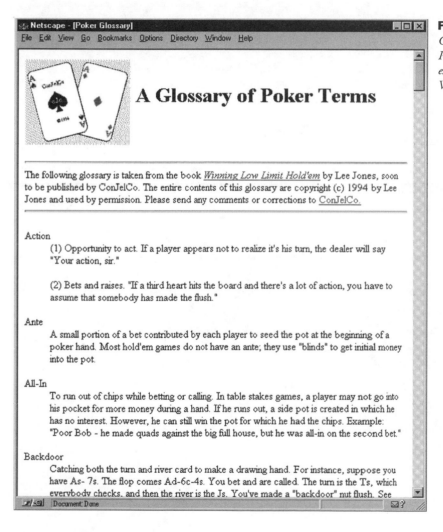

Figure 4-17.

ConJelco's Glossary of Poker Terms is a good example of a glossary Web page.

> **TECH TIP**
>
> *The glossary in Figure 4-17 is created using a plain, ordinary definition list, without any extra emphasis.*
>
> *This page uses a middle-aligned graphic followed by a level-one heading at the top of the page. Horizontal rules are used as dividers. The glossary itself is created using a plain, ordinary definition list (DL) without further ado.*
>
> *Chapter 2 covers these techniques under "Using the ALIGN Attribute in Inline Graphics," "The HR (Horizontal Rule) Tag," and "Creating Glossaries: The DL (Definition List) Tag."*

A Chronology or Timeline

Chronologies are common on the Web, perhaps because the Web itself is so young. Many of these are simply chronologies of the Web or the Internet. But a chronology can detail anything that has a history. For instance, check out the chronology in Figure 4-18.

> **TECH TIP**
>
> *There is nothing complicated about the page in Figure 4-18—just level-two headings (H2) and unordered lists, with some horizontal rules added in to dress it up a bit, which just goes to show that a page doesn't have to be fancy, just interesting. Personally, I love this kind of stuff. Forget the graphics. Just give me the facts.*
>
> *Chapter 2 covers these techniques under "Creating Lists" and "The HR (Horizontal Rule) Tag."*

Figure 4-18.
The History of Muzak Web page is a good example of an online chronology.

A Book Review

How about doing a book review? Why not! Actually, book reviews are good practice for writers. You have to be brief, concise, and yet comprehensive. A good book review can be invaluable, not only leading someone to want to read a book because it's a "good" book, but giving someone a reason to read it. Figure 4-19 shows a good example of a book review on a Web page.

Figure 4-19.

Danny Yee's book review of Civilizing Cyberspace by Steven E. Miller is a good example of an online book review.

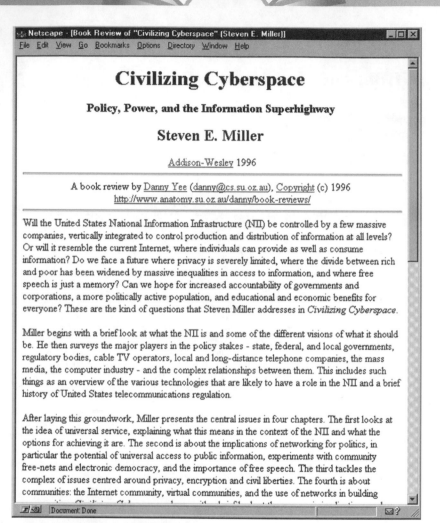

Netscape - [Book Review of "Civilizing Cyberspace" (Steven E. Miller)]

File Edit View Go Bookmarks Options Directory Window Help

Civilizing Cyberspace

Policy, Power, and the Information Superhighway

Steven E. Miller

Addison-Wesley 1996

A book review by Danny Yee (danny@cs.su.oz.au), Copyright (c) 1996
http://www.anatomy.su.oz.au/danny/book-reviews/

Will the United States National Information Infrastructure (NII) be controlled by a few massive companies, vertically integrated to control production and distribution of information at all levels? Or will it resemble the current Internet, where individuals can provide as well as consume information? Do we face a future where privacy is severely limited, where the divide between rich and poor has been widened by massive inequalities in access to information, and where free speech is just a memory? Can we hope for increased accountability of governments and corporations, a more politically active population, and educational and economic benefits for everyone? These are the kind of questions that Steven Miller addresses in *Civilizing Cyberspace*.

Miller begins with a brief look at what the NII is and some of the different visions of what it should be. He then surveys the major players in the policy stakes - state, federal, and local governments, regulatory bodies, cable TV operators, local and long-distance telephone companies, the mass media, the computer industry - and the complex relationships between them. This includes such things as an overview of the various technologies that are likely to have a role in the NII and a brief history of United States telecommunications regulation.

After laying this groundwork, Miller presents the central issues in four chapters. The first looks at the idea of universal service, explaining what this means in the context of the NII and what the options for achieving it are. The second is about the implications of networking for politics, in particular the potential of universal access to public information, experiments with community free-nets and electronic democracy, and the importance of free speech. The third tackles the complex of issues centred around privacy, encryption and civil liberties. The fourth is about communities: the Internet community, virtual communities, and the use of networks in building

Document: Done

TECH TIP

The only thing remotely fancy here is the center-aligning of the heading text at the top of the page, where different heading-levels and paragraph text are centered using the CENTER tag. Included are links to his home page, a copyright notice, and a list of other reviews he's done, as well as a "mail-to:" link to his e-mail address. Horizontal rules separate the link section from the remainder of the page.

Chapter 2 covers these techniques under "Creating Links" and "The HR (Horizontal Rule) Tag," and Chapter 3 covers them under "Text Alignment."

A FAQ (Frequently Asked Questions) Page

This is another one of those ubiquitous type pages you find all over the Web. FAQ files can be useful, especially if you're looking for an answer to a specific question that has been asked and answered many times. That's why people create FAQs in the first place—to keep from getting asked the same old questions over and over again. You get the picture. Actually, you can create an FAQ on just about anything. Figure 4-20 shows one example.

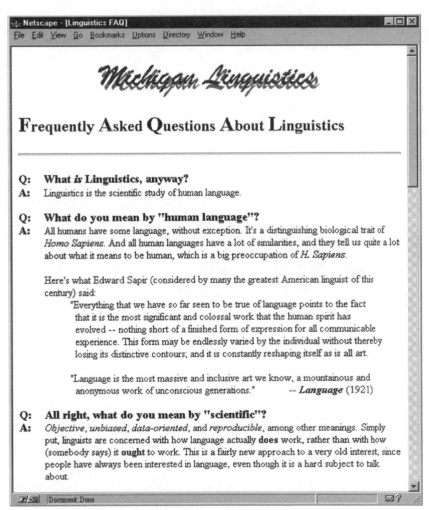

Figure 4-20.

John Lawler's Michigan Linquistics Web page from the University of Michigan is a good example of a FAQ.

TECH TIP

This page uses the COMPACT attribute in a definition list to display the definition terms (DT), which display the "Q:" and the "A:", on the same line as following definition text (DD). The graphic at the top of the page is center-aligned using the CENTER tag. It is also an "image link" with the border set to zero. The FONT tag is used to increase the size of the first letter of each word in the level-one heading (to size "6"), as well as to increase the size of the text in the definition list (to size "4"), except for the definition text following the "A:".

Chapter 2 covers these techniques under "Creating Glossaries: The DL (Definition List) Tag" and "The HR (Horizontal Rule) Tag," and Chapter 3 covers them under "Creating Image Links" and "Changing Font Sizes and Colors."

An Online Newsletter

Something else you can do is to create a newsletter. It doesn't have to be much more complicated than the basic Web page example, the one with links to subpages. Figure 4-21 shows an example of a newsletter.

TECH TIP

There is nothing terribly complicated here. The bullet items are just an unordered link list.

Chapter 2 covers this technique under "Creating Link Lists."

Figure 4-21.

The Strictly Business! WEB Online Newsletter by Online Marketing Systems is a good example of a newsletter.

Poetry

If you write poetry, why not publish it online? It's a great way to get noticed, get some feedback. Figure 4-22 shows a page of poems by Emily Dickinson.

Unfortunately, most poems on the Web aren't given any special formatting, at best usually just flushed to the left margin, at worst put in Courier using the PRE (Preformatted Text) tag. Now, this is just my opinion, but I don't think a poem should be treated exactly the same as FORTRAN output. Adding some class to the format of your poetry isn't exactly difficult. Maybe it's just a reflection of the tendency of poets to be technologically backward. Who knows?

Figure 4-22.

The Project Bartleby Web page of poems by Emily Dickinson is a good example of publishing poetry on the Web.

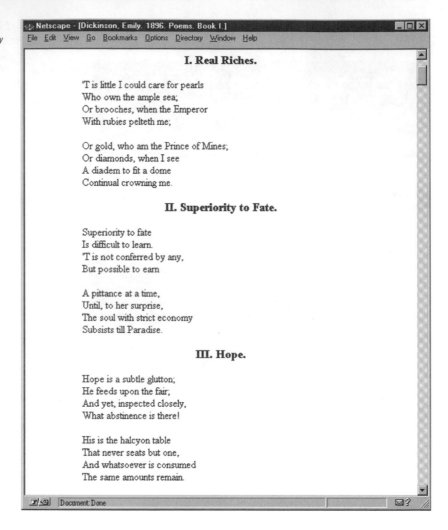

TECH TIP

The example shown in Figure 4-22 uses a Definition List (DL) nested inside another Definition List to indent the poetry. The DT's (Definition Terms) are left out and the DD's (Definition items) are used for each individual line of poetry. You can get the exact same effect in Netscape Navigator by using a BLOCKQUOTE tag nested inside a BLOCKQUOTE tag and placing BR (Line Break) tags at the end of each line of poetry.

Chapter 2 covers these techniques under "Creating Glossaries" and "The BLOCK-QUOTE (Block Quote) Tag."

A Project/Organization Description

You could just as easily replace the word "project" here with "institution," "department," "group," "company," "corporation," or something else. Figure 4-23 shows a somewhat whimsical example.

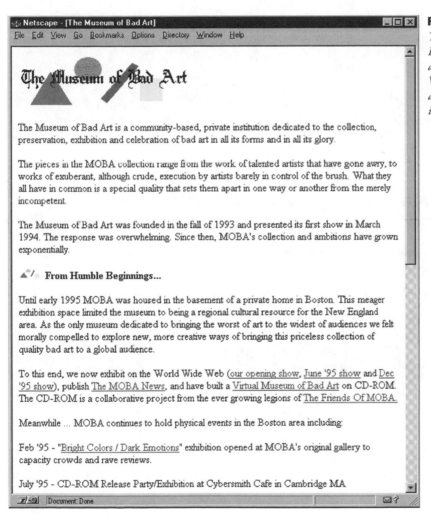

Figure 4-23.

The Museum of Bad Art Web page is a fun example of a Web page describing an organization or institution.

Once again, content is the drawing card here, not the graphics.

TECH TIP

Little in Figure 4-23 is particularly challenging, HTML-wise, which just goes to show that you don't have to use a bunch of special effects to create an effective and interesting page. The background color is set to white (#FFFFFF), which you won't even notice if you use Navigator at its default setting. If the browser window background is set to any other color, the background color here resets to white unless you've chosen to forcefully override the background colors set by Web pages with your own browser background color, something that can be done only in Netscape Navigator.

Chapter 3 covers this technique under "Setting the Background, Text, and Links Colors."

An Academic Paper or Essay

If you're a student or teacher, you might want to post a paper or essay you've written on the Web. It's a good way to get critical feedback, for one thing. An example of an academic paper is shown in Figure 4-24.

TECH TIP

This page use hardly any challenging HTML at all, which befits an academic paper, which definitely should feature content over form—mostly just different level headings and plain, ordinary paragraphs. It does, however, include some hypertext links (one to an appendix, the other to a footnote).

Chapter 2 covers all these features under "Structuring Your Web Page with Heading Level Tags" and "Creating Hypertext Links: The A (Anchor) Tag."

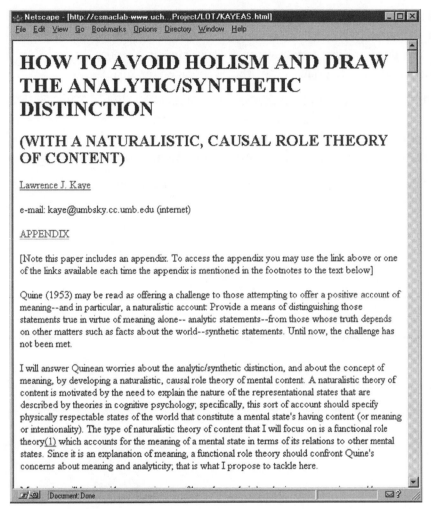

Figure 4-24.
Lawrence J. Kaye's "How To Avoid Holism and Draw the Analytic/Synthetic Distinction" is an example of publishing an academic paper on the Web

Conclusion

Before moving on to Chapter 5, "Sunday Afternoon: Creating Your First Web Page," you should have defined an objective, done an outline, and gathered and organized your materials. The latter includes writing the text for your Web page, as well as possibly also creating a banner graphic and gathering any URLs you want to use. The end product of this process should be a "mock-up text file," which you've saved and which contains the text you want to include in your Web page, references to any graphics you want to use (just a banner graphic, for creating your first Web page), as well as any URLs inserted in the positions where you want them to appear. You use this mock-up text file this afternoon as the raw material for the Web page you create.

First time through, for the purposes of this book, your mock-up should fairly closely match one of the basic Web page example formats. The actual content, however, is entirely subject to your discretion. You can copy it out of the encyclopedia, if you want, just for the sake of practice, or you can come up with something original.

Is it lunch time? Or pretty close? Take a break and have something to eat. But don't take too long. See you back soon for Chapter 5.

Sunday Afternoon:
Creating Your First Web Page

Having finished planning your Web page, you're ready to start creating it. This section is divided as follows:

1. Getting Started

2. Creating Your First Web Page

The "Getting Started" section provides general considerations that you want to take into account before you begin to create your Web page. The "Creating Your First Web Page" section then assists you step-by-step in creating your first Web page.

After you plan your Web page, you should have a good idea of what you want to do. You should have an outline, even if only a rather general one, that helps define the structure and organization of your page. You also should have some text typed in and organized according to your outline, even if you still have sections or areas you have yet to fully define.

Getting Started

You should have selected the basic Web page example (of the three presented in Chapter 4) that you want to use as your model for creating your first Web page. The first time through this process, you should start with the first or second basic Web page example: the basic Web page with a list of external links (or just a list without links) or the basic Web page with subsections. After you gain the experience of creating your first Web page using one of these models, you can try your hand at the third basic Web page example.

If you want to include a banner graphic but haven't created one yet, just use the sample banner graphic. You can create your own customized banner graphic later.

You can take many approaches to create a Web page. Nothing says you can't, for instance, fold together the planning and creating process, working directly in HTML from the start. For anything other than a fairly simple Web page, however, such an approach tends toward the impractical side. Remember, HTML works by defining *structural* elements that are common to all Web pages—so, the more logically organized and structured the material you want to tag, the better.

The process involves using the Web page example you have selected as best suited for your Web page. The sample files are available on the CD-ROM. They also are available at the Web site for this book, http://www.callihan.com/Webpage/. To save some time and typing, you can copy them to your hard drive. On the other hand, you might learn more from actually typing them in—they aren't particularly complex, so typing in the one you want to use shouldn't take too long.

You can use the basic Web page example you've selected as a template or a guide. Using it as a template means you replace the sample text with your own (delete the sample text and then cut and paste your text from your mock-up file, or just type it). If you prefer to use it as a guide, you just refer to it as an example as you apply the HTML tags to the text file (your mock-up) that you created in the last chapter.

Deciding What HTML Codes To Use

The top section (the banner graphic, level-one heading, and introductory paragraph) and the bottom section (the address block) of all three basic Web page examples are identical. You probably would include these elements on virtually any Web page you might create, except maybe the banner graphic.

The middle section of an HTML file is the part that gets interesting. Basically, you can place anything you can dream up and format in HTML in this middle section.

For the purposes of creating your first Web page, however, you need to limit your possibilities somewhat. If you don't, this chapter probably will end up looking more like a pretzel than a road map. That's why you should use one of the example files as a model for organizing and planning the material for your Web page—to try to keep things from getting too complicated too fast. The following isn't the *only* way to go about creating a Web page—it's just the best way to go about creating your *first* Web page within the time constraint of one weekend.

Copying the Example Web Page Files

Before you start, you should copy all the example files from the CD-ROM to your HTML working directory. You also can download these files from http://www.calli-han.com/webpage/. These include the basic Web page example files and any graphics that they use, as well as a number of additional graphics that are included in some of the "extra options," which are provided as you go along.

The Basic Web Page Examples

Even though the basic Web page examples are already typed out for you, you might want to go ahead and type them in yourself. You may learn more about HTML by actually typing the basic Web page example you want to use.

To use these examples and start creating your first Web page, do the following steps:

1. Run Windows Notepad. (Alternatively, you can use your word processor or an HTML editor.)

2. Load the Web page example you have selected to use, or type it in yourself (recommended). If you want to use the files already typed for you, however, they're available as BASIC1.HTM, BASIC2.HTM, and BASIC3.HTM. (BASIC3A.HTM is the subpage example file.)

3. After you load or type the Web page example you're using, resave it under a unique name, such as FIRSTPG.HTM, WEBPAGE.HTM, MYPAGE.HTM, or something like that.

4. Run another copy of Notepad (or open another window in your word processor) and load the mock-up text file you created this morning during your Web page planning session.

5. You can then copy and paste from your mock-up text file to the example Web page file, using it as a template, or you can just use the example Web page file as a guide to tagging your mock-up text file.

Here are the basic Web page examples. You can load the examples or type your own.

A Basic Web Page with External Links

If your Web page is fairly simple (doesn't include subsections), you should use this Web page example as a template or guide. You can load the version already typed (BASIC1.HTM) or type it yourself (recommended).

```
<HTML>

<HEAD>

<TITLE>A Basic Web Page</TITLE>

</HEAD>

<BODY>

<IMG SRC="webpage.gif">

<H1>A Basic Web Page</H1>

<P>This is an example of a basic web page.  It contains a banner
graphic, levelone and leveltwo headings, an introductory paragraph, a
short list of links, a horizontal rule, and an address block.  The
links are to other hypothetical web pages on the Web.  The address
block contains the hypothetical name of the author of the page, a
"mailto:" email link, and a date reference.

<H2>List of Links</H2>

<UL>

<LI><A HREF="http://www.anywhere.com/webpage1.htm">First Link</A>:
This is the first link.

<LI><A HREF="http://www.anywhere.com/webpage2.htm">Second Link</A>:
This is the second link.

</UL>

<HR>

<ADDRESS>

<STRONG>Arthur Randall</STRONG><BR>

Email: <A HREF="mailto:randall@dummy.com">randall@dummy.com</A><BR>

Last Modified: May 15, 1996

</ADDRESS>

</BODY>

</HTML>
```

If you've typed this file in, save it under a name other than BASIC1.HTM, such as EXAMP1.HTM.

Hop out and run your Web browser, then load the file you just saved. If you want, you can check it against what appears in Figure 4-5 in the previous chapter.

Go ahead now and skip to the next section, "Loading Your Mock-Up Text File."

A Basic Web Page with Subsections

If your Web page is more complicated, for instance, including a number of subsections under subheadings (level-two headings), you should use this Web page example as a template or guide. You can load BASIC2.HTM or you can type it in yourself (recommended).

```
<HTML>

<HEAD>

<TITLE>A Less Basic Web Page: Using Subheadings</TITLE>

</HEAD>

<BODY>

<IMG SRC="webpage.gif">

<H1>A Less Basic Web Page: Using Subheadings</H1>

<P>This is an example of a less basic web page.  It is similar to
the Basic Home Page, except that it has <EM>internal</EM> links
functioning as a menu to the page's subheadings.  It contains a ban-
ner graphic, a levelone heading, an introductory paragraph, a short
list of links, leveltwo subheadings, a horizontal rule, and an
address block.

<UL>

<LI><A HREF="#part1">Part One</A>: This links to the first
subheading.

<LI><A HREF="#part2">Part Two</A>: This links to the second
subheading.

</UL>

<H2><A NAME="part1">Part One</A></H2>
```

```
<P>This is the text for Part One.  When you select the menu link,
"Part One," above, you will jump to this section.  This section
would be the first part of a longer page.

<H2><A NAME="part2">Part Two</A></H2>

<P>This is the text for Part Two.  Of course, these are just dummy
headings, and dummy text, but you get the idea.  When you click on
the "Part Two" link above, you will jump to this section.

<HR>

<ADDRESS><STRONG>Arthur Randall</STRONG><BR>

*Email: <A HREF="mailto:randall@dummy.com">randall@dummy.com</A><BR>

Last Modified: May 15, 1996

</ADDRESS>

</BODY>

</HTML>
```

If you've typed this file in, save it under a new name.

Hop out and run your Web browser, then load the file you just saved. If you want, check it against what appears in Figure 4-6 in the previous chapter.

A Basic Web Page with Subpages

This is the third basic Web page example, the one that uses "local" links to subpages of your main, or "home," page. Consider using one of the other pages to create your *first* Web page. After you use one of the first two Web page examples to create your first page, however, feel free to use this example as a template or guide for creating your first multipage Web site. (Note: The word *site* here refers to any group of Web pages that are related, sharing a common theme, and linked together.)

You can load BASIC3.HTM and BASIC3A.HTM, or you can type them in yourself (recommended).

Here is the basic Web page example for the main, or home, page:

```
<HTML>

<HEAD>

<TITLE>A Less Basic Web Page: Using Subpages</TITLE>

</HEAD>
```

```
<BODY>

<IMG SRC="webpage.gif">

<H1>A Less Basic Web Page: Using Subpages</H1>

<P>This is an example of a less basic web page.  It is similar to
the Basic Home Page, except that it has <EM>external</EM> links
functioning as menu to a number (here two) of subpages.  If your
material is at all extensive, requiring a lot of scrolling to view
it in a single file, you are best off splitting your web page into a
main (or "home") page and a series of subpages corresponding to the
subsections of your document.

<UL>

<LI><A HREF="basic3a.htm">Subpage One</A>: This links to the first
subpage.

<LI><A HREF="basic3b.htm">Subpage Two</A>: This links to the second
subpage.

</UL>

<HR>

<ADDRESS><STRONG>Arthur Randall</STRONG><BR>

Email: <A HREF="mailto:randall@dummy.com">randall@dummy.com</A><BR>

Last Modified: May 15, 1996

</ADDRESS>

</BODY>

</HTML>
```

If you've typed this file in, save it under a new name, such as EXAMP3.HTM.

Hop out and run your Web browser, then load the file you just saved. If you want, check it against what Figure 4-7 shows in the previous chapter.

NOTE

You may have noticed that this Web page example is almost identical to the first Web page example. The only real difference between the two (other than the sample text) is that this example uses "local" links to subpages stored in the same directory, rather than links to Web pages that are somewhere else out on the Web.

Here's the subpage example that you can use to create subpages linked from a home page:

```
<HTML>

<HEAD>

<TITLE>A Less Basic Web Page: Subpage1</TITLE>

</HEAD>

<BODY>

<H1>Subpage One</A></H1>

<P>This is the text for the first subpage.  When you select the menu
link, "Subpage One" in the main, or "home," page, you will jump to
this web page.  This is an example of breaking up a large web page
into a main, or "home,' page and separate subpages.

<P>Return to the <A HREF="basic3.htm">Home Page</A>.

<HR>

<ADDRESS><STRONG>Arthur Randall</STRONG><BR>

Email: <A HREF="mailto:randall@dummy.com">randall@dummy.com</A>

</ADDRESS>

</BODY>

</HTML>
```

If you've typed this file in, save it under a new name, like EXAMP3A.HTM or something like that.

Hop out and run your Web browser, then load the file you just saved. If you want, check it against what appears in Figure 4-8 in the previous chapter.

Loading Your Mock-Up Text File

Run another copy of Notepad (or open another window in your word processor), then load the mock-up text file you created this morning when planning your first Web page. You now have *both* the Web page example file you've selected to use as a guide or template and your mock-up text file open.

If you choose to follow the "template" approach, you copy and paste between these two to plug the different elements and sections of your text file into the Web page example file. If you choose to follow the "guide" approach, you should use the Web page example file as a visual reference and guide to tagging your text file with the appropriate HTML tags.

Saving Your Web Page File

If you're going to use the basic Web page example you've selected as a template, then you should resave and rename the Web page example file as your new Web page file (for instance, as MYPAGE.HTM, WEBPAGE.HTM, or something that more specifically identifies the page you are creating.) If you intend to use the basic Web page example as a guide, you should resave and rename the mock-up text file you created this morning as your new Web page file.

Creating Your First Web Page

You're now ready to start actually *creating* your first Web page. You should have the basic Web page example you've chosen to use as a template or guide open in one copy of Notepad, and the mock-up text you created this morning open in another copy of Notepad.

As stressed earlier, you can use the basic Web page example as a template, into which you can plug in the pieces from your mock-up text file, or as a guide to applying the HTML tags directly to your mock-up text file. (In other words, you can insert your text into the HTML in the Web page example file or you can apply the HTML to your text.) The choice is yours. Starting out, the first time through, you might want to go the template route. Later, after you gain more experience with HTML, you directly tag your text files to create your Web pages.

Inserting the Startup HTML Tags into Your Text File

If you're going to directly tag your text file using the basic Web page example you've selected as a guide rather than as a template, you should insert the startup HTML tags into your text file.

Insert the following at the top of your text file:

```
<HTML>
<HEAD>
<TITLE>A Basic Web Page</TITLE>
</HEAD>
<BODY>
```

Insert the following at the bottom of your text file:

```
</BODY>
</HTML>
```

NOTE

The following input examples assume that you're using one of the basic Web page examples as a template rather than simply as a guide. If you use the Web page example file as a guide in directly tagging your text file, you need to interpret what is shown, realizing that instead of inserting the text into the template, as shown, you must insert the HTML codes shown in the Web page example file into your mock-up text file.

CAUTION

The "extra options" that this chapter presents require the use of an HTML 3.2 compliant Web browser, such as Netscape Navigator and the most current version of Microsoft Internet Explorer (Version 3.0). NCSA Mosaic, although it has some support for HTML 3.0 features, isn't an HTML 3.2 compliant Web browser, and so cannot be guaranteed to display all the extra options that this chapter provides. The same caution holds true for any Web browser other than Navigator or Internet Explorer that you might use.

Creating the Top Section of Your Web Page

The following section applies to all three basic Web page examples. It covers creating a title, a banner graphic, a level-one heading, and an introductory paragraph.

Creating Your Title

Creating your title is the first order of business. You should already have a pretty good idea of what you want to put in here, even if you haven't specifically included it in your text file. Feel free to just put in a provisional title for now. Including a short description with your title (no more than 40 to 50 characters) is good practice.

Delete the sample text from within the TITLE tag, then cut and paste the title you want to use from your text file (or just type it):

```
<HTML>
<HEAD>
<TITLE>Insert your title</TITLE>
</HEAD>
```

Including a Banner Graphic

You don't have to include a banner graphic at the top of your Web page, but it does add a nice touch.

> **NOTE**
>
> *If you haven't created a GIF graphic format banner file or converted a graphic file you want to use (of your company logo, for instance), you can use the sample banner graphic, WEBPAGE.GIF, which is included in the basic example templates.*

If you have created a personalized banner graphic, replace "webpage.gif" in the example templates with the name of the GIF graphic you want to use:

```
<BODY>
<IMG SRC="Insert the file name of your graphic">
```

Figure 5-1 shows what this might look like in a Web browser.

Figure 5-1.

A banner graphic is a good way to make your Web page more visually appealing.

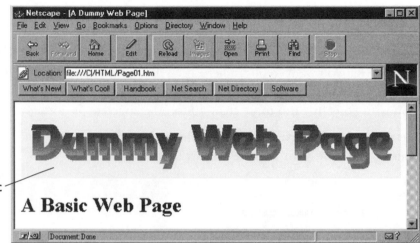

Banner graphic

NOTE

Since you're going to insert your own banner graphic and your own mock-up text, the figure illustrations in this chapter can only approximate what your Web page might look like. To see what your Web page is really going to look like, save your file and hop over to your browser to take a look. You should do so for each example, if for no other reason than to double-check and debug for errors.

If what you see in your Web browser is radically, and unpleasantly, different from what you see in the figure, you may need to double-check for an error in your Web page file. (Most errors tend to be along the lines of having only one quotation mark or angle bracket when you need two, that sort of thing.)

It also may indicate, however, that the Web browser you're using doesn't support the particular feature you're trying to use—Netscape Navigator and Internet Explorer support all the tags and features that this chapter presents, but NCSA Mosaic does not.

For more information on using a banner graphic on your Web page, see "Adding a Banner Graphic" in Chapter 3.

Creating Your Level-One Heading

The level-one heading is actually a title. You should have only one level-one heading on your page, and you probably have already thought of one for your page during this morning's planning session. If you haven't decided on a title yet, just put in a provisional title—you can always change it later. Try to keep it short, say, fewer than 30 characters. Insert your level-one heading as follows:

```
<BODY>
<IMG SRC="The name of your banner graphic">
<H1>Insert Your Level-One Heading</H1>
</BODY>
```

Figure 5-2 shows how this might appear in a Web browser.

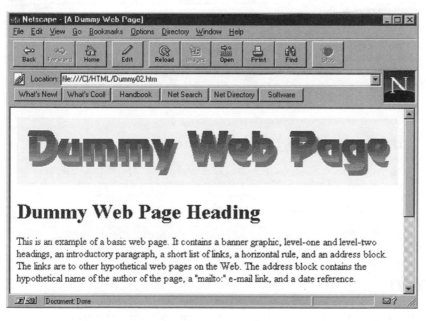

Figure 5-2.
Here is an example of a level-one heading.

Create Your Introductory Paragraph

During this morning's planning session, you probably created an introductory paragraph for your Web page. Mind you, an introductory paragraph isn't absolutely essential—skipping it doesn't violate any laws. Having an introductory paragraph is a good idea, however, and helps viewers of your page decide whether they want to linger. If you have created an introductory paragraph, insert it as follows:

```
<BODY>
<IMG SRC="The filename of your banner graphic">
<H1>Your Level-One Heading</H1>
<P>Insert your introductory paragraph text
```

Figure 5-3 shows what an introductory paragraph might look like in a Web page.

Figure 5-3.
It's a good idea to start your Web page with an introductory paragraph.

Introductory paragraph

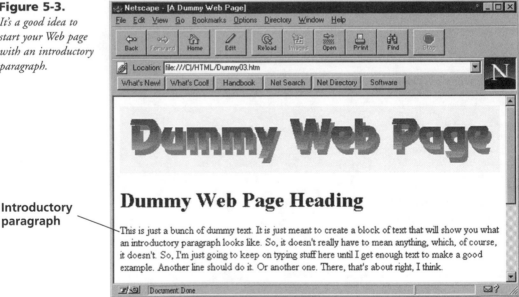

Extra Options

This section presents extra options that you might want to try in the top section of your Web page to further enhance or alter its appearance. You don't have to use these options to create your first page; feel free to skip them entirely. If you do choose to experiment with them, however, save your current Web page file, then save another version for experimentation. If you find an effect that you like, reload your original Web page file and incorporate the effect into the Web page you're creating.

> **NOTE**
>
> *Many of these extra options use features that Chapter 3 covered. If you haven't done the intermediate HTML tutorial, you might want to skip ahead here to "Creating the Middle Section of Your Web Page," and then come back and experiment with some of the suggested extra options later.*

Option #1: Centering Your Level-One Heading

Most current Web browsers support centering of headings and paragraphs. The most commonly supported centering method involves setting the ALIGN attribute in a heading or paragraph tag. To center level-one heading in the basic Web page examples, for instance, you could edit it as follows:

```
<IMG SRC="The name of your banner graphic">
<H1 ALIGN="center">Insert Your Level-One Heading</H1>
```

Figure 5-4 shows what this would look like in a Web browser that supports aligning headings.

Optionally, you also could center-align your introductory paragraph by inserting ALIGN="center" inside the paragraph tag.

For more information on center-aligning headings, paragraphs, and other elements, see "Text Alignment" in Chapter 3.

Figure 5-4.

An easy way to give your Web page a different look is to center the level-one heading.

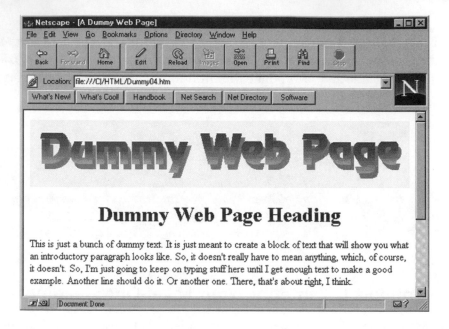

NOTE

If you're going to center your level-one heading, you probably also should center your banner graphic—even if your banner graphic extends all the way across a browser window running in 640 × 480 resolution, because you can't be certain about the resolution at which users will have their viewers set. To center your banner graphic, place it a center-aligned paragraph, like this:

```
<BODY>
<P ALIGN="center"><IMG SRC="The name of your banner graphic">
<H1 ALIGN="center">Your Level-One Heading</H1>
```

For more information on centering images, see "Aligning Images Using Paragraph Alignment" in Chapter 3.

Option #2: Add a Custom Horizontal Rule

An additional touch you can add to your Web page is to insert a regular or a custom horizontal rule between your level-one heading and your introductory paragraph. Center-alignment is the default alignment for horizontal rules, so if you want to set a percentage width for a horizontal rule, you should do it here in conjunction with a center-aligned level-one heading. To insert an unshaded horizontal rule that has a size of 10 pixels and extends across 66 percent of the browser window below a center-aligned level-one heading, for example, you would do this:

```
<IMG SRC="The name of your banner graphic">

<H1 ALIGN="center">Your Level-One Heading</H1>

<HR SIZE="10" WIDTH="66%" NOSHADE>
```

NOTE

You also can set the width of your horizontal rule in actual pixels by leaving off the percentage sign (%) at the end of the WIDTH attribute value.

Figure 5-5 shows how this looks in a browser that supports changing the size and width of a horizontal rule.

Figure 5-5.
A strategically placed horizontal rule can add a nice touch to a Web page. Here, the size, width, and shading have also been set.

Horizontal rule

For more information on setting the size, width, and shading of a horizontal rule, see "Creating Custom Rules" in Chapter 3.

Option #3: Use a Graphic Rule

For an even nicer touch, you can use a graphic rule rather than a horizontal rule. By using the HEIGHT and WIDTH attributes in the IMG tag, along with placing it in a center-aligned paragraph, you can get an effect similar what you could achieve using the horizontal rule, except that you get to add color or colors to your page. If you want, you can experiment with the sample graphic rule, RAIN_LIN.GIF, that was used in Chapter 3. For instance, you might substitute RAIN_LIN.GIF for the horizontal rule you inserted above like this:

```
<IMG SRC="The name of your banner graphic">
<H1 ALIGN="center">Your Level-One Heading</H1>
<P ALIGN="center"><IMG SRC="rain_lin.gif" WIDTH="450" HEIGHT="10">
```

For what this looks like in a Web browser, see Figure 5-6.

Figure 5-6.
A graphic rule is a good way to add extra color and graphic appeal to your Web page.

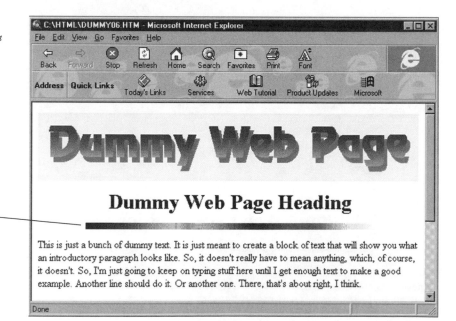

Color graphic rule

For more information on using graphic rules in your Web pages, see "Using a Graphic Rule Instead of the HR Tag" in Chapter 3.

> **NOTE**
>
> *The CD-ROM has a collection of sample graphics, including some additional graphic lines. The CD-ROM also contains additional art collections that include additional graphic rules you can use. Check Appendix A for where these are located, as well as for additional listings of where you can find Web art on the Web.*

Option #4: Wrapping Your Heading around a Graphic

The sample banner graphic included with the basic Web page examples covers the width of the browser window, if the display resolution is set to 640 × 480. Most likely, if you have created your own banner graphic, it too spans the width of the browser window. A variation here is to use a smaller left- or right-aligned graphic, taking up less than half the width of a browser window, then wrap the level-one heading around it. The graphic might be your company's logo, for instance. Just to distinguish this kind of graphic from a banner graphic, let's call it a *logo graphic*. To wrap your level-one heading around the right side of a left-aligned logo graphic, for example, edit your file like this:

```
<BODY>
<IMG SRC="The name of your logo graphic" ALIGN="left">
<H1><BR>Your Level-One Heading<BR CLEAR="left"></H1>
```

Figure 5-7 shows what this will look like in a Web browser that supports wrapping text around images.

Notice that a BR tag has been inserted at the start of the heading in Figure 5-7. That was done to move the heading down to align it more closely with the middle rather than the top of the image. Depending on the size of the logo graphic you use, you may need to add one or more additional BR tags here to move the heading down to a position that suits you. Also, at the end of the heading, another BR tag with the CLEAR="left" attribute set has been inserted to ensure that any following elements, such as your introductory paragraph, don't also try to wrap around your logo graphic.

Figure 5-7.

Instead of using a banner graphic, you can wrap your level-one heading around a left-aligned "logo" graphic.

Text wraps around graphics

You can wrap your heading around the left side of a right-aligned graphic simply by reversing the relative positions of the image and the heading, while inserting ALIGN="right" inside the heading tag. At the end of the heading, instead of <BR CLEAR="left">, you should insert <BR CLEAR="right", (or you can use CLEAR="all" in place of both).

For more information on wrapping text around left- or right-aligned images, see "Wrapping Text around Images" in Chapter 3.

NOTE

Rather than take the time right now to create a logo graphic, you can use LEFT.GIF or RIGHT.GIF, both of which are sample graphics from Chapter 3's activity. Also, if you have created a banner graphic, you also could easily pull it into your graphics editor, Paint Shop Pro or LView Pro, for instance, and simply resize it to create a smaller logo version.

Option #5: Using a Vertical Banner Graphic

A neat trick is to use a vertical *banner graphic*, a graphic that runs along the left or right side of the page. Most graphics editors let you rotate text 90 or 180 degrees, enabling you to create a graphic banner that reads vertically up or down the side of the page. To have any following elements (headings, paragraphs, and so forth) wrap around the graphic, set its ALIGN attribute to "left" or to "right." Use the HSPACE attribute to add 10 pixels to each side of the graphic. For instance:

```
<IMG SRC="Your vertical banner graphic" ALIGN="left" HSPACE="10">
<H1>Your Level-One Heading</H1>
<P>Your introductory paragraph</P>
```

The CD-ROM includes an extra "template" file that uses a vertical banner graphic (or you could download it from the Web site). To see what it looks like, hop out to your Web browser and load TEMPL4.HTM. Figure 5-8 shows what it looks like in a Web browser that supports wrapping text around left- or right-aligning images.

If you want to use the vertical banner graphic from TEMPL4.HTM in your Web page until you get around to creating a graphic of your own, just insert SRC="banner-v.gif" in the IMG tag.

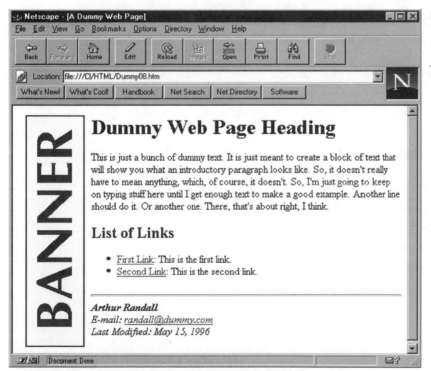

Figure 5-8.
You can use a vertical banner graphic to give your Web page a different look.

TIP

Instead of trying to create a vertical banner graphic that exactly matches the length of your Web page (which can be difficult because inserting the graphic changes the length), just create a graphic that's close in length, then include a HEIGHT attribute in the IMG tag to adjust the length of the image to match the page.

CAUTION

Be forewarned that this vertical banner trick doesn't work in all Web browsers. It doesn't make any difference to text-based Web browsers like Lynx (you might want to add an ALT attribute, however), but in a graphical Web browser that doesn't support wrapping text around left-aligned or right-aligned inline images, it's likely to look pretty bad—that is, just a long vertical opening graphic flanked by nothing but blank screen (see Figure 5-9). To get to the rest of the page, the viewer must scroll down a couple of screens to get past your opening graphic—not exactly the effect you want to produce.

So, should you use it anyway? If you don't want to turn off anyone who might view your page, then the best advice would be to simply avoid it. On the other hand, you might see no reason to cater to viewers using out-of-date Web browsers. Or you could provide an alternative page for browsers that can't handle this trick. It is legitimate HTML 3.2, however. You decide.

Option #6: Use a Typewriter Tag in Your Headings

Using a TT tag is an easy way to give your page a different look. To have your headings appear in a Courier-like monospaced font, insert a Typewriter (TT) tag inside your heading tags, like this:

```
<IMG SRC="The name of your banner graphic">
<H1><TT>Your Level-One Heading</TT></H1>
```

In the name of consistency, you also may want to insert TT tags inside any other headings you use. Figure 5-10 shows how this looks in a Web browser.

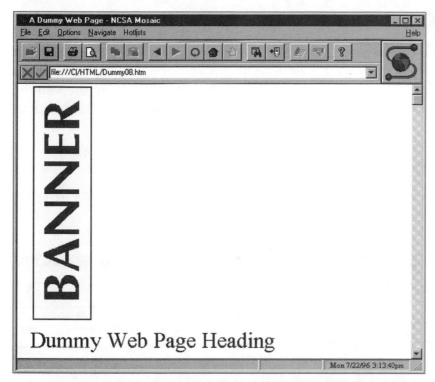

Figure 5-9.
A vertical banner graphic can look really hideous in a Web browser that doesn't support left-aligning or right-aligning inline images.

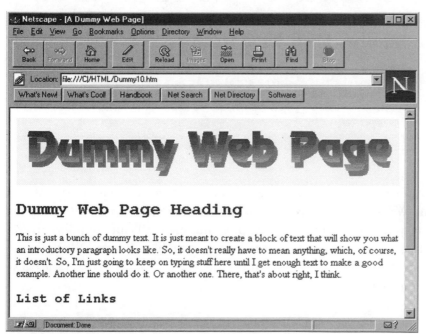

Figure 5-10.
You can insert a Typewriter (TT) tag inside your heading tags to give your Web page a different look.

Option #7: Creating a Drop Cap

There is no tag for creating a drop cap, but you can create a graphic of the first letter of your paragraph and then insert it in place of that letter. Set left-alignment in the IMG tag and following text wraps around the graphic. You can experiment with the sample drop cap graphic for the letter "T." For instance, the following inserts a drop cap "T" at the start of the introductory paragraph:

```
<P><IMG SRC="drop-t.gif" ALIGN="left">This is your introductory
paragraph text.
```

See Figure 5-11 to see what this looks like in a Web browser that supports wrapping text around a left-aligned image.

Figure 5-11.

Adding a drop cap graphic is a good way to give your Web page a distinctive look.

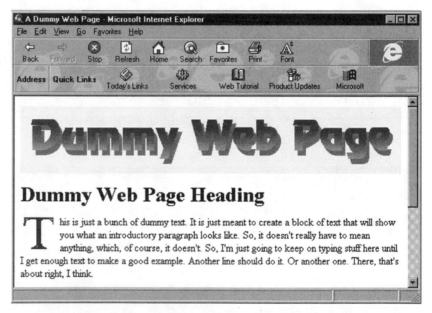

A number of collections of graphical alphabets that are great for using as drop caps also are available on the Web (see Appendix A for listings of where you can find these on the Web). Alternatively, you can use your graphics program, such as Paint Shop Pro, to create drop cap graphics and save them as GIF-format graphic files. (Note: DROP-T.GIF is 52 pixels wide and 55 pixels high.) For an added touch, use LView Pro to set the background color to transparent.

Creating the Middle Section of Your Web Page

The top and bottom sections are the same for all three basic Web page examples. The middle section, however, differs for each one. Choose the section for the basic Web page example you're using as a guide or template in creating your Web page:

- A Basic Web Page with External Links

- A Basic Web Page with Subsections

- A Basic Web Page with Subpages

Middle Section: A Basic Web Page with External Links

If you have selected the first basic Web page example (a basic Web page that has external links) as your guide or template for creating your Web page, you should proceed with this section. The Web page example file you've chosen, BASIC1.HTM, includes the following list of links:

```
<H2>List of Links</H2>

<UL>

<LI><A HREF="http://www.anywhere.com/webpage1.htm">First Link</A>:
This is the first link.

<LI><A HREF="http://www.anywhere.com/webpage2.htm">Second Link</A>:
This is the second link.

</UL>
```

The Subheading

The example includes a level-two heading (H2). Right now, this simply indicates that a list of links follows the heading. You can exclude this or you can insert the specific subheading that you want. If you're creating a Web page focused on your favorite hobby, such as stamp collecting, then the subheading here might read "Philatelist Links," or something like that. If you're including a level-two heading, insert it like this:

```
<H2>Insert Your Level-Two Heading</H2>
```

Figure 5-12 shows how this might look in a Web browser.

Figure 5-12.
You can use a level-two heading to further identify a list of links.

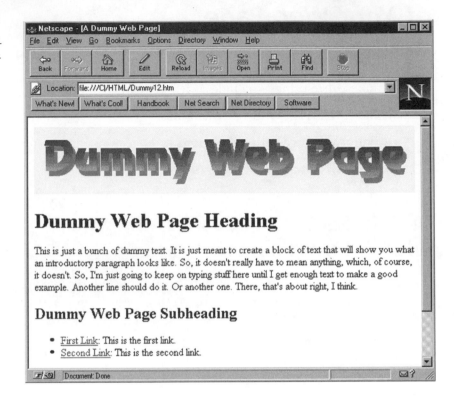

The List

The example template uses a list of hypertext links that link to other pages on the Web. For instance, you might want to create a list of your favorite links, or a list of links related to an interest, hobby, or personal expertise.

Actually, you don't have to include a list of any kind—you can completely eliminate it. Nothing says your Web page can't include just a banner graphic, a level-one heading, one or more paragraphs of text, and your address block. Nothing says you can't insert your links, in context, within your paragraph text. On the other hand, you might just want to include a list but without links, or you might want to list just the links but without explanatory or descriptive text. Or you might want to include explanations for some links but eliminate them from others that you feel are largely self-explanatory. Feel free to eliminate the descriptions, the links, or the entire list.

The following is an example for creating a link list with descriptions. (If you only want to create a list here, eliminate the links and link text. If you want to create a link list without descriptions, eliminate the link descriptions.) Follow this example to create a link list with descriptions:

```
<UL>

<LI><A HREF="Insert the URL of your first link">Insert the link
text</A>: Insert the link description.

<LI><A HREF="Insert the URL of your second link">Insert the link
text</A>: Insert the link description.

</UL>
```

Although this example includes only two link list items, a link list to other Web pages on the Web generally includes more than just two link list items. To add link list items to your link list, just duplicate either of the link list item examples shown here as many times as necessary to create your full link list, inserting the specific URLs, link text, and descriptive text for each additional link list item.

Figure 5-13 shows what a link list with links to other Web pages might look like in a Web browser.

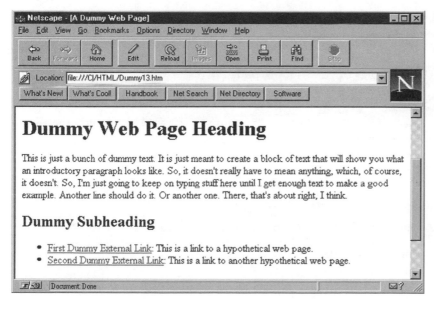

Figure 5-13.

It's a good idea to add explanations or descriptions to a link list, especially if the links are not self-explanatory.

For additional information on creating hypertext links, see "Creating Hypertext Links" in Chapter 2. For more information on creating link lists, see "Creating Link Lists" in Chapter 2.

Middle Section: A Basic Web Page with Subsections

If you have selected the second basic Web page example (a basic Web page with subsections) as your guide or template for creating your Web page, you should proceed with this section. The Web page example file you've chosen, BASIC2.HTM, includes the following list of internal links, which acts as a menu or directory to the following subsections:

```
<UL>

<LI><A HREF="#part1">Part One</A>: This links to the first subheading.

<LI><A HREF="#part2">Part Two</A>: This links to the second subheading.

</UL>

<H2><A NAME="part1">Part One</A></H2>

<P>This is the text for Part One.  When you select the menu link,
"Part One," above, you will jump to this section.  This section
would be the first part of a longer page.

<H2><A NAME="part2">Part Two</A></H2>

<P>This is the text for Part Two.  Of course, these are just dummy
headings, and dummy text, but you get the idea.  When you click on
the "Part Two" link above, you will jump to this section.

<HR>

<ADDRESS><STRONG>Arthur Randall</STRONG><BR>

Email: <A HREF="mailto:randall@dummy.com">randall@dummy.com</A><BR>

Last Modified: May 15, 1996

</ADDRESS>

</BODY>

</HTML>
```

The List

This Web page example uses a link list as a directory or menu for the following subsections. Although the example includes descriptions for each link, nothing says you can't use a link list here without descriptions. Feel free to eliminate the descriptions or to include descriptions only where you feel they are necessary. Use the following HTML code list as a guide in creating a link list to serve as a menu or directory to the following subsections:

> **NOTE**
>
> *In the following code, where it says* "Insert the anchor name of your first link target" *and* "Insert the anchor name of your second link target," *feel free to use the anchor name provided in the example,* "part1," "part2," *and so on. If you're creating a link list that links to more than two subsections, you would then continue the series of anchor names, going* "part3," "part4," *and so on. Or you can insert anchor names that more aptly describe the subsections to which you're linking. The only absolute must here is that an anchor name in the link list match the corresponding anchor name in the target anchor (in the subheading of the subsection).*

```
<UL>

<LI><A HREF="#Insert the anchor name of your first link
target">Insert your link text</A>: Insert your link description.

<LI><A HREF="#Insert the anchor name of your second link
target">Insert your link text</A>: Insert your link description.

</UL>
```

Although the above link menu contains only two link list items, you should include as many link list items as you have subsections to which you want to link. To add link list items to your link menu, just duplicate either of the link list item examples as many times as necessary to create your full link menu, inserting the specific anchor name, link text, and descriptive text for each additional link menu item.

The example also uses the text of the subheading (level-two heading) of each subsection as the link text for each link menu item. You should substitute the actual subheading text you're using. Alternatively, you might want to include shortened versions of your subheadings as the link text.

Figure 5-14 shows what your menu list might look like in a Web browser.

Figure 5-14.
A menu list functions like a directory or table of contents.

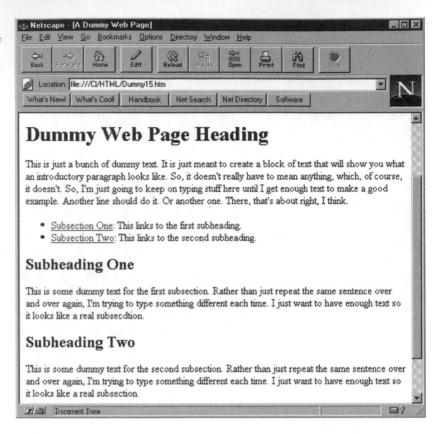

NOTE

Menu list *simply refers to a link list linking to other locations, subheadings, in the document, and not to the MENU list tag, which you're best off simply avoiding. I might, of course, refer to it as a "directory list," but then you'd be likely to confuse it with the DIR list tag, which you're also best off simply avoiding.*

For additional information on creating hypertext links, see "Creating Hypertext Links" in Chapter 2. For more information on creating link lists, see "Creating Link Lists" in Chapter 2.

The Subsections

Use the following as a guide in creating the subheadings and subsections. Note that the anchor name in each target anchor should be the same as the corresponding anchor name you use in the link list menu above ("part1" here, for instance, corresponding to "#part1" above in the link list menu, if you choose to keep the anchor names that the example supplies).

```
<H2><A NAME="Insert the anchor name of your first link"></A>Insert
Your First Level-Two Subheading</H2>

<P>Insert your first subsection paragraph

<H2><A NAME="Insert the anchor name of your second link"></A>Insert
Your Second Level-Two Subheading</H2>

<P>Insert your second subsection paragraph
```

Although the example includes only two subsections, you can have as many subsections as you want in your actual Web page. To create additional subsections, just duplicate either of the example subsections, then fill in the specific subheading and subsection text you want to use.

Figure 5-15 shows what a Web page using linked subsections might look like in a Web browser.

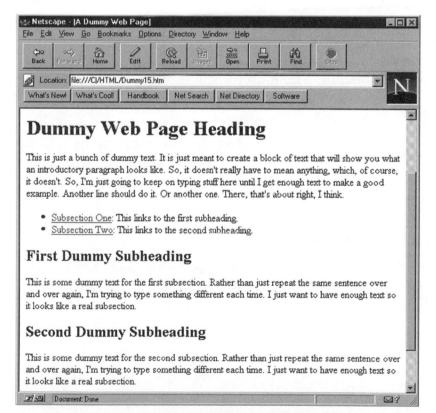

Figure 5-15.
A Web page can be divided into subsections linked to from a menu list.

Extra Options

Additional extra options that apply to the list sections of all three of the Web page examples are included, such as using an icon bullet link list rather than a regular link list. The following extra options, however, apply specifically to the second basic Web page example.

Option #1: Using a Definition List to Format Your Subsections

You can give your subsections a slightly different look by using a definition list (DL), also called a *glossary list*. Using a definition list indents your subsection paragraph text instead of displaying it flush to the left margin. Just insert your subheading on the definition term (DT) line, and use DD tags for any following paragraph tags, like this:

<DT><H2><A NAME="*The anchor name of your first link*"></A>*Your First Level-Two Subheading*</H2>

<DD>Your first subsection paragraph.

<DT><H2><A NAME="The anchor name of your second link"></A>Your Second Level-Two Subheading</H2>

<DD>Your second subsection paragraph.

To include additional subsections, just duplicate either of the preceding subsection examples, then plug in the relevant text. Also, you can include additional indented paragraphs in each subsection simply by beginning each paragraph with a DT tag rather than a P tag.

Figure 5-16 shows what a Web page using definition list subsections might look like in a Web browser.

For more information on using Definition Lists, see "Creating Glossaries" in Chapter 2.

Option #2: Including Loop-Back Links

If you're using more than just a few subsections or if your subsections are fairly long, you may want to include loop-back links that let viewers easily return to your menu list after they finish reading a subsection.

```
<UL><A NAME="menu"></A>
```

```
<LI><A HREF="#The anchor name of your first link target">Your link
text</A>: Your link description.
```

```
<LI><A HREF="#The anchor name of your second link target">Your link
text</A>: Your link description.
```

```
</UL>
```

```
<H2><A NAME="The anchor name of your first link"></A>Your First
Level-Two Subheading</H2>
```

```
<P>Your first subsection paragraph. <A HREF="#menu">Return to
Menu</A>
```

```
<H2><A NAME="The anchor name of your second link"></A>Your Second
Level-Two Subheading</H2>
```

```
<P>Your second subsection paragraph. <A HREF="#menu">Return to
Menu</A>
```

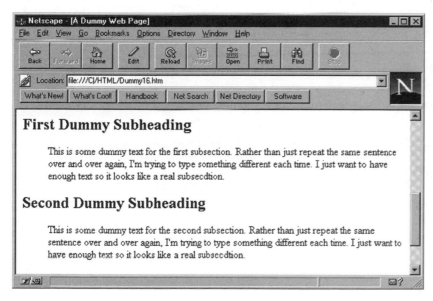

Figure 5-16.
When you use a Definition List (DL) to format subheadings and subsections, the subsection paragraphs will be indented.

Figure 5-17 shows what this might look like in a Web browser.

For additional information on creating hypertext links, see "Creating Hypertext Links" in Chapter 2.

Figure 5-17.

You can use loop-back links to allow the viewer of a Web page to easily return, loop-back, from a subsection to a menu list.

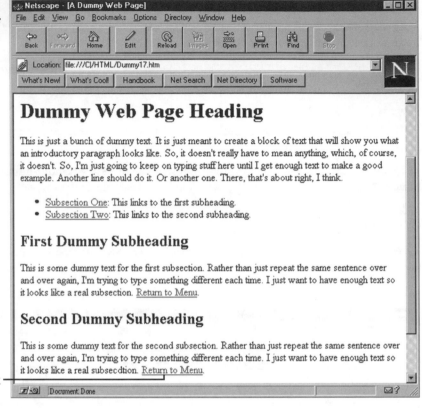

A loop-back link

Middle Section: A Basic Web Page with Subpages

If you have selected the third basic Web page example (a basic Web page with subsections) as your guide or template for creating your Web page, you should proceed with this section. The Web page example file you've chosen, BASIC3.HTM, includes the following list of internal links, which acts as a menu or directory to the following subsections:

The List

This is the link list as it appears in the example template:

```
<UL>

<LI><A HREF="basic3a.htm">Subpage One</A>: This links to the first
subpage.
```

```
<LI><A HREF="basic3b.htm">Subpage Two</A>: This links to the second
subpage.
```

```
</UL>
```

Use the following example to create the link list:

NOTE

The file names for the subpages in the example are BASIC3A.HTM and BASIC3B.HTM. You need to substitute the actual names you want to use for your subpages, either variants of your main page's name or names that are more descriptive of the subpages. The only absolute requirement here is that the file name you include in the link menu below match the actual file name of the subpage to which you want to link.

```
<UL>
```

```
<LI><A HREF="Insert the file name of the first subpage">Insert the
link text</A>: Insert the link description.
```

```
<LI><A HREF="Insert the file name of the second subpage">Insert the
link text</A>: Insert the link description.
```

```
</UL>
```

Figure 5-18 shows what this might look like in a Web browser.

NOTE

If the file for your subpage is in the same directory as your main page, you only need to insert its file name. Otherwise, you must insert either an absolute or relative URL (see the sidebar, "Using Relative or Partial URLs" in Chapter 2).

For now, though, you should store all files, including subpages, graphics, or icons, that you want to use in your working directory for creating HTML files (whichever directory you're using). After you get a better feel for how HTML works, or when a project gets large enough that you need to break it up into separate directories, then you can start using what are called relative *(or* partial*) URLs. But for now, as long as you just put everything in your working directory, you don't have to worry about that.*

Figure 5-18.

You can use link list to link to subpages of your main, or home page.

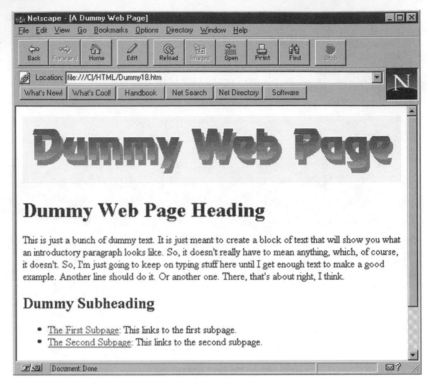

For additional information on creating hypertext links, see "Creating Hypertext Links" in Chapter 2. For more information on creating link lists, see "Creating Link Lists" in Chapter 2.

The Subpage

The following is the example subpage, BASIC3A.HTM, linked from the example home page.

```
<HTML>

<HEAD>

<TITLE>A Basic Web Page: Subpage One</TITLE>

</HEAD>

<BODY>
```

```
<H1>Subpage One</H1>
```

```
<P>This is the text for the first subpage. When you select the menu
link, "Subpage One" in the main, or "home," page, you will jump to
this web page. This is an example of breaking up a large web page
into a main, or "home," page and separate subpages.
```

```
<P>Return to the <A HREF="basic3.htm">Home Page</A>.</P>
```

```
<HR>
```

```
<ADDRESS><STRONG>Arthur Randall</STRONG><BR>
```

```
Email: <A HREF="mailto:randall@dummy.com">randall@dummy.com</A>
```

```
</ADDRESS>
```

```
</BODY>
```

```
</HTML>
```

Save a separate copy of the subpage example file for each subpage you want to create. If you have named your main page WEBPAGE.HTM, for example, you could save separate copies of this example subpage as WEBPAGEA.HTM, WEBPAGEB.HTM, and so on. Then edit each one individually to create your separate subpages, like this:

```
<HTML>
```

```
<HEAD>
```

```
<TITLE>Insert the title of your subpage</TITLE>
```

```
</HEAD>
```

```
<BODY>
```

```
<H1>Insert Your Subpage's Level-One Heading</H1>
```

```
<P>Insert the rest of your subpage
```

```
<P>Return to the <A HREF="Insert the file name of the subpage's home
page">Home Page</A>.</P>
```

```
</BODY>
```

```
</HTML>
```

Figure 5-19 shows what this might look like in a Web browser.

Figure 5-19.

A subpage is a Web page linked from your main (home) page.

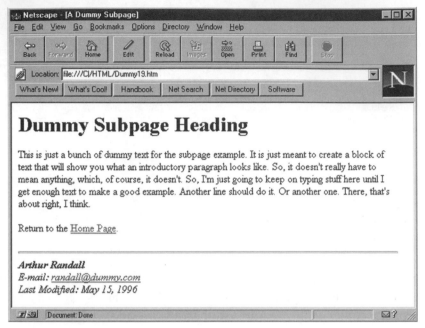

Extra Options for Subpages

You have several options for tying your subpages more closely to the main page.

Option #1: Add a Banner or Logo Graphic to Your Subpage

The example template for the subpage doesn't have a banner or logo graphic. Using a banner or logo graphic for your subpages can help tie them together, however. If you've created a banner graphic for your home page, try pulling it into a graphics editor and reducing its size or just creating a new graphic. Here's an example of inserting a banner graphic on your subpage:

```
<IMG SRC="Insert the file name of your subpage banner graphic">
<H1>Your Subpage Heading</H1>
```

Figure 5-20 shows what this might look like in a Web browser.

The subpage example includes only a single paragraph. A subpage is, of course, a full Web page in its own right. Often a home page simply functions as a directory or index to the subpages that are linked to it. So, as far as the example goes, you just have to use your imagination. The example here is extremely basic, intentionally, to illustrate linking from a home page to a subpage.

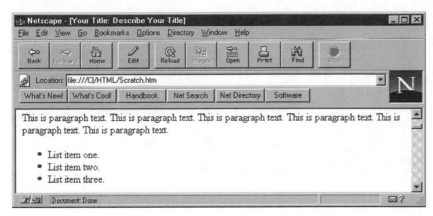

Figure 5-20.

Using a banner or logo graphic on subpages can give your Web pages a common look—use a smaller version of your main banner graphic, for instance, to reduce loading time.

NOTE

The subpage example includes a loop-back link at the bottom of the page. It provides a means, a navigational device, to loop back from the subpage to its home page. Including a loop-back link on subpages is important because you don't know how somebody is going to end up at a subpage—they don't have to go through your home page to get to it, but can jump in from anywhere as long as they have its URL. If someone comes to your subpage via a search engine, for example, pressing your Web browser's Back button returns them not to your home page, but rather, to the search engine list.

Option #2: Use Navigational Icons

Navigational icons are a way to visually indicate a link without having to spell it out. Generally, a leftward pointing arrow indicates that the viewer can click on the icon to return to the home page or to the previous page in a sequence of pages. The following example uses the navigational icon graphic of a leftward pointing arrow, BACK.GIF (from Chapter 3). Try replacing the loop-back link with a navigational icon, as shown here:

```
<H1>Your Subpage Heading</A></H1>

<P>Your subpage text. Your subpage text. Your subpage text.

<A HREF="The file name of your home page"><IMG SRC="back.gif"
ALT="Return to Home Page"></A>
```

Figure 5-21 shows what this might look like in a Web browser.

Figure 5-21.

You can use a navigational icon to visually represent an action, such as returning to the home page.

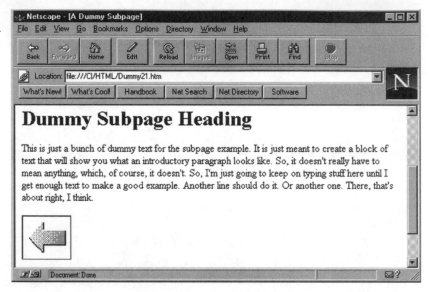

NOTE

If you're creating a series of subpages that visitors should view in sequence, such as the chapters of a book, you could use a rightward pointing arrow or hand to indicate a link to the next subpage in the series. A leftward pointing arrow would then indicate a loop back to the previous page. An upward pointing arrow could then indicate a link back to the home page. Also, sometimes an icon of a house indicates a link back to the home page. The main thing is simply that the icons be unambiguous.

Notice also that the example uses the ALT attribute in the IMG tag to identify the navigational icon. You should always use an ALT attribute with navigational icons, because a navigational icon offers no other indication of the graphic's purpose.

For more information on using navigational icons, see "Using Navigational Icons" in Chapter 3.

Creating a Link List

This extra option applies to the middle section of all three basic Web page examples: creating an icon link list.

Rather than use a regular unordered (or bulleted) list to create a link list, you can use bullet icons create an icon link list and thereby enhance the appearance of your Web page.

Because an icon link list doesn't use an unordered list, you need to first delete the UL start and end tags, and all the LI tags, so that the text for your link list looks like this:

> **NOTE**
>
> *In the following,* URL *refers to the first basic Web page example;* anchor name *refers to the second basic Web page example; and* subpage file name *refers to the third basic Web page example.*

```
<A HREF="The URL, anchor name, or subpage file name for your first
link">The link text</A>: The link description.

<A HREF="The URL, anchor name, or subpage file name for your second
link">The link text</A>: The link description.
```

Now, to create an icon link list, you need to add 1) a paragraph tag at the start of the list, 2) a graphic icon bullet at the start of each list line, and 3) a BR tag with the CLEAR="left" attribute value set. To do this, edit the text for your link list like this:

> **NOTE**
>
> *The example that follows uses the icon bullet, REDBALL.GIF, which served to illustrate creating icon link lists in Chapter 3. You can substitute another icon bullet, though. The CD-ROM includes a number of icon bullets in the collection of sample Web graphics. If you want to use any of them, just copy them to your working directory.*

```
<P><IMG SRC="redball.gif" ALIGN="left" HSPACE=5 VSPACE=5>
```

<A HREF="The URL of your first link">The link text</A>: The link description.**<BR CLEAR="left">**

```
<IMG SRC="redball.gif" ALIGN="left" HSPACE=5 VSPACE=5>
```

<A HREF="The URL of your second link">The link text</A>: The link description.**<BR CLEAR="left">**

Figure 5-22 shows how an icon link list might look applied to the first basic Web page example.

Figure 5-22.

A good way to add extra punch to your Web page is to use an icon link list.

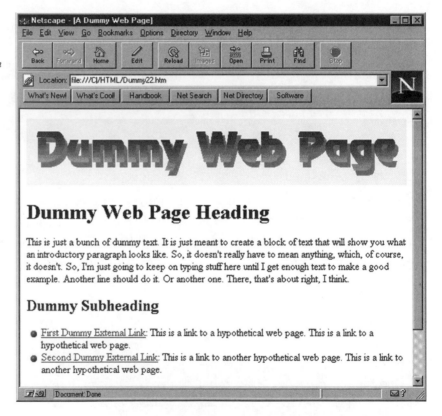

For more information on creating icon link lists, see "Creating Icon Link Lists" in Chapter 3.

Creating the Bottom Section of Your Web Page

The bottom section of the Web page example contains the address block and is the same for all of the basic Web page examples. This is the address block in all three basic Web page examples, including the </BODY> and </HTML> end tags that conclude the Web page:

```
<HR>

<ADDRESS>

<STRONG>Arthur Randall</STRONG><BR>

Email: <A HREF="mailto:randall@dummy.com">randall@dummy.com</A><BR>

Last Modified: May 15, 1996

</ADDRESS>

</BODY>

</HTML>
```

Follow this example to create your Address block:

```
<HR>

<ADDRESS>

<STRONG>Insert your name</STRONG><BR>

Email: <A HREF="mailto:Insert your e-mail address">Insert your e-mail
address again</A><BR>

Last Modified: Insert the date

</ADDRESS>
```

Figure 5-23 shows what this might look like in a Web browser. For more information on creating an address block, see "Signing Your Work" in Chapter 2.

Figure 5-23.

In an address block, you can identify yourself, let others know how to contact you, and date your work.

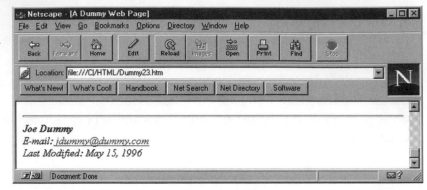

Extra Options

You can do a number of different things to vary the look of your address section.

Option #1: Vary the Height and Shading of the Horizontal Rule

You can change the height and shading of the horizontal rule. For instance, to use a 10-pixel high unshaded rule as a separator between the rest of your Web page and your address block, do the following:

<HR [NEW] **SIZE="10" NOSHADE** [END NEW]>

<ADDRESS>

<STRONG>*Your name*</STRONG>

Email: <A HREF="mailto: *Your e-mail address*">*Your e-mail address again*</A>

Last Modified: *The date*

</ADDRESS>

Figure 5-24 shows what this might look like in a Web browser.

Figure 5-24.
You can vary the height and shading of a horizontal rule, but it has different effects, or no effect at all, depending on the browser.

Option #2: Use a Graphic Line In Place of a Horizontal Rule

You can add more color and pizzazz to your page by using a graphic line rather than a horizontal rule as a separator. The example here uses the same graphic rule image, RAIN_LIN.GIF, as was used in the extra option for inserting a graphic rule between the level-one heading and the introductory paragraph. The width of the graphic rule is the same width as the banner graphic, 595 pixels, and its height is 10 pixels, as shown here:

```
<IMG SRC="rain_lin.gif" WIDTH="595" HEIGHT="10">
```

<ADDRESS>

<STRONG>*Your name*</STRONG>

Email: <A HREF="mailto: *Your e-mail address*">*Your e-mail address again*</A>

Last Modified: *The date*

</ADDRESS>

Figure 5-25 shows what this might look like in a Web browser.

Figure 5-25.
You can use a graphic line in place of a horizontal rule to make your Web page more aesthetically appealing.

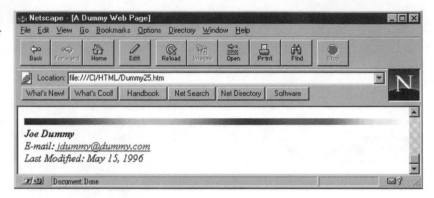

Option #3: Center Your Address Block

You don't have to use a left-flush address block. You can center it for Web browsers that can read the <CENTER> and </CENTER> tags. For instance:

<HR>

<ADDRESS>

<CENTER><STRONG>*Your name*</STRONG>

Email: <A HREF="mailto: *Your e-mail address*">Your e-mail address again</A>

Last Modified: *The date***</CENTER>**

</ADDRESS>

Figure 5-26 shows what this might look like in a Web browser.

Figure 5-26.
You can use the CENTER tag to center an address block, but not all Web browsers recognize this tag.

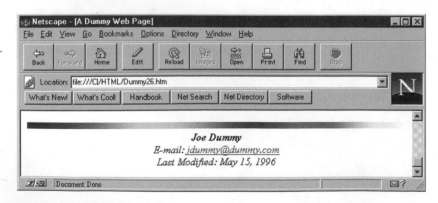

> **NOTE**
> *You also could insert a center-aligned paragraph at the start of the address block, but this has the effect of moving the address text further down from the horizontal rule.*

If you're creating a home page with subpages, you should create an address block for each page. Signing and dating all your pages is a good idea. Remember, you don't know how somebody is going to get to a particular page—they don't have to go through your home page to get to one of your subpages. Some search engines, for instance, use robot agents, sometimes called *worms* or *spiders*, to scan and index the Web. So, you don't have to actually list your page for someone to arrive at it; for example, via a Webcrawler search.

Extra Options for the Whole Page

This section contains a series of extra options that you can use to impact the overall look and feel of your Web page. They include changing the background and text colors and using a background image.

Option #1: Changing the Background and Text Colors

You can add significant impact to your Web page just by changing the background and text colors. The text colors here include not just the text color (TEXT) but also the color of links (LINK), visited links (VLINK), and activated links (ALINK), which are links where you have pressed but not released the mouse button. To change the colors for your background and text, all you have to do is add some color attributes to the <BODY> tag. Here's an example that looks pretty good:

```
<HTML>

<HEAD>

<TITLE>Your title</TITLE>

</HEAD>

<BODY BGCOLOR="#004080" TEXT="#ffff00" LINK="#00ff00" VLINK="#a4c8f0"
ALINK="#ff8000">
```

Figure 5-27 gives some idea of what this might look like in a Web browser (to see the actual colors, you need to hop over to your Web browser, though).

Figure 5-27.

To give your Web page a whole new look, assign colors to the background, text, and links.

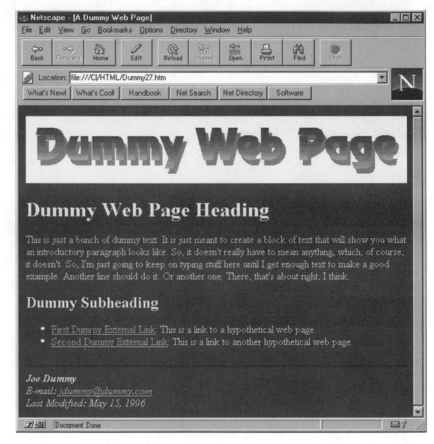

Many HTML editors provide color charts from which you can just pick and click the colors you want to use. Appendix A also offers pointers to various color selection charts and utilities available on the Web. To see exactly how a color will look, however, you must check it out in a browser. How a color looks in one browser has no real bearing on how it will look in another browser.

For more information on assigning background, text, and link colors, see "Setting the Background, Text, and Links Colors" in Chapter 3.

Option #2: Change Font Sizes and Colors

Besides setting the background, text, and links colors, another thing you can do to radically alter the look of your Web page is to change the size and color of sections of your text. You can use the BASEFONT, FONT, BIG, and SMALL tags to change the size of a section of text. You can use the FONT tag to change the color of a section of text. This example uses the BASEFONT to change the overall size of the text font to "4" (the regular default font size is "3") and uses the FONT tags to change the size of the level-one and level-two headings to "7" and "6" and their colors to "aqua" (one of the 16 color names that you can use to specify a color). The first basic Web page example is used here, but if you're using one of the other two examples, you should have no trouble adapting it to the example you're using.

```
<BODY BGCOLOR="#004080" TEXT="#ffff00" LINK="#00ff00" VLINK="#a4c8f0"
ALINK="#ff8000">
```

`<BASEFONT SIZE="4">`

`<IMG SRC="`*`Your banner graphic`*`">`

`<H1>`**`<FONT SIZE="7" COLOR="aqua">`**`Your Level-One Heading`**`</FONT>`**`</H1>`

`<P>`*`Your introductory paragraph. Your introductory paragraph. Your introductory paragraph. Your introductory paragraph.`*

`<H2>`**`<FONT SIZE="6" COLOR="aqua">`**`Your Level-Two Subheading`*`[NEW]`* **`</FONT>`**`</H2>`

Figure 5-28 shows what this might look like in a Web browser.

For more information on changing font sizes and colors, see "Changing the Font Size" and "Changing the Font Color" in Chapter 3.

Option #3: Using a Background Image

You can add a background image to your Web page by using the BACKGROUND attribute in the <BODY> tag. For instance, the image MOTTLE.GIF (included with the sample graphics) is used as a background:

```
<HTML>
<HEAD>
<TITLE>Your title</TITLE>
</HEAD>
<BODY BACKGROUND="mottle.gif">
```

Figure 5-28.

Changing the size and color of your text font can give your Web page a radically different look.

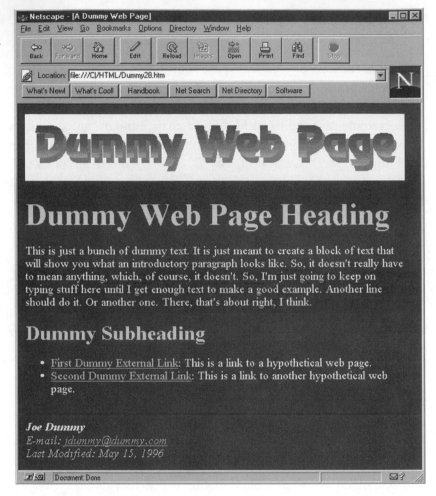

Figure 5-29 gives some idea of what this might look like in a Web browser (since this includes some color, you need to hop over to your Web browser to see what it really looks like).

For more information on using background images, see "Using a Background Image" in Chapter 3.

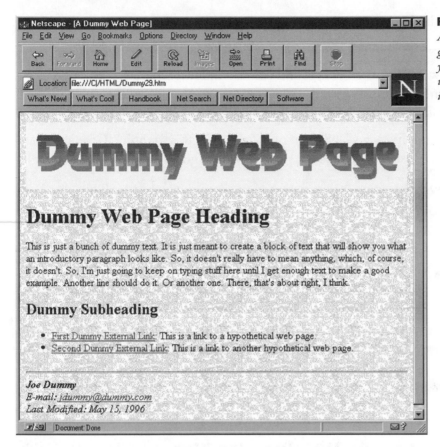

Figure 5-29.
Another way to add graphical appeal to your Web page is to use a background image.

Option #4: Using a Transparent Background Color

When you set the background of your banner graphic to transparent, it appears to float on top of whatever background color or background image you use. A number of utilities can do this, but the easiest way is to use LView Pro. Here are instructions for using LView Pro to create a transparent background color:

1. Run LView Pro and load the GIF graphic you're using for your banner graphic.

2. Choose **O**ptions.

3. Enable the Save **G**IFs interlaced check box.

4. Select Bac**k**ground color.

5. Click on the Dropper button.

6. Click the dropper in the color area you want to be transparent.

7. If you now recheck the Background colors window (choose **O**ptions and Bac**k**ground colors), you see the non-transparent areas of your graphic masked in black (assuming Black is the chosen mask selection).

8. Save your graphic as a GIF89a graphic (*not* a GIF87a graphic). Give it a new name (you must change the name of the banner graphic in your HTML file).

Figure 5-30 shows what using a transparent banner graphic might look like in a Web browser.

Figure 5-30.

Another way to add a nice touch to your Web page is to use a transparent banner graphic set against a background color or image.

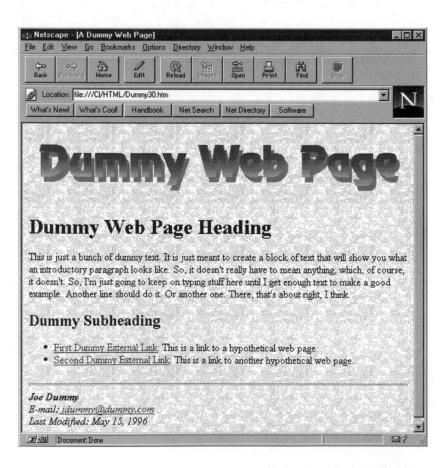

Option #4: Pulling Out All the Stops

This option combines many of the "extra options" that have been presented here in one example, including using a background image, assigning text and link colors, setting the base font size, using a transparent banner graphic, center-aligning headings, setting the font size and color of headings, creating centered graphic rules with custom widths and heights, and creating an icon link list. The example that follows uses the first basic Web page example as the base. The italics indicate text you have already inserted, or must now to insert, in place of the example text.

<HTML>

<HEAD>

<TITLE>*The title of your web page*</TITLE>

</HEAD>

<BODY **BACKGROUND="mottle.gif" TEXT="#804040" LINK="green"**>

<BASEFONT SIZE="4">

<IMG SRC="***Insert file name of transparent banner graphic*** **ALIGN="center"**>

<H1 **ALIGN="center"><FONT SIZE="7" COLOR="#205AB3">**￼*Your Level-One Heading*</FONT></H1>

<P [NEW]**ALIGN="center"><IMG SRC="rain_lin.gif" WIDTH="450" HEIGHT="10">**[END NEW]

<P>Your introductory paragraph. Your introductory paragraph. Your introductory paragraph. Your introductory paragraph. Your introductory paragraph. Your introductory paragraph.

<H2 **ALIGN="center"><FONT SIZE="6" COLOR="#205AB3">**￼*Your Second-Level Heading***</FONT>**</H2>

<P><IMG SRC="redball.gif" ALIGN="left" HSPACE=5 VSPACE=5><A HREF="URL, anchor name, or local file name of first link">Link text</A>: Link description.**<BR CLEAR="left">**

<IMG SRC="redball.gif" ALIGN="left" HSPACE=5 VSPACE=5><"URL, anchor name, or local file name of second link">Link text">Link text.</A>: Link description.**<BR CLEAR="left">**

<CENTER><IMG SRC="rain_lin.gif" WIDTH="400" HEIGHT="10"></CENTER>

<ADDRESS>

```
<CENTER><FONT SIZE="5" COLOR="red"><STRONG>Your
name</STRONG></FONT><BR>

Email: <A HREF="mailto:Your e-mail address">Your e-mail address
again</A><BR>

Last Modified: The date</CENTER>

</ADDRESS>

</BODY>

</HTML>
```

Figure 5-31 shows how this might appear in a Web browser.

Figure 5-31.

You can get creative, pulling out all the stops, by using all the options at once.

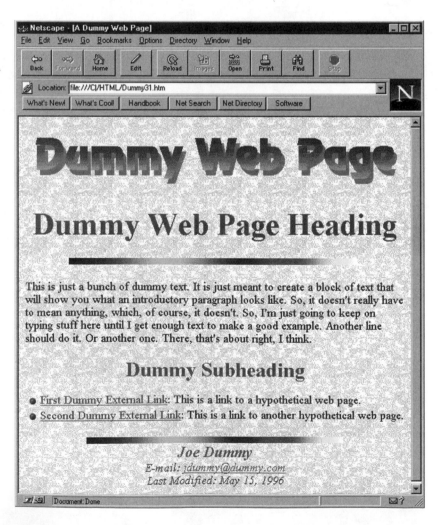

Conclusion

You should now have fully created your first Web page. You may have stuck to creating a basic Web page, which uses only tags and features from Chapter 2, or you may have incorporated a number of the suggested "extra options," most of which are based on tags and features from Chapter 3.

So what do you do now? Here are some ideas:

- If you haven't completed the intermediate HTML tutorial in Chapter 3, you may want to go back and do that next.

- If you've been using the sample graphics provided as placeholders, you now can create your own customized banner or logo graphic. See Appendix A for references to where you can find graphics resources on the Web and on the enclosed CD-ROM disk.

- If you have created a customized banner graphic, you can spend more time enhancing and fine-tuning it and other graphics you may want to use. See Appendix A for references to resources on the Web for additional information and reference material on creating graphics on the Web.

- If you have created a single Web page using one of the first two basic Web page examples, you can now go back and use the third basic Web page example to create a multipage Web site—a home page linked to a number of subpages.

- When you feel ready for "showtime," visit the Web site for this book (http://www.callihan.com/webpage/) for additional information and guidelines on actually putting your Web page up on the Web, including a list of budget Web hosts, an updated Web publishing resources list, information on maintaining and promoting a Web page or site on the Web, and more.

The next section of this book, Appendix A, provides an extensive listing of Web publishing resources that are available on the Web, as well as resources that are available on the enclosed CD-ROM disk. It has many pointers to areas of HTML that this book hasn't had the time and space to cover or that simply are too advanced for a beginning to intermediate Web publisher to handle right out of the gate, including information and instructions for creating tables, forms, frames, GIF animations, CGI scripts, and more. Also, the Web site for this book maintains a current and updated version of the listings furnished in Appendix A.

Appendix A:
A Resource Directory

This directory of resources includes pointers to resources that are available on Web browsers, HTML editors and converters, graphics editors and converters, Web art collections, and many different types of software tools. It also includes pointers to Web locations for all the sample graphics and templates used in the tutorials.

- **The Web.** The Resource Directory includes pointers to many additional tools and resources available on the Web that aren't on the CD-ROM.

- **The Web Site.** Because of the dynamic nature of the Web, any listing of current tools and resources becomes dated very fast. Therefore, I maintain a continuously updated list of resource links at the Web site for this book:

  `http://www.callihan.com/webpage/`

  All sample graphics and templates used in the book also are available for download. Additionally, information and resource materials are available on actually putting your Web page up on the Web, including finding an affordable Web host, placing and updating your Web pages on a server, and announcing and promoting your Web page.

This appendix contains the following sections:

1. **Your Web Page: Graphics Tips and Tricks.** This section includes pointers to general graphics resources, as well as information on using interlaced/transparent GIFs, image sizing/scaling, bandwidth conservation, backgrounds, and Web art.

2. **Putting It Up on the Web: Placing, Maintaining, and Promoting Your Web Page.** When you have a final page ready to go, you're going to want to put it up on the Web. This section contains some pointers to resources that can help you place, maintain, and promote your Web page.

3. **Web Publishing Resource Materials.** This section gives you pointers to just about everything and anything you want to know about HTML and Web publishing, including HTML guides, tutorials, references, style guides, and more.

4. **Web Publishing Tool Chest: Programs and Utilities.** This section provides pointers to a slew of programs and utilities that can assist you in your Web publishing endeavors, including browsers, HTML editors, converters, templates, word processor add-ons, graphics editors and utilities, and more.

Enhancing Your Web Page: Graphics Tips and Tricks

While learning basic HTML and planning and creating your first Web page, you didn't have much time to get into the graphics end of it. The idea was to learn how to create your first Web page first, and then learn how to graphically improve and enhance your Web page later. The following list of resources covers just about anything and everything you might graphically want to do with a Web page.

General Graphics Resources

Creating High-Impact Documents by Netscape

http://home.netscape.com/assist/net_sites/impact_docs/index.html

Netscape's page on interlaced GIF images, JPEG images, image sizing, percentage autoscaling, and the percentage low/high resolution flip trick.

Jonathan E. Adair's Neat Tricks Page

http://keywest.csee.usf.edu:1111/adair/neat-tricks.html

An excellent rundown on interlaced GIF images, transparent GIF images, sizing your images, image maps, and browser dependence.

Inline Images Frequently Asked Questions by Brian Patrick Lee

http://galway.informatik.uni-kl.de/./comp/Mosaic/inline-images.html

An excellent overall treatment of inline image issues.

Graphics FAQ by The Aldridge Company

http://www.aldridge.com/faq_gra.html

Another FAQ that offers good information on GIFs, interlacing, miscellaneous graphic formats, and JPEGs.

DiP: A Guide to Digital Pictures & More

http://www.algonet.se/~dip/minimal1.htm

Links, tips, and tricks for Painter, PhotoShop, Kai's Power Tools and other graphics programs, plug-ins, and utilities.

Tom's Tips for Web Designers by Tom Karlo

http://the-tech.mit.edu/KPT/Toms/index.html

Tips on using Adobe Photoshop to create Web art.

Creating Interlaced and Transparent GIFs

An interlaced GIF is loaded in more than one pass, giving a "venetian blind" effect when viewed using a Web browser capable of viewing interlacing. A transparent GIF has a transparent background (not a background that is simply the same color of your browsers background). The following resources on the Web can guide you in creating interlaced and transparent GIFs for your Web pages.

Appendix A: *A Resource Directory*

The Transparent/Interlaced GIF Resource Page

http://dragon.jpl.nasa.gov/~adam/transparent.html

http://www.put.poznan.pl/hypertext/Internet/faq/t-gif/transparent.html

An excellent "clearing house" page for all manner of information on transparent and interlaced GIF graphics. Should be the first stop for anyone seeking information and guidance in these areas.

Creating Transparent Background Images by Kerry Keogan

http://www.magi.com/~kk/tbi2.html

An excellent step-by-step tutorial for using LView Pro 1.B to create transparent background images. Actually, you can use LView Pro to make any GIF image transparent, not just background images. For Windows users, LView Pro is the preferred tool for creating transparent images.

Transparent and Interlaced Gifs: How to Do It—Where to Get the Tools You Need by Bruce Morris

http://www.awa.com/nct/software/transgif.html

An article from *NCT Web Magazine*. Offers side-by-side interlaced and non-interlaced GIFs to demonstrate how they differ when loading.

Tutorials: Transparent Gifs by QuaLitty Design

http://www.qualitty.com/trans.html

Another step-by-step tutorial on using LView Pro to create transparent GIFs.

Moss' Transparent GIF Tutorial: Creating Transparent Gifs with LView Pro

http://lahs.losalamos.k12.nm.us/%7Etempletm/transtut.html

Yet another tutorial on using LView Pro to create transparent GIFs; but this one makes abundant use of screen grabs to illustrate the steps.

Transparent Background Images by The HTML Guru (Chuck Musciano)

http://members.aol.com/htmlguru/transparent_images.html

Treats creating transparent background images largely from a Unix perspective, but still applies to the Windows or DOS platforms.

The JPiG Project by Thomas Lindstrom and Ed Scott
http://www.algonet.se/~dip/jpig_1.htm

An interesting page on the quest for the non-existent graphics format, the transparent JPEG format. It discusses the possibilities of developing the JPiG graphics format, which would be a 24-bit JPEG format with soft-edge transparency (as opposed to hard-edge transparency, as is the case with transparent GIFs). The proposal is that this be implemented as a pair of plug-ins, one for Adobe Photoshop for creating the actual image, and the other for Netscape Navigator for viewing the image as an inline image on a Web page.

See **Creating High-Impact Documents** in the "General Graphics Resources" section earlier in this appendix for additional information on creating interlaced and transparent GIFs.

Image Sizing and Scaling

Percentage Auto-Scaling by Netscape
http://home.netscape.com/assist/net_sites/impact_docs/auto-scaling.html

See **Creating High-Impact Documents** and **Jonathan E. Adair's Neat Tricks Page** in the "General Graphics Resources" section earlier in this appendix for information on image sizing and auto scaling.

See **Creating High-Impact Documents** in the "General Graphics Resources" section earlier in this appendix for information on how to do the "low/high resolution flip trick," an image sizing and scaling method that combines low- and high-resolution versions of the same banner graphic to create a "fade-in" effect, allowing a viewer to get a much quicker look at what a graphic contains, but with a slightly longer overall loading time.

Color Depth Optimization and Bandwidth Conservation

You can reduce the number of colors used to display a graphic to reduce the bandwidth, or size, of the graphic, which can significantly speed up loading of the graphic, often without significant loss of image quality.

Appendix A: *A Resource Directory*

The Bandwidth Conservation Society

`http://www.infohiway.com/faster/index.html`

Learn how to make your images load faster. Excellent information and tutorials on how to reduce the bit-depth (the number of colors in the palette) of GIF and JPEG graphics to reduce file size. Also offers information on creating background images that conserve bandwidth.

Backgrounds

Netscape introduced the capability to display background colors and images, but most other major graphical Web browsers have followed suit. The following resources can assist you in creating background colors and images for your Web pages.

Tutorials: Web Page Backgrounds by QuaLitty Design

`http://www.qualitty.com/bgrnd.html`

A rundown on background images, as well as assigning colors to backgrounds, text, and links.

The background FAQ by Mark Koenen

`http://www.sci.kun.nl/thalia/guide/color/faq.html`

Everything, and I do mean everything, you might want to know about backgrounds.

Controlling Document Backgrounds by Netscape

`http://home.netscape.com/assist/net_sites/bg/`

Netscape's page on document backgrounds.

So You Want a Background, huh? by Joe Burns

`http://www.cs.bgsu.edu/~jburns/backgrnd.html`

A good page on using background images and colors.

Making Seamless Backgrounds from Any Graphic by Thomas Karlo and Josh Hartmann

`http://the-tech.mit.edu/KPT/Makeback/makeback.html`

Advice on how to create "seamless" background graphics.

Web Art

Tons of Web art and other clip art is available for you to download and use in your Web pages. This section lists some pointers on where to find it.

GNNpress Clip Art

http://www.gnnhost.com/publish/clip-art/gnnclip.htm

A set of icons, bullets, rules, backgrounds, arrows, and other Web art that you can download and use in your Web pages.

Icons and Graphics by Julie A. Duncan

http://www.cameron.edu/~julie/creation/graphics.html

Bullets, balls, bars, buttons, and backgrounds.

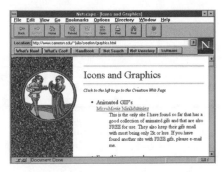

Horizontal Rules/Bars by Craig Clark

http://www.psy.uwa.edu.au/iconshr.htm

Horizontal rules and bars adjusted to use a subset of Windows 8-bit system palette.

Planet Earth Home Page: Images Section

http://www.nosc.mil/planet_earth/images.html

Tons of image links.

Appendix A: *A Resource Directory*

The Background Generator by Daniel Prust

`http://east.isx.com/~dprust/Bax/index.html`

A neat online utility that generates a background image that you create yourself. Requires a Java-capable browser, such as Netscape Navigator Gold for Windows 95.

Clip Art brought to you by Deep Visions (formerly known as Sandra's Clip Art Server)

`http://www.n-vision.com/panda/c/`

An index to many, many clip art links. Includes links to many large clip art libraries and collections.

Barry's Clip Art Server

`http://ns2.clever.net/~graphics/clip_art/clipart.html`

Another omnibus clip art site.

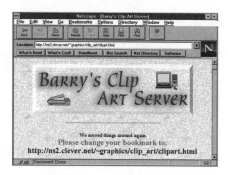

Funet Collection (brought to you by Barry's Clip Art Server)

`http://ns2.clever.net/~graphics/clip_art/funet.html`

The whole Funet collection of clip and Web art from Finland. One of the biggest collections of clip art anywhere.

Rose's Backgrounds

`http://www.wanderers.com/rose/backgrou.html`

An A-to-Z index of links to background collections and libraries all over the Web.

The Virtual Image Archive by Brian Casey

`http://imagiware.com/via.cgi`

Lots of image links.

Gifs (alphabetically)

`http://www.acm.uiuc.edu:80/rml/Gifs/`

A good collection of GIFs.

Swedish University Network (SUNET) FTP Archive

`ftp://ftp.sunet.se/pub/pictures/`

A big FTP archive of clip art broken down into category directories.

The Image Server by Alan Messer

`http://web.cs.city.ac.uk/archive/image/image.html`

A collection of photos in various categories. No statement made about copyright, however, so if you want to use you might want to query first. Good photos, though.

Backgrounds

`http://www.ncsa.uiuc.edu/SDG/Software/WinMosaic/Backgrnd/`

An anonymous collection of some very nice background images.

The Clip Art Connection: Your Clip Art Treasure Chest by Eric Force

`http://www.acy.digex.net/~infomart/clipart/`

Loads and loads of image links.

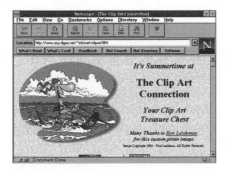

Textures for HTML 3.0 Clients

`http://www.baylor.edu/textures/`

A collection of background textures.

MacDaddy's Background Sampler and Tutorial

`http://flamestrike.hacks.arizona.edu/~macdaddy/backgrounds.html`

A tutorial on background colors and images, and a collection of more than 100 background images.

Dr. Zeus' Textures

`http://www.best.com/~drzeus/Art/Textures/Textures.html`

A small collection of somewhat surreal background textures.

Paul's More Backgrounds

http://www.niagara.com/~pmarquis/backgr.html

A collection of 161 backgrounds, including stone, wood, paper, marble, and more.

Paul's Ruled Lines and Bars

http://www.niagara.com/~pmarquis/free.html

A large collection of graphic rules and bars.

Paul's Directional Devices, Menu Bars, and Misc. Icons

http://www.niagara.com/~pmarquis/free2.html

Some more of Paul's stuff.

Laurie McCanna's Free Art Website

http://www.mccannas.com/

Tips, tricks, and Web art.

Ender Design: Realm Graphics

http://www.ender-design.com/rg/

Big collection of backgrounds, bullets, buttons, icons, and lines.

Public Domain Icons

http://www.eit.com/web/gopher.icons/gopher.html

Originally made for Mosaic for X, the first version of Mosaic.

The Backgrounds Archive by Tom Karlo and KPT Online

http://the-tech.mit.edu/KPT/bgs.html

An archive of seamless background images.

Putting It Up on the Web: Placing, Maintaining, Promoting, and Validating Your Web Page

After you create and graphically enhance your Web page, you're going to want to put it up on the Web. This involves finding a Web server to host your pages, then maintaining and promoting your Web pages after you put them up on the Web. Validating your Web page has two aspects: validating your HTML and validating your hypertext links (which have a habit of "going out" like lights on a Christmas tree). An additional, but important concern, in the general area of putting materials up on the Web is copyright, ensuring that you both protect your own copyright while not infringing on the copyright of others.

Visit the Web Site for This Book

At the Web site for this book (http://www.callihan.com/webpage/), you can find a list of affordable Web hosts (also called *presence providers*), to assist you in finding a host for your pages, as well as continuously updated information on placing, maintaining, and promoting your Web page.

Placing Your Web Page on a Server

After you create your Web page to your satisfaction, the first thing you need to do is find a server to host it. Here are some places to start looking.

The Budget Web Host List

http://www.callihan.com/budget/

My list of budget Web hosts, which is the online version of a list of affordable presence providers I published in my article, "Web Site on a Budget," in the April 96 issue of *Internet World.*

The Budget Web Index by Alex Chapman

http://budgetweb.com/budgetweb/index3.shtml

When I created my list, I hadn't realized that Alex had already done something similar. Still, minimal duplication exists between the two lists.

Free WWWeb Space Providers by Barry B. Floyd

http://www.angelfire.com/pages0/floydb/freespac.html

The Free Pages Page by Peter da Silva

http://starbase.neosoft.com/~peter/freepages.html

Providers by the Web Developer's Virtual Library

http://www.stars.com/Vlib/Misc/Providers.html

Web Presence Providers by Yahoo!

http://www.yahoo.com/Business_and_Economy/Companies/Internet_Services/Web_Presence_Providers/

The grandaddy of all presence provider lists—actually, several lists under this one heading.

Appendix A: *A Resource Directory*

Promoting Your Web Page

Just putting your page up on the Web isn't enough. You want people to notice it. A couple of the following services will register your Web page with all the major search engines and indexes. This list also includes some pointers to information on search engines and how to get your page to the top of the list, as well as on a link exchange service.

Submit It!
http://www.submit-it.com/

Allows you to submit your Web page to 15 different search engines and indexes by filling out just one form. Submit your Web page to Yahoo, Open Text, Infoseek, Webcrawler, Lycos, Alta Vista, and others.

SubmitAll by the HOME TEAM
http://www.hometeam.com/tools/submital.htm

A service quite similar to Submit It!.

META Tagging for Search Engines by Alan and Lucy Richmond
http://www.stars.com/Search/Meta.html

Covers how to use the META tag to snag search engines. Invaluable information on how to get your page to the head of the list.

How Search Engines (Say They) Work by Danny Sullivan
http://www.maxonline.com/webmasters/work.htm

A good rundown on what the different search engines say about their own indexing criteria.

The Internet Link Exchange
http://www.linkexchange.com/

A free service in which you agree to display a revolving banner ad, and, in return, your banner ad is displayed on other participating Web pages. The number of times your banner ad is displayed is directly proportional to the number of banner ads you display on your own Web page—so, the higher your number of hits, the more exposure you get. They claimed 580,000 ads a day are running on over 30,000 different Web pages.

Validating Your Web Page

Validating your Web page can means two things: 1) checking that your HTML is legal, and thus likely to display correctly on the browsers for which it is intended (for example, HTML 2.0 browsers, HTML 3.2 browsers, and so on) and 2) checking that your links are alive and well.

HTML Validation Tools

http://www.khoral.com/staff/neilb/weblint/validation.html

Lists many links to validation services available on the Web.

Doctor HTML by Thomas Tongue and Imagiware

http://www2.imagiware.com/RxHTML/

Online service that will retrieve your Web page and run several tests on it, including for spelling errors, image bandwidth and syntax, document, table, and form structure, dead links, and command hierarchy. Site Doctor, a commercial service that allows you to validate a whole Web site is also available.

Web Law and Copyrights

Web Law FAQ by Oppedahl and Larson

http://www.patents.com/weblaw.sht

Excellent FAQ on legal issues related to use of information and materials on the Web. Discusses many gray areas.

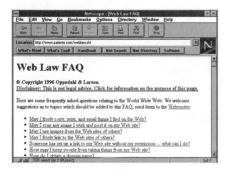

---

10 Big Myths about copyright explained by Brad Templeton

http://www.clari.net/brad/copymyths.html

A good discussion of copyright issues on the Web.

The Mystery Behind the (c) by Christopher B. Skvarka

http://www.pitt.edu/%7Eskvarka/education/copyright/

Another good discussion of copyright issues on the Web.

Web Publishing Resource Materials

The following sections provide pointers to various kinds of Web publishing resource materials and other information that are available on the Web, including HTML reference materials (guides, tutorials, and references), style guides, general Web publishing information, templates, example Web pages, and the Microsoft-Netscape war.

HTML Guides, Tutorials, and References

This section lists guides, tutorials, and references, ranging from the simple to the more comprehensive, to help you more fully explore using HTML.

Demonstration of Basic and Advanced HTML Tags by Kristina Ross

`http://www2.utep.edu/~kross/tutorial/`

More of a demonstration of HTML than a how-to or tutorial. It provides, however, a good resource of example HTML from the simple to the advanced. Advanced areas covered include image maps, tables, and forms.

The Bare Bones Guide to HTML by Kevin Werbach

`http://werbach.com/barebones/barebone_table.html`

A good rundown in table form of HTML currently in use. As the title indicates, it's a "bare bones" guide. Not so much a how-to as a handy and quick reference.

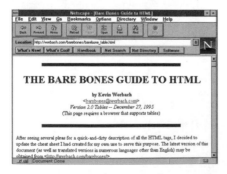

Hands-On HTML by @LearnSkills.com

`http://www.learnskills.com/hohtml/hin_01.htm`

Outline and materials for a course on HTML that you can actually sign up for and take. You don't have to sign up to use the materials though.

Appendix A: *A Resource Directory*

Hypertext Markup Language - 2.0 (Sept 22, 1995) by T. Berners-Lee and D. Connolly

http://www.w3.org/hypertext/WWW/MarkUp/html-spec/html-spec_toc.html

A comprehensive rundown of HTML 2.0 from the W3 Consortium. One of the coauthors is the godfather of HTML, himself, Tim Berners-Lee, often referred to as "the inventor of the Web"—the horse's mouth, in other words.

Crash course on writing documents for the Web by Eamonn Sullivan

http://www.pcweek.com/eamonn/crash_course.html

Originally written as a quick and dirty guide for people in the *PC Week* Labs for creating Web pages on their server.

HTML Overview by Russ Jones

http://www.ora.com/gnn/bus/ora/features/html/index.html

As the title indicates, an overview, not an in-depth review, of HTML.

A Beginner's Guide to HTML by NCSA

http://www.ncsa.uiuc.edu/General/Internet/WWW/HTMLPrimer.html

NCSA is the home of Mosaic and, as such, if not exactly the horse's mouth, then one of its teeth. This is an excellent guide to HTML 2.0 with a couple extra HTML 3.0 tags thrown in.

HTML Quick Reference by Michael Grobe

http://kuhttp.cc.ukans.edu/lynx_help/HTML_quick.html

A fairly comprehensive but concise rundown on using HTML.

HyperText Mark-up Language Quick Reference by H. Churchyard

http://uts.cc.utexas.edu/~churchh/htmlqref.html

Another quick reference. Apart from the basic stuff, also includes information on reducing color depth and forms.

HTML, the complete-ish guide by Sunil Gupta

http://www.cis.ksu.edu/~jfy/html.reference.html

A fairly comprehensive, if brief, guide to HTML. Written as a guide for creating documents for X-Mosaic, but should apply across the board to other platforms.

Introduction to HTML by Peter Flynn

http://www.ucc.ie/~pflynn/books/ch7-8.html

An excerpt from the book, *The World Wide Web Handbook*, by Peter Flynn. Contains a good rundown on the ins and outs of HTML specifications, DTDs, and so on, as well as an introduction to HTML markup.

Appendix A: *A Resource Directory*

Introduction to HTML by Eric A. Meyer and Case Western Reserve University

http://www.cwru.edu/help/introHTML/toc.html

The most novel aspect of this site are the interactive quizzes that follow after each chapter—you get to select answers to multiple choice questions, then submit your answers for immediate feedback.

Intermediate HTML by Eric A. Meyer and Case Western Reserve University

http://www.cwru.edu/help/interHTML/toc.html

A continuation of Eric A. Meyer's *Introduction to HTML*, covering intermediate to more advanced HTML. Primary focus is on creating forms.

HTML Reference Manual by Sandia National Laboratories

http://www.sandia.gov/sci_compute/html_ref.html

A comprehensive online reference to HTML, past, present, and future. Note that the real goodies here, the descriptions of the HTML elements, are buried in the inconspicuous link, list of elements.

A Guide to HTML Commands by Richard Rutter

http://www.woodhill.co.uk/html/html.htm

A fairly complete A-to-Z HTML reference, covering almost all HTML tags.

Introduction To HTML by Ian Graham

http://www.utoronto.ca/webdocs/HTMLdocs/NewHTML/htmlindex.html

Excellent A-to-Z reference, from the author of the book, *The HTML Sourcebook*.

HTML EXAMPLE (Level 2.0) by Christian Sandvig

http://www.dcn.davis.ca.us/~csandvig/ip/example.htmluses

Uses a side-by-side approach, using tables, to show HTML code on the left and the results as they will appear in a browser on the right.

Compendium of HTML Syntax

http://www.winternet.com/%7Erlkelog/WIP/CompendHTML.html

The HyperText Markup Language: Netscape Version 2.02

http://www.best.com/%7Emcguirk/gavito/html-spec.html

A rundown on HTML up to Netscape 2.02.

HTML Reference by Microsoft

http://www.microsoft.com/workshop/author/newhtml/htmlr018.htm

Microsoft's rundown on the current state of HTML, including use of its own extensions. (Microsoft seems to want to keep moving this page around, or changing its name, without leaving any forwarding address. Hopefully, this one will stay put. If it doesn't, then try its home page:

http://www.microsoft.com/workshop/author/newhtml/

W3Writer: A Basic HTML Tutorial by Gordon Hake

`http://hake.com/gordon/w3-index.html`

Basic tutorial on creating HTML documents.

HTML Style Guides

An HTML reference can tell you what HTML is and what it's supposed to do, but it can't necessarily tell you how to use it to the best effect. To find out, listen to the sage advice of those who have been there before you.

What is good hypertext writing? by Jutta Degener

`http://www.cs.tu-berlin.de/~jutta/ht/writing.html`

An excellent common-sense style guide for writing good hypertext text.

How to Make Great WWW Pages! by Carlos L. McEvilly

`http://www.c3.lanl.gov/~cim/webgreat/first.html`

Contains an excellent collection of tips and just plain practical advice on how to make your Web page successful on the Web.

Composing Good HTML by Eric Tilton

`http://www.cs.cmu.edu/~tilt/cgh/`

An excellent style guide written by the one of the authors of *Web Weaving*, a book on HTML. Full of good practical advice.

The Ten Commandments of HTML by Sean Howard of Visionary Designs

`http://www.visdesigns.com/design/commandments.html`

Good common-sense pointers on using HTML.

Appendix A: *A Resource Directory*

Setting Up a Web Site by Anonymous

`http://freethought.tamu.edu/~meta/setup-guide.html`

A highly ironical, and funny, guide to doing all the right—I mean wrong—things in setting up your Web site.

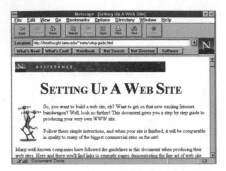

The Hall of Shame by FLUX

`http://www.meat.com/netscape_hos.html`

Not really a style guide, but rather a gallery of bad style, and I mean really, really bad style. Worth checking out to see how *not* to do it.

Hints for Web Authors by Warren Steel

`http://www.mcsr.olemiss.edu/~mudws/webhints.html`

Good style guide that treats the subjects of Web authorship, portability, and Netscape 2.0.

Guide to Web Style by Sun Microsystems

`http://www.sun.com/styleguide/`

A style guide from one of the major players in the Web game.

Advice for HTML Authors by the HTML Writers Guild

`http://ugweb.cs.ualberta.ca/~gerald/guild/style.html`

The result of a discussion on an HTML Writers Guild mailing list.

Style Guide for online hypertext by Tim Berners-Lee

http://www.w3.org/pub/WWW/Provider/Style/Overview.html

Wise words from the inventor of the Web.

HTML Bad Style Page by Tony Sanders

http://www.earth.com/bad-style/

Some HTML *don'ts*. A bit on the "purist" side, but has some good advice.

Web Style Manual by Patrick J. Lynch

http://info.med.yale.edu/caim/StyleManual_Top.HTML

The style guide used internally by the Yale Center for Advanced Instructional Media.

General Web Publishing Information

The HTML Writers Guild List of HTML Resources

http://www.hwg.org/resources/html/

A page to many more HTML links.

The Web Developer's Virtual Library

http://WWW.Stars.com/

Offers links to *everything*.

Bob Allison's Web Master's Home Page

http://gagme.wwa.com/%7Eboba/masters1.html

A compendium of resources and information on creating a Web presence.

Word Wide Web FAQ by Thomas Boutell

http://www.boutell.com/faq/

A compendium of all manner of information on the WWW, including Web publishing and authoring information.

WWW FAQ: What newsgroups discuss the Web? by Thomas Boutell

http://www.boutell.com/faq/ngroups.htm

Listing and discussion of Web publishing and authoring related newsgroups.

Search the AWEBS News archives

http://www.awebs.com/news_archive/

Allows you to do a search of archives of Web publishing and authoring oriented newsgroups. At time of writing, search included only current month, but plans are to include previous months, too.

Appendix A: *A Resource Directory*

Microsoft Internet Explorer Author's Guide and HTML Reference (Microsoft Site Builder Workshop)

http://www.microsoft.com/workshop/author/newhtml/

Microsoft's omnibus Web authoring site.

D.J. Quad's Ultimate HTML Site

http://www.quadzilla.com/

D.J. Quad's omnibus Web site on all things HTML.

Web Page Templates

Web page templates can be handy as out-of-the-box solutions or as starting points for further elaboration. You can plug your own text into them or use them as guides for tagging your text.

Netscape Web Page Templates by Netscape

http://home.netscape.com/assist/net_sites/starter/samples/templates/index.html

Part of the Netscape Gold Rush Tool Chest. An excellent collection of templates covering a wide range of different kinds of Web pages.

Templates for Homepages by Christian Mogensen

http://www-pcd.stanford.edu/mogens/intro/templates.html

A selection of Web page templates, including plain, generic, and free-form pages, as well as resume and project description pages. These are pretty basic, at best starting points, not finished designs.

HTML Templates for Courses from the University of Maryland at College Park

http://www.inform.umd.edu:8080/EdRes/Faculty_Resources_and_Support/template/

Includes templates for course descriptions and supplementary readings.

HTML 2.0 Templates by Jim Hurley

http://www.webcom.com/~hurleyj/article/templates.html

Includes a "standard head template" and a "standard trailer template," covering standardizing the header and address sections of your Web pages.

Web Page Templates by Lansing Community College

http://www.lansing.cc.mi.us/title3/sample.htm

A collection of Web page templates developed for use at Lansing Community College, including templates for List of Links, Divisional, Departmental, Personal, Newsletter, Staff Directory, and Conference/Seminar Web page templates.

Example Web Pages from Chapter 4

This section lists Web pages that were used in Chapter 4 to illustrate different kinds of Web pages that you can create, such as a personal page, a resume, a list of links, an informational page, a glossary, an FAQ, a newsletter, and so on. If you want to check them out for yourself, here are the links.

Charles Stuart's Hairy Human Homepage

http://www.luna.co.uk/%7Echarles/

Chun K. Lee's online resume

http://128.173.41.74/~chunlee/resume1.html

Marv Vendehey's Dance Directory

http://www.cyberspace.com/vandehey/dance.html

Internet Stats and History by Mike Bray

http://www.oir.ucf.edu/~mike/statistics.html

The Online Communicator: Writing by Rich Wilson

http://www.communicator.com/writing1.html

Spam Facts by Polly Esther Fabrique

http://www.cusd.claremont.edu/~mrosenbl/spamfacts.html

The World's Best Bubble Wrap Homepage

http://members.gnn.com/rfernie/bubblewrap.html

Camping in Hawaii by the Hawaii Visitor's Bureau

http://www.visit.hawaii.org/activity/camping.html

Glossary of Poker Terms by ConJelco

http://www.conjelco.com/pokglossary.html

History of Muzak

http://www.seanet.com/Vendors/muzak/MLP/HISTORY.HTML

Appendix A: *A Resource Directory*

Danny Yee's book review of Civilizing Cyberspace by Steve E. Miller
http://www.anatomy.su.oz.au/danny/book-
reviews/h/Civilizing_Cyberspace.html

Michigan Linguistics FAQ by John Lawler
http://www.ling.lsa.umich.edu/lingfaq.html

Poems by Emily Dickinson published by Project Bartleby at Columbia University
http://www.columbia.edu/acis/bartleby/dickinson/dickinson1.html#1

The Museum of Bad Art
http://www.glyphs.com/moba/

How to Avoid Holism and Draw the Analytic/Synthetic Distinction by Lawrence J. Kaye
http://csmaclab-www.uchicago.edu/philosophyProject/LOT/KAYEAS.html

The Microsoft-Netscape War

Microsoft Declares War by Michael Neubarth (Internet World March/96)
http://www.iw.com/1996/03/microware.html

Browser Battle by Gus Vemditto (Internet World July/96)
http://www.iw.com/1996/07/battle.html.

An Account on Browsers and Machines
http://www.thru.com/online/
A good running account of the Microsoft-Netscape brouhaha.

Advanced and Other HTML Features

The following resources can guide you in the implementation of many "advanced" HTML features, as well as other specific features of HTML that bear mentioning, including the Netscape and Microsoft extensions, HTML 3.2, character entities, tables, colors, forms, image maps, frames, GIF animations, CGI programming, Java, Shockwave, and RealAudio.

Netscape Extensions

Extensions to HTML 2.0 by Netscape

`http://home.netscape.com/assist/net_sites/html_extensions.html`

Word on the Netscape extensions to HTML 2.0 from the horse's mouth.

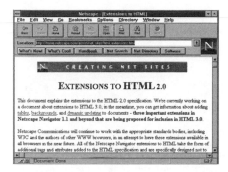

Extensions to HTML 3.0 by Netscape

`http://home.netscape.com/assist/net_sites/html_extensions_3.html`

The How to Manual of Really Cool HTML

`http://home.teclink.net/~rets/indy.html`

Covers a number of things you can do using Netscape's extensions.

How Do They Do That With HTML? by Carl Tashian

`http://www.nashville.net/%7Ecarl/htmlguide/index.html`

Covers many HTML tips and tricks, primarily using Netscape's extensions, including background and text colors, transparent and interlaced GIFs, font size and color changes, GIF animation, access counters, dynamic documents, browser detection, background sounds, frames, and tables.

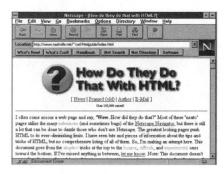

HTML 3.0 and Netscape 3.0: How to tame the wild Mozilla by Webreference.com
http://webreference.com/html3andns/

A good discussion of Netscape HTML (NHTML) and its relation, and non-relation, to HTML. 3.0.

Mozilla DTD by Webtechs
http://www.webtechs.com/sgml/Mozilla/DTD-HOME.html

Microsoft Extensions

HTML Reference by Microsoft
http://www.microsoft.com/workshop/author/newhtml/local018.htm

Includes descriptions of all of Microsoft's extensions to HTML, as well as a pretty complete rundown on the rest of HTML. (Note: Microsoft has a nasty habit of moving their reference pages around without providing forwarding links. Hopefully, this one will stay put.)

Microsoft IE DTD by Webtechs
http://www.webtechs.com/sgml/IE/DTD-HOME.html

HTML 3.2

HTML 3.2 is the latest specification for HTML, supplanting HTML 2.0 and superceding HTML 3.0. Want to know what is included? Check out the following sites.

The W3 Consortium Announces HTML 3.2 by W3C (the World Wide Web Consortium)
http://www.w3.org/hypertext/WWW/MarkUp/Wilbur/pr7may96.html

The press release (May 7, 1996) announcing HTML 3.2. HTML 3.2 supercedes HTML 3.0.

The Structure of HTML 3.2 Documents by W3C
http://www.w3.org/hypertext/WWW/MarkUp/Wilbur/features.html

The dope on HTML 3.2 from the horse's mouth.

HTML 3.2 DTD by W3C
http://www.w3.org/hypertext/WWW/MarkUp/Wilbur/HTML3.2.dtd

A Web site for those who want to get into the real nitty-gritty. May be too technical for some, however (DTDs are like that).

Hyper Text Markup Language v3.2 Reference
http://www.wvitcoe.wvnet.edu/~sbolt/html3/

W3C Activity: Hypertext Markup Language (HTML) by W3C

http://www.w3.org/pub/WWW/MarkUp/Activity

Answers questions about HTML 3.2 and current direction of the HTML standard.

Character Entities and the ISO-8859-1 Character Set

The extended, or special, characters that you can use in Web pages are defined by the ISO-8859-1 character set, also sometimes called the ISO-Latin1 character set.

Pointers to information about ISO-8859 by A. J. Flavell

http://ppewww.ph.gla.ac.uk/~flavell/iso8859/iso8859-pointers.html

Excellent rundown on issues involved with ISO-8859 character set.

Character code coverage - browser report by A. J. Flavell

http://ppewww.ph.gla.ac.uk/~flavell/iso8859/browser-report.html

Reports on support among browsers for ISO 8859-1 characters.

8 bit ASCII codes (for ISO-Latin1 character set) by W3C

http://www.w3.org/pub/WWW/MarkUp/Wilbur/latin1.gif

Provides a table of all ASCII numeric codes and corresponding displayable characters for the ISO-Latin1 character set.

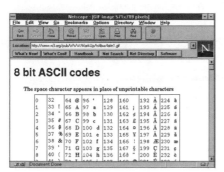

ISO Latin1 Text Entities

http://info.arc.com/docs/lynx/lynx_help/ISO_LATIN1_test.html

Lets you see how your Web browser displays named character entities in the ISO Latin1 character set.

Appendix A: *A Resource Directory*

ISO Latin1 Character Codes

http://www.pact.srf.ac.uk/~nathan/chars.html

A listing of both named character entities and ASCII character codes.

W3Writer: HTML Special Characters by Gordon Hake

http://hake.com/gordon/w3-spec.html

An excerpt from the HTML 2.0 specification edited and simplified for beginners.

ISO8859-1 Table by Martin Ramsch

http://ecsdg.lu.se/iso8859-1.html

ISO 8859-1 National Character Set FAQ by Michael K. Gschwind

ftp://rtfm.mit.edu/pub/usenet/news.answers/internationalization/
iso-8859-1-charset

Discusses how to use European (Latin American) national character sets on UNIX-based systems and the Internet.

Tables

The following resources are tutorials and references on including tables in your Web pages.

HTML Table Tutorial by Urban A. LeJeune

http://www.charm.net/~lejeune/tables.html

An excellent tutorial on creating tables; focuses on Netscape Navigator.

NCSA Mosaic(tm) Tables Tutorial

http://www.ncsa.uiuc.edu/SDG/Software/Mosaic/Tables/tutorial.html

NCSA's tutorial on tables.

TableMaker by Sam Choukri

http://www.missouri.edu/~c588349/tablemaker.html

A neat online utility that allows you to enter your table data into a form, then creates the HTML table for you.

The Table Sampler by Hagan Heller

http://www.netscape.com/people/hagan/html/tables1.html

A "by example" tables tutorial.

So You Want A Table, Huh? by Joe Burns

http://www.cs.bgsu.edu/~jburns/table.html

Another Joe Burns "So You Want . . ." page, this one on creating tables.

Setting Colors

You can set the color of the background of your Web page, as well as for foreground text and links, including regular links, already visited links, and activated links (links on which you have pressed down the mouse button but not yet released it). You also can use the COLOR attribute of the FONT tag to assign different colors to sections of text within a Web page. Originally introduced by Netscape, many other Web browsers now support these capabilities.

Colors by InfiNet

http://www.infi.net/wwwimages/colorindex.html

An excellent resource for information on setting colors for your backgrounds, text, and links. Includes a listing of colors and their hex codes that you can click on to see what they are going to look like.

Hypertext Handbook: Color Chart by Multimedia Productions

http://world.std.com/~ldjackso/5colors.htm

Extensive display of full range of colors and their hex codes. Organizes colors into different shades and hues of reds, oranges, yellows, greens, blues, indigos, and violets.

The Hex Color Guide

http://www.cranfield.ac.uk/docs/hex/

Includes a table of hex codes for different colors.

Weber "Color" Chart by Ray Weber

http://felix.scvnet.com:80/~weber/colorweb.html

A chart of hex values displayed in their resulting colors.

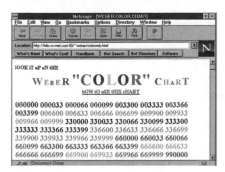

Appendix A: *A Resource Directory*

RGB Hex Triplet Color Chart by Doug Jacobson

http://www.phoenix.net/%7Ejacobson/rgb.html

An excellent chart of hex codes and their corresponding colors. Chart is a GIF file that can be downloaded (in Netscape Navigator, click on it with the right mouse button).

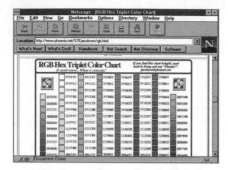

X11 based RGB color table

http://nickel.as.arizona.edu:8080/cgi-bin/color_table.pl

Allows you to submit an X11 color name, then returns results of matching colors in a RGB database. A search for "red" returned 26 different matches, form "indiared" to "violetred4." Color names are displayed in their corresponding colors, along with their hex codes. A great resource.

The Color Specifier for Netscape by HYPE Electazine

http://www.users.interport.net/~giant/COLOR/hype_color.html

Lists the names of colors and their ASCII and Hex RGB values, with a link from each color name to a page using it as a background color. Actually, this will specify colors for any browser capable of viewing background, text, or font colors, not just Netscape (Netscape did introduce this, however, so...).

ColorMaker by Sam Choukri

http://www.missouri.edu/~c588349/colormaker.html

From the same source as the TableMaker utility. Lets you point and click to specify colors for the background, text, and links, then specify a Web page, and then shows you the new colors applied to the page.

Decimal<—>HEX Convertor

http://www.sci.kun.nl/thalia/guide/color/dec-hex.html

Entering decimal values for Red, Green, and Blue will return corresponding hex numbers. Entering hex values will return corresponding decimal numbers.

Victor Engel's No Dither Netscape Color Palette

http://www.onr.com/user/lights/netcol.html

Discusses strategies and provides color chart for getting best color display results, especially in Netscape Navigator.

The Joy of Hex (Get Hexed!) by Pequod

http://www.stardot.com/%7Elukeseem/hexed.html

This is a handy form-based online utility that allows you to enter RGB decimal values (0-255) for background, text, link, and visited link colors, then see your results displayed in the colors you have specified, along with the RGB hex codes you need to insert in your Web page to get the same effect.

Forms

Forms are an advanced feature of HTML 2.0. They can be used to create customer response or order forms, for instance.

Introduction to Web Forms by the Information Technology Division Emory University

http://www.cc.emory.edu/INFODESK/MM/FORMS/

Assumes a good working knowledge of Unix (being able to copy files, change the permissions on files, use a text editor, and so on).

A Tour of HTML Forms and CGI Scripts by Sanford Morton

http://www.halcyon.com/sanford/cgi-tour.html

Assumes some familiarity with Perl.

Carlos' FORMS Tutorial by Carlos Peros

http://robot0.ge.uiuc.edu/~carlosp/cs317/ft.1.html

Aimed more at the beginning to intermediate user.

HTML Forms for Feedback by Bill Jenkins

http://www.englib.cornell.edu/instruction/www/email-forms-class.html

A good tutorial on forms aimed at the beginning to intermediate user.

HTML Forms examples by Michael Grobe

http://kuhttp.cc.ukans.edu/cwis/people/Michael.Grobe/examples.html

A set of forms examples.

Appendix A: *A Resource Directory*

Mosaic for X version 2.0 Fill-Out Form Support by NCSA

http://www.ncsa.uiuc.edu/SDG/Software/Mosaic/Docs/fill-out-forms/overview.html

Written relative to Mosaic for X, but should apply to other browsers that support forms.

HTML forms refresher course

http://www.itp.tsoa.nyu.edu/~student/jamie/help/cgi-perl/forms.html

Uses a table to give side-by-side illustrations of specific form examples and their HTML coding.

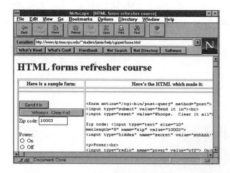

HTML Forms Table by Curt Robbins

http://ftp.clark.net/pub/cargui/formchrt.html

A handy table-based quick reference to forms tags and their attributes.

HTML Form-Testing Home Page by Glenn Trewitt of Digital Equipment Corporation

http://www.research.digital.com/nsl/formtest/home.html

Allows you to test different browsers for their forms compatibility. Your test then becomes part of the overall test results, which are updated every 15 minutes and reviewable online.

So, You Want A Form, Huh? by Joe Burns

http://www.cs.bgsu.edu/~jburns/forms.html

Another Joe Burns contribution, this time on creating forms.

Image Maps

You can use image maps to define an image to act like a menu, on which you can click in different areas of the image to activate different hypertext links.

NCSA Imagemap Tutorial
http://hoohoo.ncsa.uiuc.edu/docs/tutorials/imagemapping.html

A step-by-step tutorial for creating image maps.

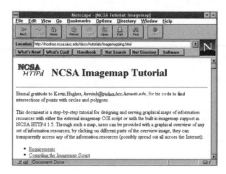

Imagemap Help Page by Steve Rogers for Hiway Techologies
http://www.hway.net/ihip/

A good resource for information on image maps.

Constructing an Image Map for your Home Page by Mark Rasmussen
http://www.et.byu.edu/resources/imagemap.html

Good basic information on constructing image maps.

Clickable Image Maps by Russ Jones
http://www.ora.com/gnn/bus/ora/features/miis/index.html

A concise explanation of how image maps work, excerpted from the book, *Managing Internet Information Services.*

Creating Clickable Images in CNC Web Pages
http://www.cris.com/help/web/clickimage.html

Targets the beginning to intermediate user.

So you want an image map, huh? by Joe Burns
http://www.cs.bgsu.edu/~jburns/imagemap.html

Excellent tutorial aimed at the non-techie. An NBNSOFT Content Award Winner.

Appendix A: *A Resource Directory*

Implementing Client-Side Image Maps by Spyglass

http://www.spyglass.com/techspec/tutorial/img_maps.html

Step-by-step instructions on how to create client-side image maps.

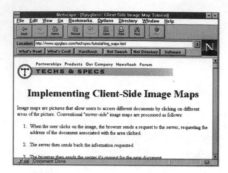

Frames

Netscape originally introduced frames, but Microsoft has since supported them, too. Frames enable you to divide the browser window into "frames," with different Web pages active in each frame.

Frames: An Introduction by Netscape

http://home.netscape.com/assist/net_sites/frames.html

Netscape's own rundown on the feature it introduced.

Netscape Frames by Charlton Rose

http://sharky.nomius.com/frames/menu.htm

A great page on using frames. Makes effective use of graphic illustrations.

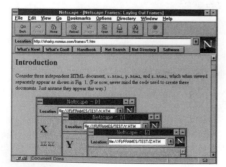

FrameShop! by Sam Choukri

http://www.missouri.edu/~c588349/frameshop/index.html

From the same source as TableMaker and ColorMaker. An interesting online utility that enables you to enter information for main frames and subframes into forms. It then automatically creates the codes for the frames for you. It can create up to three main frames and up to three subframes for each main frame.

Introduction to Frames by Webspinners

http://www.spunwebs.com/sites2c/frmtutor.html

An excellent tutorial on creating frames, as well as three templates.

Framing the Web by Webreference.com (Dan Brown)

http://www.webreference.com/dev/frames/

Another good rundown on creating frames. Includes a cheat sheet.

GIF Animation

The GIF89a standard for GIF images allows for the creation of animated GIF files—an image file containing several separate images which are displayed rapidly in turn. Here are some pointers to where you can find out more.

Wilson's GIF Animation Tutorial by Wilson Chan Wai Shing

http://www.comp.polyu.edu.hk/%7Ec4075231/gif.html

Everything you want to know about GIF animation.

Appendix A: *A Resource Directory*

Samiel's GIF Animation Page

http://www.fastlane.net/~samiel/anim.shtml

Another good page on GIF animations.

GIF Animation on the WWW by Royal E. Frazier

http://www.reiworld.com/royalef/gifanim.htm

Lots of stuff on GIF animations. Includes a tutorial. Also includes the 1st Internet Gallery of GIF Animation.

Counters and Statistics

So You Want A Counter, Huh? by Joe Burns

http://www.cs.bgsu.edu/~jburns/counter.html

Another in Joe Burns' excellent series.

WebCounter

http://www.digits.com/

A source for free counters, as well as information and guidance on using counters.

Internet Audit Bureau

http://www.internet-audit.com/

A sponsor-provided free service that will compile usage statistics for you on your page or pages.

So, why can't we find out exactly how many people are hitting our Web site? by Organic Online Services

http://www.organic.com/Home/Services/traffic-analysis.html

Some caveats on Web statistics.

CGI and Perl

The Common Gateway Interface by NCSA
http://hoohoo.ncsa.uiuc.edu/cgi/

An authoritative rundown on CGI.

Decoding FORMs with CGI by NCSA
http://hoohoo.ncsa.uiuc.edu/cgi/forms.html

Aimed at advanced users.

CGI Tutorial by Nik Silver
http://agora.leeds.ac.uk/Perl/Cgi/start.html

Assumes knowledge of Perl.

Perl Tutorial by Nik Silver
http://agora.leeds.ac.uk/Perl/start.html

Java and JavaScript

Brewing Java: A Tutorial by Elliotte Rusty Harold
http://sunsite.unc.edu/javafaq/javatutorial.html

An excellent tutorial on using Java.

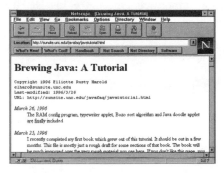

Beyond Java: Distributed objects on Web by Eamonn Sullivan
http://www.pcweek.com/navigator/1218/nav1218.html

JavaScript Outpost
http://intergalactinet.com/javascript/

A compilation of links to Web pages on JavaScript.

Appendix A: *A Resource Directory*

Introduction to JavaScript by Stefan Koch

http://rummelplatz.uni-mannheim.de/%7Eskoch/js/script.htm

A comprehensive JavaScript tutorial.

Java Technology Update from Personal Computer Magazine

http://www.vnu.co.uk/bc/pcm/603java.htm

A good discussion of Java and its potential, as well as its drawbacks. Has an interesting section on "Java's rival and friends," including discussion of the Java positions, pro or con, of Macromedia, Silicon Graphics, Borland, Microsoft, Netscape, IBM/Lotus, and Symantec.

The Java Developers Kit by JavaSoft

http://java.sun.com/products/JDK/1.0.2/index.html

Besides letting you download the latest version of the Java Developers Kit, offers lots of information online about Java.

JavaScript Tutorial: Intermediate Level by Intergalactinet

http://intergalactinet.com/javascript/JSIntTutor.html

Multimedia

Shockwave by MacroMedia

http://www.macromedia.com/

Shockwave is a set of plug-in authoring tools for for Authorware, Director, and Freehand and a Netscape plug-in that allows display of streaming animation. You can download the software at this site.

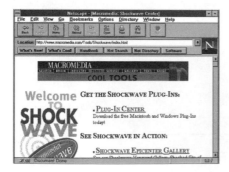

RealAudio: Audio on Demand for the Internet by Progressive Networks

http://www.realaudio.com/

Includes two products, RealAudio Play and Real AudioServer. Enables playing and delivering of on-demand streaming audio. You can download the software at this site. Requires a 16-bit sound card. Works with numerous Web browsers.

Miscellaneous Advanced and Other HTML

Advanced HTML programming by Sky Coyote

http://www.intergalact.com/hp/part2/part2.html

Rundowns on image maps, forms, and CGI.

Hypertext links in HTML by Murray Maloney (SoftQuad)

http://www.sq.com/papers/Relationships.html

Discusses use of the REL and REV attributes of the LINK and A (Anchor) tags.

A Proposed Convention for Embedding Metadata in HTML by Stuart Weibel

http://www.oclc.org:5047/~weibel/html-meta.html

Discusses a proposed convention for including metadata using the META tag in HTML documents.

General Web Resources

This section lists useful Web-related resources that can help Web publishers.

Glossaries

Guide to Web Terminology by Information Innovation

http://www.euro.net/innovation/Web_Word_Base/Dictionary.html

A good glossary of Web terms, with links.

Hypertext Handbook: Glossary of Terms by Multimedia Productions

http://world.std.com/~ldjackso/hthb5.htm

A list of links to definitions.

The Websurfer's Handbook: The Web-to-English Dictionary by The Asylum

http://asylum.cid.com/handbook/handbook.html

A funny compilation of hip Web slang. I contributed the "link rot" entry, by the way.

Online Magazines

This section lists some online magazines that target Web developers and publishers.

Web Developer Magazine

http://www.webdeveloper.com/

By the publishers of *Internet World*. You can do a keyword search of articles from back issues.

WebMaster Magazine: The Executive Resource for Doing Business on the Net

http://www.cio.com/WebMaster/wmhome.html

Case studies, interviews, how-to strategies, and new products and services. Aimed at IT executives, senior managers, and corporate webmasters, with the slant definitely on doing business, making money, but a good information source for anyone wanting to make an impact on the Web.

WEBsmith: the How-To Magazine for technicians of the World Wide Web

http://www.smithing.com/

A resource for Web-related developers.

Web Professionals' Digest

http://www.littleblue.com/webpro/

The Web Developer's Journal

http://nctweb.com/nct/software/eleclead.html

Appendix A: *A Resource Directory*

Web Tools Review

http://www-swiss.ai.mit.edu/wtr/

An online journal for Web developers.

Web Success

http://www.kdcol.com/~ray/index.html

An online magazine that focuses on Web marketing and resources to promote commerce on the Internet.

Web Site Promotion Newsletter

http://www.meh.com/meh/about.html

Reports monthly on methods and resources for publicizing Web sites.

WWWiz Magazine

http://wwwiz.com/

Read the latest issue, browse through back issues, or read late-breaking news.

Web Week Magazine

http://www.webweek.com/

Read the premier weekly magazine for all matters that are Web related. Back issues are also available for browsing.

TechWeb: The Technology Information Source

http://techweb.cmp.com/

WebTechniques: Solutions for Internet and Web Developers

http://www.webtechniques.com/

The Spider's Web

http://www.incontext.com/spidweb/index.htm

Aimed at Web developers and designers.

Navigate! The Online Magazine for Netscape Users

http://www.netscapepress.com/zine/

Off the Net

http://home.mcom.com/assist/net_sites/off_the_net.html

Another Netscape-originated online publication.

Netscape World

http://www.ntscpwld.com/

Another Netscape-oriented online publication, but this one isn't by Netscape.

Appendix A: *A Resource Directory*

Word Wide Web Journal by O'Reilly/W3C

http://www.w3.org/pub/WWW/Journal/

The journal of the Word Wide Web Consortium, published by O'Reilly and Associates. Not the full version of the journal, which is available only through subscription, but contains excerpts.

Internet/Web History and Statistics

Internet Statistics: Web Growth, Internet Growth by Matthew Gray

http://www.mit.edu/people/mkgray/net/

Internet Facts by Parallax Webdesign

http://www.echonyc.com/~parallax/interfacts.html

Statistics on size/growth and demographics of the Net.

Internet statistics by Vincent O'Keefe

http://webnet.mednet.gu.se/computer/internet-statistics.txt

Internet Stats and History by Mike Bray

http://www.oir.ucf.edu/~mike/statistics.html

A page of links to many other Web pages on statistics and history of the Net.

Internet Evolution (GIF graph) by A.M. Rutkowski and the Internet Society

ftp://ftp.isoc.org/isoc/charts/history-gifs/timeline.gif

Project 2000 by Hoffman, Novak, and Kalsbeek

http://www2000.ogsm.vanderbilt.edu/baseline/internet.demos.july9.1996.html

Report on Internet and Web use in the U.S.

Hobbes' Internet Timeline by Robert H. Zakon

http://info.isoc.org/guest/zakon/Internet/History/HIT.html

A Brief History of the Internet and Related Networks by Robert H. Zakon

http://info.isoc.org/guest/zakon/Internet/History/
Brief_History_of_the_Internet

Short History of the Internet by Bruce Sterling

http://info.isoc.org/guest/zakon/Internet/History/
Short_History_of_the_Internet

A Timeline of Network History by Stan Kulikowski II
http://info.isoc.org/guest/zakon/Internet/History/
Timeline_of_Network_History

Internet Statistics—Estimated by Internet Solutions
http://www.netree.com/netbin/internetstats

CyberStats by FAS CyberStrategy Project
http://www.fas.org/cp/netstats.htm

Web Publishing Tool Chest: Programs and Utilities

Web Browsers

Don't already have a Web browser? Thinking of switching? Want to assemble a collection of Web browsers you can use to check your pages? The following are pointers to general information on Web browsers, as well as where you can find and download many Windows Web browsers.

General Information on Web Browsers

Picking the Perfect Web Browser by C/NET
http://www.cnet.com/Content/Reviews/Compare/Browsers/
Includes reviews of 28 browsers for Windows, Macintosh, and OS/2.

BrowserCaps: A catalog of the HTML support provided by different Web browsers by David Ornstein
http://objarts.com/bc/
These are survey results on how different browsers handle HTML. You can participate, submitting your browser to the test.

Appendix A: *A Resource Directory*

BrowserWatch

http://www.browserwatch.com/

Offers breaking news in the browser and plug-ins industry.

Web Browser Test Page

http://www.uky.edu/~magree00/TestPage.html

Tests your browser's capability to display GIFs and JPEGs, as well as tests for MPEG, QuickTime, WAV, and AU players.

Windows Web Browsers

These are Web browsers you can download from the Web. They are freeware, shareware, and demoware.

> **NOTE**
>
> *A demoware product is a time-limited or feature-limited ("cripple-ware") version of a commercial software product. It may stop working once the evaluation period is up or may simply pester you with nag screens.*

Netscape Navigator

http://home.netscape.com/

Download the latest versions of Navigator for Windows 3.1 or Navigator Gold for Windows 95 or Windows NT.

Appendix A: *A Resource Directory*

NCSA Mosaic

http://www.ncsa.uiuc.edu/SDG/Software/WinMosaic/HomePage.html

Versions are available for Windows 3.1, Windows 95, and Windows NT. Windows 3.1 version requires Win32s (available at site).

Microsoft Internet Explorer

http://www.microsoft.com/

Download the latest version of Internet Explorer for Windows 3.1, Windows 95, or Windows NT.

Emissary by Attachmate

http://www.twg.com/emissary/emiss1.html

At the time of this writing, the Emissary 2.0a Beta version was available for download. It's a full-feature Web browser with support for frames, tables, Shockwave, Netscape Plug-Ins, and HTML 3.0. Also features a USENET news reader, multimedia e-mail, file transfer and management, and a WYSIWYG HTML editor.

HotJava by Sun

http://java.sun.com/

A "preBeta" version is available for free download for Windows 95. From the makers of Java and JavaScript.

Cello by the Legal Information Institute at Cornell Law School

http://www.law.cornell.edu/cello/cellotop.html

A Windows 3.1 browser. Although I don't recommend you use it as your main browser, it can be useful as a test browser to see how your pages appear in more than one browser.

Spyglass Mosaic

http://www.spyglass.com/home.html

A 30-day evaluation copy of Spyglass Mosaic is available for download. Didn't say whether it actually stops working after 30-days, or just pesters you with nag screens. Supports tables, background colors and images, center and right alignment, text wrap, border controls and other HTML 3.0 proposed formatting extensions.

Appendix A: *A Resource Directory*

PowerBrowser by Oracle

`http://www.oracle.com/products/websystem/powerbrowser/html/index.html`

More than just a browser, PowerBrowser includes a Web server, an integrated BASIC scripting environment, Java support, plus Database Wizard to help you create database-enabled applications. Supports all the major proposed extensions to HTML, including frames, tables, and GIF animations. Available for Windows 3.1, 95, and NT.

SPRYNET Mosaic

`http://www.spry.com/sos/net_tools/internet/browsers/`

A tables-capable Windows 3.1 Web browser. (Note: The link for downloading the browser is hidden at the bottom of the page.)

Cyberjack for Windows 95 by the Delrina Corporation

`http://www.cyberjack.com/`

The Online Trial version is available for download.

WebSurfer by NetManage

`http://www.netmanage.com/netmanage/`

Software is available free, with no time-out feature or expiration date. Versions are available for Windows 3.1 and Windows 95/NT. Newest versions support inline video, RealAudio, True Speech, plus tables, backgrounds, fonts, text wrap around graphics, and more.

I-View Off-line HTML Browser by Talent Communications

`http://www.talentcom.com/iview/iview.htm`

This is a good offline Web browser, which is useful if your online Web browser cannot be run easily, or at all, offline. Also useful if you want to create Web pages but don't have an Internet connection.

SlipKnot by MicroMind, Inc.

`http://plaza.interport.net/slipknot/slipknot.html`

This is a graphical Web browser that will work with a shell account and does not require a SLIP/PPP account.

Video On Line Internet Browser

http://www.vol.it/VOLB/browser.html

Can be freely duplicated and/or distributed without any restriction. Latest version is available in multiple languages, including Czech, Egyptian, Finnish, French, German, Greek, English, Italian, Maltese, Norwegian, Polish, Spanish, Swedish, Turkish. Earlier versions available in Arabic, Danish, Hungarian, Dutch, Portuguese, and Russian.

Accent Multilingual Mosaic

http://www.accentsoft.com/

Lets you browse in 30 different languages under any language version of Windows (including 95). Browse pages in Russian, Arabic, Greek, or Japanese, even while using the U.S. version of Windows. Evaluation copies are available for download.

Quarterdeck Mosaic

http://arachnid.qdeck.com/qdeck/demosoft/QMosaic/

Trialware version was available to June 30, 1996. Check to see whether offer has been renewed (with a new expiration date).

Webview Offline Web Browser by South Pacific Information Services, Ltd.

http://www.spis.co.nz/webcentr/webview.htm

Another offline Web browser that supports most of HTML 2.0, plus some additional HTML 3.0 features, such as tables and font size changes. Registration is $35 (New Zealand dollars).

The Other Internet Package by Pixelogic

http://www.theother.com/

Includes a Web browser that supports forms, tables, frames, and most Netscape 2.0 extensions. Also includes e-mail and news reader software. At the time of this writing, a free beta version (0.903) was available for download. Both 16-bit (Win 3.1) and 32-bit versions (Win 95/NT) available. A version in French is slated for release soon.

Opera by Opera Software

http://www.fou.telenor.no/opera/opera.html

English, Norwegian, and Swedish evaluation versions are available for download. Optimized for keyboard browsing. Supports frames, tables, text wrap around images, and more. Registration is $30.

HTML Editors, WP Add-Ons, Convertors, and Templates

Here are software tools to help you create and edit your HTML files, including HTML editors, word processing add-ons, convertors, and templates.

HTML Editors

After you learn some HTML, you might want to try out one or more of these HTML editors to make your HTML coding life easier.

HoTMetaL by SoftQuad

http://www.sq.com/products/hotmetal/hm-ftp.htm

HoTMetaL Free Free Version 2.0 is a non-commercial evaluation version for Windows 3.1 that is available for download. The price for the commercial version, HoTMetaL Pro 3.0, is $159 U.S. and $199 Canadian.

HotDog by Sausage Software

http://www.sausage.com/

Demonstration copies of 16-bit Standard and Pro Versions and 32-bit Standard and Professional Versions (written specifically for Windows 95) are available for download. Evaluation periods are for 14 or 30 days, after which the software will stop working, but you can e-mail for an extension of the trial period. Prices for the registered versions are $29.95 for HotDog Standard 2 (Win 3.1), $39.95 for HotDog Standard 32-Bit (Win 95), $99.95 for HotDog Professional 2 (Win 3.1), and $99.95 for HotDog Pro 32-Bit (Win 95).

HTMLed by Internet Software Technologies

http://www.ist.ca/htmled/

Both a 16-bit version for Windows 3.1 and a 32-bit version for Windows 95 or Windows NT are available for download. The registered version is $29 U.S. and $35 Canadian.

HTML Assistant Pro 2 for Windows by Brooklyn North Software Works

http://www.brooknorth.com/

A freeware version is available for download. The registered version is $99.95 U.S. and $139 Canadian.

<Live Markup> by My Software Company

http://www.mediatec.com/

The 16-bit version is available for download for a 14-day free evaluation, after which the software will stop working. Registered versions (16-bit and 32-bit) are $49. The 32-bit version is for both Windows 95 and NT.

Web Weaver by McWeb Software

http://www.tiac.net/users/mmm/webweav.html

This is the evaluation version. The registered version is $12.

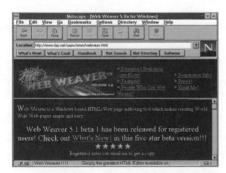

Web Wizard: The Duke of URL by ARTA Software Group

http://www.halcyon.com/artamedia/webwizard/

Both the 16-bit and 32-bit (Win 95/NT) are available for download. No pricing information mentioned. Webber by Cerebral Systems Development Corp. at http://www.csdcorp.com/webber.htm. Evaluation version is available for downloading. Registered version is $30 U.S. and $40 Canadian. Versions are for Windows 3.1.

Appendix A: *A Resource Directory*

HTML NotePad by Cranial Software

http://www.cranial.com/software/htmlnote/

Shareware version available for download. Registration is £24 or U.S. $45.

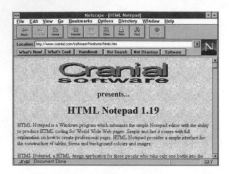

Aardvark Pro by Functional Business Systems of Australia

http://www.fbs.aust.com/aardvark.html

Two versions are available for download. A free version and a shareware version. Registration of the shareware version is $59 U.S. and $89 Australian.

Arachnid by Tim Long

http://rhwww.richuish.ac.uk/resource.htm

No pricing information mentioned.

EdWin by Michael Sutton

http://www.vantek.net/pages/msutton/edwin.htm

16-bit non-commercial download version is available. Registration cost is $35 for 16-bit and 32-bit (Win 95/NT) versions.

GNNpress by GNN Hosting Service

http://gnn.com/gnn/netizens/gnnpress/index.html

Available for free from GNN Hosting Service.

Gomer HTML Editor by Stoopid Software

http://clever.net/gomer/

Registration is $15.

HTML Handler by Jonathan Reinberg

http://happypuppy.com/digitale/hthand.html

Freeware. Both 16-bit and 32-bit (Win 95) versions are available for download.

HTML Easy! Pro by Joe Lin (Basic Concept Studio)

`http://www.trytel.com/~milkylin/`

Both English and Chinese language versions are available for download. No pricing information mentioned.

Kenn Nesbitt's WebEdit

`http://www.nesbitt.com/`

Both 16-bit and 32-bit (Win 95/NT) 30-day trial versions are available for download. Registration is $39.95 for both 16-bit Personal/Education version and 32-bit Standard edition, and $79.95 for 16-bit Commercial version and 32-bit Professional version.

WebPen by Informatik Inc.

`http://www.execpc.com/~infothek/webpen.html`

Both the Standard and Pro versions (both Win 3.1) are available for download. Registration is $19 for the Standard version and $39 for the Pro version. Standard version includes an offline browser and an OLE-link to MS-Word spellchecker. The Pro version includes WinCopy screen ·capture, GifWeb transparent GIFs tool, and Hotspots Imagemaps tool.

TC-Director by Tashcom Software

`http://pages.linkstar.com/tashcom-software/index.html`

Both 16-bit and 32-bit versions are available for download. Registration is $25 for 16-bit version and $30 for 32-bit version.

WebMania by Q&D Software Development

`http://www.q-d.com/`

Supports creation of frames, forms, and client-side image maps. A download version is available. Registration is $34.95 for WebMania Standard and $49.95 for WebMania Pro.

DerekWare HTML Author

`http://shell.masterpiece.com/derek/derekware/`

Free Windows 95 HTML editor that supports HTML 2.0 and Internet Explorer extensions.

Appendix A: *A Resource Directory*

HTML Builder by FLFSoft

http://www.execpc.com/~flfsoft/HTMLBuilder.html

$30. A 32-bit HTML Editor (Windows 3.1 requires Win32s).

WinHTML by Gulf Coast Software

http://www.gcsoftware.com/winhtml.html

16-bit and 32-bit versions available. $25/49.

InContext Spider

http://www.incontext.com/products/spider1.html

$79. 30-day evaluation version is available (expires after 30 days).

Web Ed for Windows

http://www.ozemail.com.au/~kread/webed.html

Free.

The Web Media Publisher

http://www.wbmedia.com/publisher/

$30. A 32-bit HTML editor. Includes FTP upload and internal Web browser. Evaluation version available for download.

Microsoft FrontPage

http://www.microsoft.com/frontpage/

$149. $109 for users of Microsoft Office for Windows 95 applications. No demo or beta version available for download.

CMed

http://www.iap.net.au/~cmathes/

A 32-bit HTML editor for Windows 95/NT. Supports HTML 2.0 and 3.0, Netscape and Microsoft extensions. CMed is shareware. A 30-day evaluation version available for download. Registration is $25 (U.S.) and $30 (AU).

WebThing by Paul Lutus

http://www.arachnoid.com/lutusp/webthing.htm

A Windows 95 HTML editor that supports drag and drop conversion of word processing files, tables, outlines, and so on, to HTML. Supports frames and JavaScript. This software is described as being "Careware." The author doesn't want money, but a demonstration of "care," such as stopping whining for a week. Otherwise, WebThing can be freely copied and distributed.

Word Processor Add-Ons

If you want to use your favorite word processor for editing HTML files, here are some add-on HTML editors for Word for Windows and WordPerfect for Windows.

Internet Assistant for Microsoft Word for Windows

http://www.microsoft.com/msword/internet/ia/default.htm

Internet Assistant is available for free from Microsofft in both 16-bit (Win 3.1) and 32-bit (Win 95) versions.

HTML Author for Microsoft Word for Windows 6.0

http://www.salford.ac.uk/iti/gsc/htmlauth/summary.html

Does not work with Microsoft Word for Windows 7.0 (Win 95), but a 32-bit version is projected for the future. Registion is 28 pounds sterling, with other currencies acceptable provided you add 10% to your local equivalent based on the exchange rate at the time of posting.

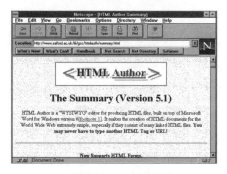

Internet Publisher for WordPerfect 6.1 for Windows

Since Novell sold WordPerfect to Corel, Novell has dropped the Web page for Internet Publisher. However, you can still download Internet Publisher (free) at any of these addresses:

http://www.wpmag.com/Windows/1996/apr/WPIPZIP.EXE

http://www.schaft.com/ftp/HTML_Stuff/wpipzip.exe

ftp://ftp.esva.net/pub/win31/wpipzip.exe

HTML Convertors and Templates

Convertors are handy if you have a bunch of files you want to convert to HTML. Templates are used in Word for Windows to create HTML files from your word processing files.

Appendix A: *A Resource Directory*

ANT_HTML.DOT

http://mcia.com/ant/antdesc.htm

A document template for Microsoft Word 6.0. Works in Word for Windows, NT, and 95 (and Word for Macintosh), and international versions of Word 6.0 and above. Includes support for HTML 2.0 plus the Netscape extensions. Has a customizable toolbar for user-added tags. Includes a WYSIWYG previewer. A demo version is available for download. Registration is $39, plus an additional $3 if you're in Texas.

CU_HTML.DOT by Anton Lam

http://www.cuhk.hk/csc/cu_html/cu_html.htm

A document template for Microsoft Word for Windows 6.0 and 2.0. WYSIWYG creation of HTML files inside Word. There is no registration fee. Software is provided without warranty or support.

GT_HTML.DOT by the Georgia Tech Research Institute

http://www.gatech.edu/word_html/

Provides what it terms a "psuedo-WYSIWYG authoring environment" for creating HTML files in Word f6.0 (Windows or Macintosh). It should also work with Word for Windows 95, but no absolute promises are given. A version also is available for Word for Windows 2.0. Freeware.

Wp2Html

http://www.res.bbsrc.ac.uk/wp2html/

Conversion/template package for WordPerfect. Converts WordPerfect files to HTML. Runs stand-alone and is designed for the batch conversion of multiple existing WP documents. Can convert tables, text, styles, and most formatting codes. Can handle equations and figures, subject to the limitations of HTML (Netscape). Evaluation kit, which is an earlier version of the software and works with WordPerfect 5.1 or 5.2 files, is available for download. Registration is 5 UK pounds.

WPTOHTML 2.0 by Hunter Monroe

http://www.lib.ox.ac.uk/~hunter/wptohtml.htm

Conversion/template package for WordPerfect for DOS. Versions available for 5.1 and 6.0. Can also be used with WordPerfect 5.2/6.0/6.0a for Windows, as well as any other version of WordPerfect that can use the same printer drivers and style files. Supports conversion of special characters and equations to transparent inline images (.XBM format). Freeware.

WPTOHTML 1.0 by Hunter Monroe

http://www.coast.net/SimTel/msdos/wordperf.html

Download WPT51d10.ZIP for 5.1 version and WPT60D10.ZIP for 6.0 version. Older version than 2.0, but supports conversion of tables of contents, cross-references, indexes, end notes, and WP 6.0 hypertext links to HTML hypertext links. Available for WordPerfect 5.1 and 6.0 for DOS. Freeware.

EasyHelp/Web by Eon Solutions Ltd.

http://www.eon-solutions.com/easyhelp/easyhelp.htm

Converts Word for Windows documents to either Windows Help files or HTML files. Two versions are available for download, one for Word 6/7/NT (which includes both 16-bit and 32-bit versions) and the other for Word for Windows 2.0. Required version 3.10.505 (extended) or later of the Microsoft Help Compiler if you want to compile Help files. Registration is $140.

AmiWeb by Steve Belleguelle

http://www.cs.nott.ac.uk/%7Esbx/amiweb.html

This is a combination of macros, stylesheets, and a convertor program for creating HTML files from Ami-Pro for Windows. (Note: Ami-Pro has since become Word-Pro, and it is not specified whether this package will work with the Word-Pro versions.) AmiWeb supports the creation of tables. See also the set of macros, FORMS.ZIP, by Ashley Bass, available at the same site for creating forms using AmiWeb. Although it is not specifically stated, this appears to be freeware. No pricing information is mentioned.

Advantage HTML-ASCII Convertor

http://www.demon.co.uk/advantage/files.htm

Shareware that strips HTML codes.

DBF to HTML Convertor by Ronald A. "Andy" Hoskinson

http://www.demon.co.uk/advantage/files.htm

$20. Shareware. Converts dBase/XBase files into HTML.

ForeFront ForeHTML

http://www.ff.com/pages/forehtm.htm

$169. WinHelp to HTML convertor. Windows 3.1 and Windows 95 versions available. Demo versions available for download (demo versions limit you to 10 topics).

WebWorks Publisher by Quadralay

http://www.quadralay.com/Publisher/

$895. Calls itself the premier FrameMaker-to-HTML convertor. 30-day evaluation versions available for download (Windows 3.1 requires Win32s).

KEYview: The Universal Viewer by FTP Software

http://www.ftp.com/mkt_info/keyv2.html

Works as a file viewer and convertor. Can convert multiple different formats to HTML. Also functions as a Netscape plug-in for viewing multiple file formats on the Web. 30-day evaluation version available for download. Cost: $49.95.

RTFtoHTML by Chris Hector

`http://www.w3.org/pub/WWW/Tools/rtftohtml-3.0.html`

The latest version of RTFtoHTML (3.0), incorporating RTFtoWEB features. Converts between RTF (Rich Text Format) and HTML. Supports tables, Netscape and Microsoft extensions, splitting long documents into smaller files. Supports coversion from RTF export from Microsoft Word, WordPerfect, Next, Claris Works, Framemaker, and any other word processor capable of exporting RTF files. Shareware. Price not mentioned (other than its being "small").

WebMaker by Harlequin

`http://www.harlequin.com/webmaker/`

Converts between FrameMaker and HTML. Offers customizable conversion of text, graphics, tables, and equations. Evaluation version available for download. Evaluation version is not time-restricted. The only feature limitation is that you can only create up to five separate HTML pages from any one FrameMaker document. Registration is $99.

Automated Page Creators, Site Managers, and Web Authoring Suites

Do you think you might need more than just an HTML editor to help manage your HTML files? Planning on setting up a large Web site? For an "industrial strength" solution, check out the following pointers to automated page creators, site managers, and Web authoring suites.

Web Publisher 1.1 by SkiSoft

`http://www.skisoft.com/skisoft/`

An automated Web page production tool. Allows you to seamlessly convert and enhance documents with from Word, WordPerfect, AmiPro, and FrameMaker into Web pages. Automatically converts images to GIFs, builds tables, builds tables of contents with links to headings, converts numbered and bulleted lists, and places signatures, mailto URLs, and corporate images/logos into your documents. Includes batch conversion of multiple documents. A free 30-day trial version is available for download. This is a fully functional version, not a demo or limited-function version. Registration is $495 for the Standard Edition and $990 for the Professional Edition (which includes the Long Document Utility which can take a long document and break it up into HTML subpages).

QuickSite by Deltapoint

`http://secure.deltapoint.com/qs/`

A Web site development and management system. Requires no HTML coding. Automatically establishes all links to your pages. It is project- and database-oriented. Supports embedding of forms. Transfers finished files to your site via FTP. A 30-day evaluation version is available for download. Registration is $79 (Internet: Unlock Code Only) and $99 (Retail: Box, Manuals, and Disk).

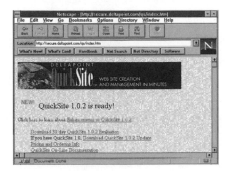

HTML Transit by InfoAccess

`http://www.infoaccess.com/`

Automates production of HTML electronic publications. Allows direct import of native formats of most major world processors and most graphic formats. Automatic generation of table of contents and index hypertext links, linked navigation icons. Handles HTML 2.0, 3.0, and browser-specific extensions. An evaluation version is available for download, but will stop working after 15 days. However, if you order before the 15 days are up, you can save $100 off the purchase price (you must however fill out the download form in full). The registered version is $495, but has a 30-day no-risk guarantee.

WorldDoc by SPI Inc.

`http://www.spii.com/`

Allows point-and-click creation of Web pages without having to learn HTML. A trial version is available for download, but is time-limited to 15 days. Registration is $49.

Dr. Web's Internet ListKeeper

http://www.drweb.com/lkeeper/

Designed for the user who knows absolutely nothing about the Internet but wishes to maintain a frequently changing Web page. It automatically generates Web pages and then, at the click of a button, FTPs them to your server. Provides default styles or can be customized for custom Web pages. A 30-day demo version is available for download. Registration is $49.

Internet Creator: The Web Site Builder

http://www.forman.com/ic3/ic3.htm

$189. 15-day trial version available for download. Build and maintain unlimited number of Web sites with no need to learn HTML.

Macromedia Backstage Designer Plus

http://www.macromedia.com/software/backstage/index.html

$79. 30-day trial version of Backstage Designer (not Plus) is available for download. Word processing-like HTML editing, automates plugging in Shockwave and Java applets, professional image editing. Project-level management system and site maintenance tool.

8Legs Web Studio by Foghorn Software

http://www.fogsoft.com/~fogsoft/index.htm

Integrated project management and Web editing application. 14-day evaluation version for Wndows 95/NT is available for download—it stops working after the evaluation period is over, but you can temporarily extend the evaluation period via e-mail. Registration is $59.

Corel Web.Designer

http://www.provantage.com/PR_10372.HTM

$99. Retail only. Suite of tools comprises complete HTML authoring package for Web page creation; includes 7500+ Internet-ready clipart images. Offers: WYSIWYG HTML authoring; 120+ professionally designed templates; graphics/text file conversion; effortless publishing of existing documents to the Web; much more. No HTML knowledge required.

LinkStar Site Launcher

http://www.linkstar.com/linkstar/bin/tools

Free. Available in 16-bit and 32-bit versions. First create your Web page, then post and promote it with LinkStar Site Launcher.

Dummy by Sausage Software

http://www.sausage.com.au/dummy.htm

HTML editing for dummies (or the non-technically gifted). Provides step-by-step guide to Web page creation using pre-generated style templates. Supports Netscape Navigator tags. Fully functional version for Windows 95 available for download. Registration is $25.

4W Publisher by Information Analytics

http://www.4w.com/4wpublisher/index.html

A database tool for developing and storing Web pages. Current version is a 16-bit version, but a 32-bit version is promised soon. A demo version is available for download, but is limited to five database records. Registration is $250.

SiteMan by GreyScale Systems

http://www.morning.asn.au/siteman/index.html

An offline site management tool that will check links, analyze HTML files, do global search/replace, and find orphans in multiple-directory Web sites. Available in three versions, SiteMan 2 for Windows 3.1 (for single directory Web sites), and SiteMan 3-16 for Windows 3.1 and SiteMan 3-32 for Windows 95/NT (both for multiple-directory Web sites). SiteMan 2 is $30 (AUS$35) and SiteMan 3 is $50 (AUS$60). A free trial version is available for download.

CyberSpyder Link Test by Aphrodite's Software

http://www.cyberspyder.com/cslnkts1.html

$25. Shareware. Checks the links of your Web site to see if they are still good.

Graphics Editors, Viewers, and Convertors

LView Pro by MMedia Research Corp.

http://world.std.com/~mmedia/lviewp.html

A 16-bit version is available for Windows 3.1 (Ver. 1.B) and a 32-bit version is available for Windows 95, Windows NT 3.51, and Windows 3.1 w/Win32s. In addition to other image-editing features, LView Pro's main claim to fame is its capability for easily creating transparent GIFs. A must have for any Web publisher. Registration is $30.

Appendix A: *A Resource Directory*

Paint Shop Pro by JASC, Inc.

http://www.jasc.com/pspdl.html

It is available in two versions, a 16-bit version for Windows 3.1 and a 32-bit version for Windows 95/NT. Supports over 30 image formats. Also supports Adobe Photoshop plug-ins. This is a full-feature paint program. Also a must have for any Web publisher. Registration is $69, and $99 for the Paint Shop Pro Power Pack which also includes Kai's Power Tool's SE CD-ROM.

GIF Construction Set for Windows by Alchemy Mindworks

http://www.mindworkshop.com/alchemy/gifcon.html

Can create transparent GIFs and GIF animation files, as well as add non-destructive text to images. It is available in a 16-bit version for Windows 3.1 and a 32-bit version for Windows 95.

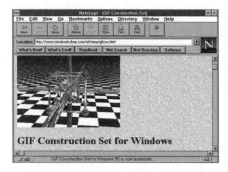

Graphic Workshop for Windows by Alchemy Mindworks

http://www.mindworkshop.com/alchemy/gww.html

From the makers of the GIF Construction Set. Converts files between a wide range of differnt file firmats, including file formats from Ventura Publisher, Paintbrush, PageMaker, Word, WordPerfect, CorelDraw, Deluxe Paint, and more. It can also reverse, rotate, flip, crop, and scale images, as well as dither color images into halftones, dither color images, reduce color depth, and manipulate and adjust color, contrast, brightness, sharpness, softness, and such. Can be run in batch mode for converting multiple files. It's available in two versions, a 16-bit version for Windows 3.1 and a 32-bit version for Windows 95. Registration is $40.

VuePrint by Hamrick Software

http://www.hamrick.com/

An image viewer for Windows that claims to use a special form of color dithering to produce high-quality pictures. It can also view UUEncoded images and MIME/Base 64 images. It is available in two versions, a 16-bit version for Windows 3.1 and a 32-bit version for Windows 95, Windows NT, and Windows 3.1 w/Win32s (available for download at the site). Registration is $40.

Appendix A: *A Resource Directory*

WebImage by Group42
http://www.group42.com/webimage.htm

Allows you to define and view transparent GIFs, create and edit image maps (including client side, NCSA,or CERN compliant map files), interlace GIF and PNG images, as well as a broad assortment of other operations, including image optimization and color depth reduction. Also allows you to apply a variety of "Web effects" to images, including buttonizing images, adding borders and text, creating button bars, and embossing tiled backgrounds. Supports a wide range of different file formats. Can decode and encode UUEncoded files. Two versions are available, a 16-bit version for Windows 3.1 and a 32-bit version for Windows 95, Windows NT, and Windows 3.1 w/Win32s. Demo versions are available for download that you can test out for 10 days (it isn't specified whether they actually stop working at that time, but I would assume so). Two versions are available. Registration is $39.95.

GraphX Viewer by Group42
http://www.group42.com/graphx.htm

A graphics viewer for Windows 3.1 from the makers of WebImage. Allows you to view and convert a wide range of different image formats, including BMP, FAX G3/G4, GIF, JPEG, PCX, PNG, SunRaster, TARGA, TIFF, and XWD. Also can export to PostScript. Can also encode and decode UUEncoded files. Can also cut and paste, crop, color reduce, resized, rotate, and mirror images, as well as adjust brightness, contrast, sharpness, gamma, and so on. GraphX Viewer is provided as freeware for private, non-commercial use. For commercial use (such as using it at work), registration is $29.95.

PolyView Graphics Viewer/Converter by Polybytes
http://198.207.242.3/authors/polybytes/default.html

A graphics viewer, conversion, and printing utility for Windows 95 or NT. It uses multithreading to allow, for instance, reading and writing of muliple image files at the same time. It includes image appearance manipulation, copy and paste, and DDE execution capabilities. Registration is $20.

GIFTOOL by Home Page, Inc.
http://www.homepages.com/tools/

An MS-DOS utility that does interlacing and transparency, batch conversion of multiple images, and more. It is also available for various UNIX platforms. Home Page, Inc. is a Web authoring consulting firm and, since no pricing information is given for GIFTOOL, my assumption is that it is free.

Painter 4 by Fractal Design
http://www.fractal.com/

Apart from a wide range of other high-end paint features, also includes the capability to create interlaced and transparent GIFs and image maps. It is available in versions for Window 3.1 and Windows 95. A demo version is available for download, but for Windows 95 only (that's a switch—usually it's the other way around). It is a biggy though—over 8 MB. It contains all the features of the regular program except the capability to save, print, paint across a network and work with frame-by-frame animation. All the Natural-Media tools are available for your use. No time-limit is mentioned for the demo version. Registration is $549 (includes CD-ROM).

VuGrafix by Informatik, Inc.

http://www.execpc.com/~infothek/vugrafix.html

Can view 10 different graphics formats, including GIF, TIFF, JPEG, WMF, WPG, BMP, PCX, and DCX. Can view thumbnails and slide shows. Features include rotation, scaling, inversion, color adjustments, mirroring, and copy and paste. Registration is $19.

3DEnvMap by Thanassis Tsiodras

http://manolito.image.ece.ntua.gr/~ttsiod/

A 3D renderer from Greece. Requires WinG, which you can find at
http://manolito.image.ece.ntua.gr/~ttsiod/wing10.zip

PhotoImpact GIF/JPEG SmartSaver by ULead Systems

http://ulead.iready.com/

A plug-in program for the 32-bit versions of Adobe PhotoShop and Ulead PhotoImpact. Paint Shop Pro also can use PhotoShop plug-ins, but you'll have to test it out to see if it works. It allows dynamic WYSIWYG optimization of JPEG and GIF images to get the best balance possible between image size and quality. Non-Ulead PhotoImpact users can us the software for a 30-day trial period only (although it doesn't say whether the software actually stops working, I suspect that would be the case).

Dr. Jack's HTMLView

http://www.drjack.com/htmlview/welc2.htm

$10. 9-day evaluation period. Available in 16-bit and 32-bit versions. An image browser that allows you to batch view graphic files, even in different directories.

TC-Image by Tashcom Software

http://www.linkstar.com/page/tashcom-software/tc-image.html

Lets you view, crop, grab, and print images. Registration is $20.

Miscellaneous Web Publishing Tools

Image Map Utilities

These are programs that can help automate the process of creating clickable image maps.

Map This

http://www.ecaetc.ohio-state.edu/tc/mt/

A freeware image map utility written to run under Windows 95 or NT, or Windows 3.1 w/Win32s (available for download). Also supports client-side image maps.

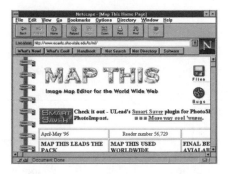

MapEdit by Boutell.Com, Inc.

http://www.boutell.com/mapedit/

Available in 16-bit (Windows 3.1) and 32-bit (Windows 95/NT) versions. Includes support for client-side image maps, as well as support for frames and toolbars. An evaluation copy is available that is good for 30 days, plus a 10-day grace period. My assumption is the software stops working at the end of the evaluation and grace periods. At any rate, it is stated that you need to register the software before the evaluation period (and grace period) expires. Registration is $25.

Forms Utilities

Forms can add interactivity to your Web pages, but many shy away from them because they are difficult to set up, require CGI script support, and so forth. And once you've set up a form, you've got to extract the form responses from the rest of your e-mail before you can read them, as well as organize and keep track of them. It would be nice if there was something available to automate all this, and there is.

WebForms by Q&D Software Development

http://www.q-d.com/

From the makers of the HTML editor, WebMania. Allows creation of forms to accept orders for products, conduct surveys, and so on. The program comes in two modules, WebForms Forms Generator and WebForms Response Reader. The first creates the forms. The second reads the responses from any WebForms form. If you are using a standard POP3 mail server, it will dial directly into your mailbox and download all your forms responses, automatically separating them from other e-mail, importing them into the WebForms database. WebForms comes in two version. Registration of WebForms Standard is $21.95. Registration of WebForms Professional is $34.95.

Tables Utilities

So you've got some data that you want to display as a table, but the idea of handcoding it with Table tags is just too daunting. No problem. Here are a couple utilities that can covert data from Excel or a table from Word for Windows 6.0 into an HTML table.

XL2HTML.XLS by Jordan Evans

http://rs712b.gsfc.nasa.gov/704/dgd/xl2html.html

This is a Visual Basic macro for Microsoft Excel. It can be used with Excel 5.0 for Windows or Macintosh, as well as Excel 7.0 for Windows 95. It allows you to specify a range of cells and convert them to an HTML table. This is unsupported freeware.

hcTableToHtml by Yuri M. Lesiuk

http://www.w3.org/hypertext/WWW/Tools/hcTableToHtml.html

This is a freeware WinWord 6.0 table to HTML convertor.

Frames Utilities

The use of Frames is proliferating rapidly on the Web. Want to get into the act? No problem. Here's a utility to make it all easy.

Frame-It by GME Systems

http://www.iinet.net.au/~bwh/frame-it1.html

Uses a point-and-click inteerface to generate frames. Both Windows 3.1 and Windows 95 versions are available. Registraton is $15.

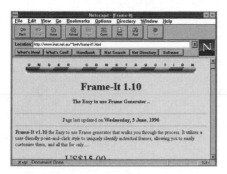

Color Utilities

Hate Hex? Do you find that finding just the right colors for your Web page is an unnecessarily difficult process? No problem. Here are some utilities that you can use to find just the right combination of colors for your Web page.

HTML Color Scheme Designer by Wolf Spider Web Architects

http://www.sound.net/%7Ewolfs/htmlcsd/

Allows you to easily test text, link, and background color combinations. When you find the combination you want, you can copy the complete tag line to the Clipboard for pasting into your HTML file. A Beta version is available for download. No pricing information was mentioned.

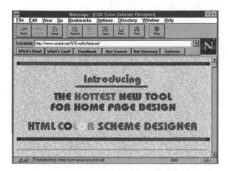

Appendix A: *A Resource Directory*

Colour Buster by Tashcom Software

`http://www.linkstar.com/page/tashcom-software/index.html`

By the makers of TC-Director HTML Editor. It does color to hex code conversions. Click on the color and Buster calculates the right hex code to insert in your HTML file. This is freeware.

Color Machine

`http://ucunix.san.uc.edu/~hamilte/colors.html`

Free. Small utility that automates insertion of hex color codes.

Color Picker for HTML by Vector Development

`http://www.cjnetworks.com/~vecdev/vector/`

Freeware. Another utility for inserting color hex codes.

Software Collections

These are software collection sites where you can find many additional programs and utilities of interest to Web publishers.

TUCOWS: The Ultmate Collection of Winsock Software by Scott A. Swedorski

`http://tucows.phx.cox.com/index.html`

The place to go to find anything and everything in winsock software, including browsers, HTML editors, graphics editors, and much, much, more. An absolute must for anyone's bookmark list or hotlist.

Stroud's CWSApps List

`http://www.cwsapps.com/cwsa.html`

Another omnibus site where you can find just about any Web or Net-related software program or utility.

Randy's Windows 95 Resource Center

http://206.151.75.235/html.tools.html

This one focuses on Windows 95 software.

FTP and Telnet Software

When you get around to putting your Web pages up on the Web, as well as maintaining your Web pages once they're up on a server, you're going to need a way to do it.

FTP Software

FTP software allows you to remotely (from your own computer) maintain and update your Web pages on a Web server.

WS_FTP by Junod Software

http://www.csra.net/junodj/default.htm

Once you get around to wanting to put your Web page or pages up on the Web, you'll need a way to do it. It is available in both a 16-bit version (Windows 3.1 and a 32-bit version (Windows 95/NT). Registered versions are available for $37 from Ipswitch at http://www.ipswitch.com/pd_wsftp.html.

CuteFTP by Alex Kunadze

http://www.cuteftp.com/

This is another FTP client that you can use to upload files to or download files from the Net. Registration is $30.

Integrated Internet FTP by Kent D. Behrens

http://www.aquila.com/kent.behrens/

$25.

Telnet Software

Telnet software allows you to log onto a server (a Unix Web server, for instance) where you have an account and then run their software to update and maintain your Web pages.

NetTerm for Windows by IntraSoft International, Inc.

http://starbase.neosoft.com/~zkrr01/

You might prefer using a Telnet client to update your pages on the Web, or your Web host may not provide FTP access. NetTerm includes a Telnet client and more. It is available in both 16-bit and 32-bit versions. Registration is $20.

Trumpet Telnet by Trumpet Software International

http://www.trumpet.com.au/

Software, however, is not available for download from Trumpet's site. Download (ftp) it from ftp://papa.indstate.edu/winsock-l/telnet/trmptel.zip. This is freeware.

UW Term by Brad Greer

ftp://papa.indstate.edu/winsock-l/telnet/uwterm097g.zip

An unsupported freeware telnet client for Windows.

Net and Web Automation Tools

Auto WinNet Version 2.0

http://www.webcom.com/autownet/

Automates FTP, Web browsing, e-mail, and USENET News. FTP automation allows you to download files by the truckload, hammering at busy sites until they open, or scheduling downloads for late at night. If you want to vacuum stuff off the Net, this is the tool to do it with. WWW automation allows downloading of Web pages while you sleep, then viewing them offline. Downloads Web pages and all associated files. E-mail automation allows mailing list management. Send announcements, newsletters, and more, to hundreds of recipients. USENET News automation allows reading and editing of posts offline. The evaluation version only includes the FTP capabilities. This is not the easiest programs in the world to figure out how to use, but if you need to download a bunch of files off the Net, there's nothing else like it. Registration is $49.

Web Whacker by Forefront

`http://www.ffg.com/whacker.html`

Allows automatic downloading (or "whacking") of Web pages, complete Web sites, including text and images, for offline browsing. Whacked Web pages are relinked on your local hard drive. Free trial versions are available for Windows 3.1 and Windows 95. Registration is $49.95.

Browser Buddy by Softbots

`http://www.softbots.com/bb_home.htm`

Calls itself a "prefetching agent." Helps you organize your URLs and automates downloading of Web site files so they can be viewed offline from your local hard drive. 30-day evaluation versions are available for both Windows 3.1 and Windows 95. Registration is $39.

URL Grabber 95

`http://www.brooknorth.com/grabr95.html`

This doesn't grab the whole page, just the URL. Great for grabbing URLs you want to include in your Web pages. Freeware version available—limits the number of URLs that can be saved before restarting. Registration is $19.95.

Miscellaneous Software

These are programs and utilities of general use to Web publishers.

Anti-Virus Scanners

While downloading software from company sites or from major software collections is generally not a risk, pulling stuff down from an FTP directory that anybody can post to might expose you to the risk of catching a virus. Here are a couple anti-virus programs that can give you some protection.

Thunderbyte Anti-Virus

`http://www.thunderbyte.com`

Both Windows 3.1 and Windows 95 versions available. Can be downloaded from http://tucows.phx.cox. com/files/tbavw701.zip.

McAfee VirusScan for Windows

`http://www.mcafee.com/`

Both Windows 3.1 and Windows 95 versions available. Can be downloaded from http://tucows.phx. cox.com/files/wsc-22fe.zip.

File Viewers and Managers

The material that goes into a Web page doesn't necessarily come from only one source, but might include files in different word processing, spreadsheet, database, and graphics formats. It would be nice if there was one utility that would let you view all of these. Well, there is.

Drag and View by Canyon Software

http://www.canyonsw.com/

A multipurpose file viewer for Windows that can view files, and display them as they will appear in their native applications, across a broad spectrum of different file types, such as word processing, spreadsheet, database, archive, and bitmapped and vector graphic files. Versions are available for Windows 3.1 and Windows 3.1. Registration is $35.

File Compressors/Decompressors and Decoders

Most software programs and graphics collections that you can download from the Web are compressed to conserve space and download times. After you download something, you need to be able to uncompress it. The following utilities should cover all the bases.

WinZip by Nico Mak Computing, Inc.

http://www.winzip.com/

If you are going to download ZIP, TAR, or virtually any other compressed file from the Web, you need WinZip. An evaluation version is available for download. Register the software to get rid of the nag screens. A 16-bit version (Windows 3.1) and a 32-bit version (Windows 95/NT) are available. Registration is $29.

Stuffit Expander for Windows

http://tucows.phx.cox.com/files/sitex10.exe

A shareware compression/decompression utility that can handle "stuffed" SIT files and so on.

Wincode

http://tucows.phx.cox.com/files/wc271b16.zip

Encodes and decodes UUEncoded files.

Appendix B:
What's on the CD?

The CD-ROM that accompanies this book contains numerous tools and utilities to make creating your first Web page a productive experience, including HTML editors, graphics, Web browsers, Windows utilities, and more. You also can find all the examples and templates used in this book on the CD-ROM.

Running the CD

There is no install routine, so running the CD is a breeze, especially if you enable autorun. Simply insert the CD in the CD-ROM drive, close the tray, and wait for the CD to load.

If you disable autorun, place the CD in the drive and follow these steps:

1. From the Start menu, select Run.

2. Type *d:\primacd.exe* (where *d:* is the CD-ROM drive).

3. Select OK.

You don't have to run an install procedure, you copy whichever files you want to your hard disk, and that's all.

The Prima User Interface

Prima's user interface is designed to make viewing and using the CD contents quick and easy. It contains six category buttons, four options buttons, and a display window. Select a category button to show a list of available titles in the display window. Highlight a title in the window and choose an option button to perform the desired action.

Category Buttons

- **HTML Tools.** A large collection of HTML editors and other tools, including Hot Dog, HTML Assistant, and Internet Assistant for Word.

- **Multimedia.** Cool Edit, LView Pro, and a variety of other graphics and WAV editors.

- **Internet Tools.** Internet Explorer and Cute FTP top this list.

- **Utilities.** Both the 16- and 32-bit versions of WinZip are included.

- **Book Examples.** Samples, templates, and tutorials from the book.

- **Images.** Hundreds of images and icons you can use in your Web pages.

Options Buttons

- **Install/Run.** If the highlighted title contains an install routine, selecting this option begins the installation process. If the title has no install procedure but contains an executable file, that executable is run. If neither an install nor an executable file is present (as in the case of a graphics library), the folder that contains the information is shown.

NOTE

You can install some of the shareware programs that do not have installation routines by copying the program files from the CD to your hard drive and running the executable file.

- **Information.** Information about the selection is shown, if available. This information is usually in the form of a readme or help file.

- **Explore.** This option allows you to view the folder that contains the program files.

- **Exit.** When you're finished and ready to move on, select Exit.

The Software

This section gives you only a brief description of some of the software and things you'll find on the CD. As you browse the CD, you will find much more.

- **Aardvark Pro.** An HTML editor; essentially, an ASCII editor not unlike a turbo-charged version of Notepad.

- **Frame-IT!.** A feature-packed HTML frame generator, which allows you to generate complex HTML frames, using only your mouse.

- **Gomer.** An easy-to-use HTML editor.

- **HTML Assistant Pro.** A simple Web publishing tool for creating HTML Web pages.

- **Mapedit.** A WYSIWYG (What You See Is What You Get) editor for image map files.

- **Paint Shop Pro.** The popular bitmap image editor from JASC, Inc.

- **PolyView.** A multi-threaded 32-bit Microsoft Windows 95 and Windows NT application that provides viewing, file conversion, and image manipulation support for most popular graphics image format files.

- **Web Whacker.** A 32-bit program that grabs and downloads entire Web pages or groups of Web pages for browsing on the local desktop.

- **WinZip.** One of the leading file compression utilities for Windows 95, NT, and 3.1.

For additional software for keeping your Web site exciting and on the cutting edge, don't forget to stop by the book's Web site:

`http://www.callihan.com`

In addition to all the examples and software that his book covers, you can find updated links to many more valuable resources and tons of free stuff to download and use for creating cool Web pages.

Appendix C:
A Basic Tables Tutorial

Although tables are included in the new HTML 3.2 specification, the intermediate tutorial wasn't the place to deal with them, owing to time and space restraints. Tables, however, are a significant feature that isn't that difficult to implement in your Web pages. Therefore, this appendix serves as a tutorial on creating "basic" tables here as an appendix. As the word basic implies, the tutorial doesn't tell you *everything* there is know about tables, but rather, focuses on telling you just what you need to know to get started on using them effectively in your Web pages. Appendix A provides pointers to where on the Web you can find additional material and information on creating tables.

Getting Started

To get started, run your text editor, word processor, or HTML editor. Load your starting template, START.HTM, that you saved in Chapter 2. It should look like this (if you didn't save a starting template, go ahead and type this now):

```
<HTML>
<HEAD>
<TITLE>Your Title: Describe Your Title</TITLE></HEAD>
<BODY>
</BODY>
</HTML>
```

Save this as C:\HTML\TABLE.HTM.

The Basic Tables Tutorial

You can do this tutorial in two ways: 1) create just one table and then insert the bolded insertions into your table for each example, and 2) make a fresh copy of your table for each example and then insert the bolded insertions into each copy, which then gives you one table for each example. (One example also uses "strikethrough" to mark example text you need to delete.)

Feel free to save your file after each example and hop over to your Web browser to see what it looks like.

The TABLE Tag

The TABLE tag needs to bracket your table. Enter this nested in the BODY tag:

```
<BODY>
<TABLE>
</TABLE>
</BODY>
```

Create Columns and Rows

You can use the TR (Table Row) and TD (Table Data) tags to create a grid of columns and rows:

```
<TABLE>
<TR><TD>1A</TD><TD>1B</TD><TD>1C</TD><TD>1D</TD></TR>
<TR><TD>2A</TD><TD>2B</TD><TD>2C</TD><TD>2D</TD></TR>
</TABLE>
```

Notice the <TR> start tag and the </TR> end tag bracket in each row. See Figure C-1 to see what the above looks like in a table-compatible Web browser.

Figure C-1.
A table can be just columns and rows.

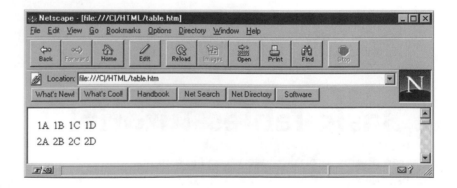

Add a Border

A table hardly looks like a table without a border. Including a BORDER attribute inside the TABLE tag does the trick:

```
<TABLE BORDER>
<TR><TD>1A</TD><TD>1B</TD><TD>1C</TD><TD>1D</TD></TR>
<TR><TD>2A</TD><TD>2B</TD><TD>2C</TD><TD>2D</TD></TR>
</TABLE>
```

See Figure C-2 to see what this change looks like in a table-compatible Web browser.

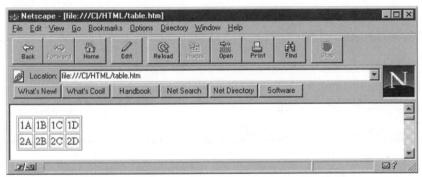

Figure C-2.
The BORDER attribute will add a border to a table.

Add Column Headings

What's a table without column headings, right? So, add some. Use the TH (Table Heading) tag, which works just like the TD (Table Data) tag, except it defines a "cell" as a heading cell rather than as an ordinary data cell. To create a row of headings at the top of the table, you need to use the TR tag to define a row and then, instead of using TD tags, insert TH tags to define the cells, like this:

```
<TABLE BORDER>
<TR><TH>A</TH><TH>B</TH><TH>C</TH><TH>D</TH></TR>
<TR><TD>1A</TD><TD>1B</TD><TD>1C</TD><TD>1D</TD></TR>
<TR><TD>2A</TD><TD>2B</TD><TD>2C</TD><TD>2D</TD></TR>
</TABLE>
```

As Figure C-3 shows, table headings are automatically bolded and centered.

Figure C-3.
Table headings are automatically bolded and centered.

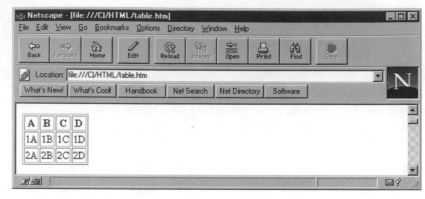

Add Spacing and Padding

Your table looks a bit cramped, don't you think? The CELLSPACING attribute adds space between cells, while the CELLPADDING attribute adds space within each cell. Add six pixels or so of space and padding:

```
<TABLE BORDER CELLSPACING="6" CELLPADDING="6">
```

Figure C-4 shows that, with the border turned on, the CELLSPACING attributes increases the thickness of the border.

Figure C-4.
You can add space between cells and padding within cells.

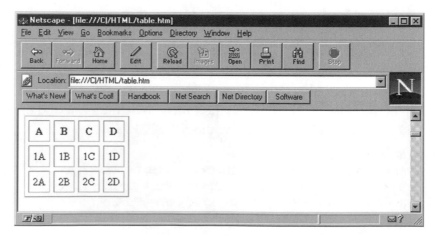

Add a Caption

Every table needs a caption, right? Add one:

```
<TABLE BORDER CELLSPACING="6" CELLPADDING="6">
<CAPTION>I. Table Example</CAPTION>
```

As you can see in Figure C-5, a caption appears above the title by default. (Include ALIGN="bottom" in the CAPTION tag to display the caption beneath the table.)

Other than centering, no special formatting is added to the caption. Feel free here to add some highlighting, using I (Italic) or B (Bold), for instance. Or tag it with, say, an H3 tag to make it really stand out.

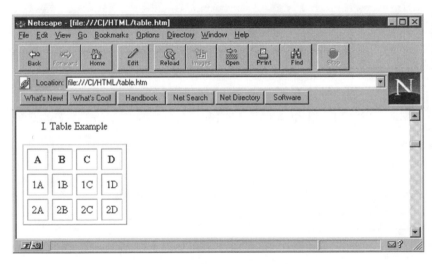

Figure C-5.
You can add a caption to a table.

Set the Table Width and Height

You can include WIDTH or HEIGHT attributes to specify the width and size of your table. You can use either absolute values (number of pixels) or relative values (percentages). For instance, specify a width of 75 percent like this:

```
<TABLE BORDER CELLSPACING="6" CELLPADDING="6" WIDTH="75%"
```

Figure C-6 shows the table now occupying 75 percent of the browser window.

Figure C-6.
The WIDTH attribute can be used in the TABLE tag to set the width of a table to either a percentage of the browser window or to a specific number of pixels.

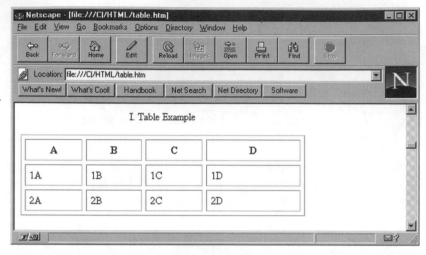

Add Row Headings

You've already added some column headings. Now add some row headings. To create a row heading, you just add TH cell (instead of a TD cell) at the start of a table row, like this:

```
<TABLE BORDER CELLSPACING="6" CELLPADDING="6" WIDTH="75%">
<CAPTION>I. Table Example</CAPTION>
<TR><TH></TH><TH>A</TH><TH>B</TH><TH>C</TH><TH>D</TH></TR>
<TR><TH>Row 1:</TD><TD>1A</TD><TD>1B</TD><TD>1C</TD><TD>1D</TD></TR>
<TR><TH>Row 2:</TD><TD>2A</TD><TD>2B</TD><TD>2C</TD><TD>2D</TD></TR>
</TABLE>
```

As Figure C-7 shows, row headings are formatted just like column headings (they are both TH tags)—centered and bolded.

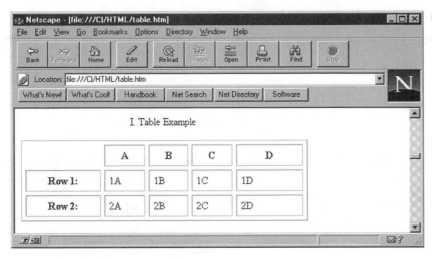

Align Cell Contents

Although it's fine for your column headings, you don't really want to center your row headings. Add an ALIGN="right" attribute to the TH tags of your row headings, like this:

```
<CAPTION>I. Table Example</CAPTION>
<TR><TH></TH><TH>A</TH><TH>B</TH><TH>C</TH><TH>D</TH></TR>
<TR><TH ALIGN="right">Row
1:</TD><TD>1A</TD><TD>1B</TD><TD>1C</TD><TD>1D</TD></TR>
<TR><TH ALIGN="right">Row
2:</TD><TD>2A</TD><TD>2B</TD><TD>2C</TD><TD>2D</TD></TR>
```

See Figure C-8 to see the new alignment for the row headings.

You can use the ALIGN attribute to align the contents of a HD (Heading Data) or TD (Table Data) cells by assigning "left," "center," or "right" as the ALIGN value. (Center-alignment is the default for HD cells, while left-alignment is the default for TD cells.)

Set Column Width and Height

The only problem with your table now is that when you set the width of the table, the width of the columns come out different (at least in Navigator, anyway). To make them the same, set each row to a width of 20 percent (since you have five rows), by inserting a WIDTH="20%" attribute value in each of the heading cells, like this:

Appendix C: *A Basic Tables Tutorial*

```
<CAPTION>I. Table Example</CAPTION>
<TR><TH WIDTH="20%"></TH><TH [END]WIDTH="20%">A</TH><TH
WIDTH="20%">B</TH><TH
WIDTH="20%">C</TH><TH WIDTH="20%">D</TH></TR>
```

See Figure C-9 to see what this looks like.

You can use either percentages or a pixel amount to specify column widths.

Figure C-8.
You can set the alignment of table heading (TH) cells and table data (TD) cells to "left," "center," or "right," Here, the table row headings are set to right-alignment.

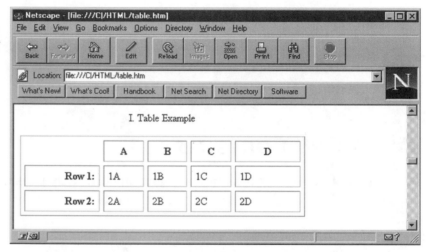

Figure C-9.
By setting the widths of the top row cells, you can control the width of the columns in a table.

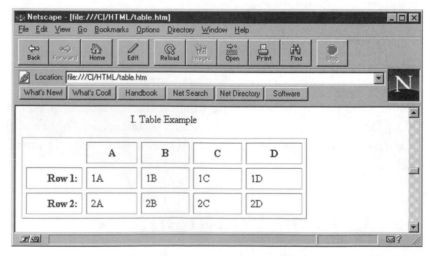

Centering a Table

It would be nice if you could center the table. To do so, just put it inside a CENTER tag, like this:

```
<CENTER>
<TABLE BORDER CELLSPACING="6" CELLPADDING="6" WIDTH="75%">
<CAPTION>I. Table Example</CAPTION>
<TR><TH WIDTH="20%"></TH><TH WIDTH="20%">A</TH><TH WIDTH="20%">B</TH><TH
WIDTH="20%">C</TH><TH WIDTH="20%">D</TH></TR>
<TR><TH ALIGN="right">Row
1:</TH><TD>1A</TD><TD>1B</TD><TD>1C</TD><TD>1D</TD></TR>
<TR><TH ALIGN="right">Row
2:</TH><TD>2A</TD><TD>2B</TD><TD>2C</TD><TD>2D</TD></TR>
</TABLE>
</CENTER>
```

Figure C-10 shows how the above will look.

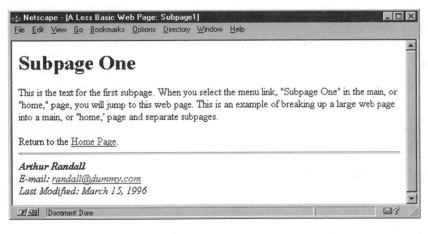

Figure C-10.
You can center a table by putting it inside a CENTER tag.

TIP

To indent a table, rather than center it, use BLOCKQUOTE above instead of CENTER.

Inserting an Image

You can insert an image inside a table cell. The following inserts one of the graphics used in the HTML tutorials (so it should already be available), ONE.GIF, inside the upper left corner cell:

```
<TR><TH WIDTH="20%"><IMG SRC="one.gif"></TH><TH WIDTH="20%">A</TH><TH
WIDTH="20%">B</TH><TH
WIDTH="20%">C</TH><TH WIDTH="20%">D</TH></TR>
```

As Figure C-11 shows, a graphic image of the number "1" has been inserted in the upper right cell.

Figure C-11.
You can insert an image into a table cell.

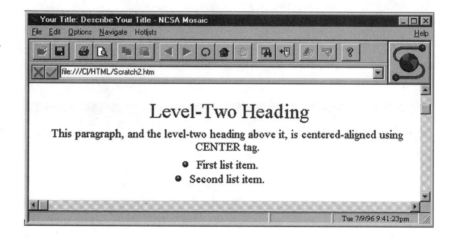

Spanning Columns

The COLSPAN attribute lets you create that which span across columns. Add a row to your table that includes two cells that span across two columns each, like this:

```
<CAPTION>I. Table Example</CAPTION>

<TR><TH WIDTH="20%"><IMG SRC="one.gif"></TH><TH WIDTH="20%">A</TH><TH
WIDTH="20%">B</TH><TH

WIDTH="20%">C</TH><TH WIDTH="20%">D</TH></TR>

<TR><TH></TH><TH COLSPAN="2">A & B</TH><TH COLSPAN="2">C & D</TH></TR>

<TR><TH ALIGN="right">Row

1:</TH><TD>1A</TD><TD>1B</TD><TD>1C</TD><TD>1D</TD></TR>
```

Figure C-12 shows the result of inserting a new row including three cells, a blank cell in the first column, then two following cells spanning two columns each.

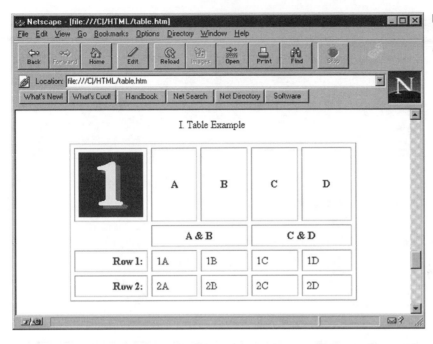

Figure C-12.
Table cells can span columns.

To span additional columns, just specify the number with the COLSPAN attribute. Just make sure that you don't exceed the total number of columns. For instance, the above amounts to three cells spanning 1 + 2 + 2 = 5 columns.

Spanning Rows

You not only can create cells that span columns, you can create cells that span rows. To create a cell that spans a row, use the ROWSPAN attribute to specify the number of rows to span. Now this gets just a little tricky: the cells to be spanned need to be removed from any following rows. In the following example, the cell that you need to delete is marked with strikethrough.

```
<CAPTION>I. Table Example</CAPTION>
<TR><TH WIDTH="20%" ROWSPAN="2"><IMG SRC="one.gif"></TH><TH
WIDTH="20%">A</TH><TH WIDTH="20%">B</TH><TH
WIDTH="20%">C</TH><TH WIDTH="20%">D</TH></TR>
<TR><TH </TH><TH COLSPAN="2">A & B</TH><TH COLSPAN="2">C &
D</TH></TR>
```

As Figure C-13 shows, the cell with the graphic "1" in it now spans two rows.

Figure C-13.

Table cells can also span rows.

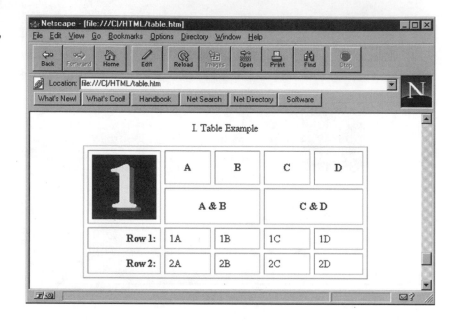

Setting Font Sizes and Colors

You can't set the overall font size or color, but you can set them for each individual cell (at least in Navigator). Set the font size to "7" and the color to "blue" for just one of the cells:

```
<CAPTION>I. Table Example</CAPTION>
<TR><TH WIDTH="20%" ROWSPAN="2"><IMG SRC="one.gif"></TH><TH
WIDTH="20%"><FONT SIZE="7" COLOR="blue">A</FONT></TH><TH
WIDTH="20%">B</TH><TH
WIDTH="20%">C</TH><TH WIDTH="20%">D</TH></TR>
<TR><TH COLSPAN="2">A & B</TH><TH COLSPAN="2">C & D</TH></TR>
```

As Figure C-14 shows, your first row heading now has grown considerably, and is blue (you should check the color out in your own browser, though).

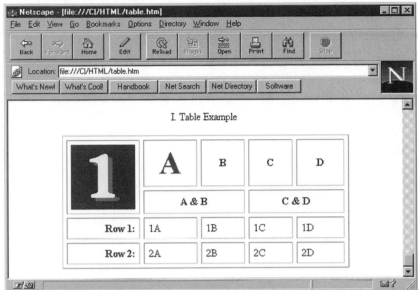

Figure C-14.
You can set the font size and color for each individual cell, but not for the table as a whole.

Appendix D:
Getting Your Web Page Noticed

The basic HTML tutorial briefly covered the TITLE tag, stressing the importance of keeping your title relatively short but making it descriptive. The idea is that your title is your welcome mat, the sign on your front door, and thus an important influence on whether somebody is liable to want to visit your page.

This appendix covers some things you may want to consider that can enhance the likelihood of getting visitors to your Web page. It includes a style guide for creating titles and a section on using the META tag to add additional information and keywords to your page which can help to snag even more visitors to your page.

Titles: A Style Guide

The following is a style guide for creating titles. Remember, however, that rules are made to be broken. There are no absolutely hard and fast rules. What is right for you depends on your specific goals.

Keep Titles Short but Descriptive

This is the primary point that this morning's tutorial made. If you were creating the All about Dogs home page, for example, your title and title description might be something like "All about Dogs: Dogs from A to Z." The main thing is that you want your title to concisely convey what your page is all about. You also might want to try to include in your title one or more possible "keywords" that users might use to search for your Web page.

Try to keep your title to less than, say, 50 characters. If you can keep it to less than 40 characters, that's even better. There really is no hard and fast rule here, but if your title is too long, search engines are likely to truncate it. The Webcrawler search engine, for instance, truncates any title longer than 57 characters. (Also, if you want to make sure that your title is not truncated when displayed on a browser's title bar, you should probably try to keep your title to less than 40 characters—browsers differ considerably on how much of a title they will display.)

Be Specific

If you want to attract people who are interested specifically in what you have to offer, be specific. For instance, "The All-American Yo-Yo Catalog" will attract people who are specifically interested in buying yo-yos. "The History of the Yo-Yo" will attract people who are specifically interested in, or looking for information on, the history of yo-yos but people who just want to buy yo-yos will go somewhere else.

If Not Descriptive, at Least Make It Evocative

Titles don't have to be descriptive. They can be evocative. One of the most successful sites on the Web simply calls itself "The Asylum," for instance. But you want to make sure that the spirit of your page matches what your title is trying to evoke. No false advertising, in other words. And while people love a mystery, having your page be a complete mystery probably is not a good idea. Your title should be evocative of something, in other words (otherwise it's not being evocative of anything). For the best of both worlds, make your title evocative and descriptive.

Don't Make False Promises or Over-Hype Your Page

Nothing irks a visitor to a Web page more than false promises. Surfers consume bandwidth, clicks on the clock, just to get to your page. So be accurate and honest, and don't over-hype your page. If you want them to visit your page more than once, for instance, don't create a title like "The Greatest Page on Earth: Thrills, Thrills, Thrills." Not only does that make promises you can't possibly keep, it says absolutely nothing about your page. Remember, also, that you don't want to attract visitors who aren't really interested in what you have to offer. You want to meet the people who want to meet you.

Avoid Titles That Don't Say Anything

The other thing you want to avoid is a title that says absolutely nothing, such as "Welcome!" or "News of the Week." What do they say? They provide no information, have no allure. Many "personal" pages just identify themselves as something like "Jimmy Brown's Page," for instance. The title conveys no information, leaves no impression. Now, "Jimmy Brown: Weekend Magician," says something. Or "Jimmy Brown: Amateur Sleuth."

Don't Shout in My Ear

On the Internet, using ALL CAPS generally is considered somewhat impolite, because it denotes shouting, yelling, or screaming. So, unless you want to convey that impression, don't use ALL CAPS. In fact, even if that is the impression you want to convey, don't use All CAPS. Don't use ALL CAPS, period. Now, while surfing the Web, using search engines, and so on, you've probably noticed many titles that use ALL CAPS. Not most, thankfully, but still a good many. It's their authors' attempt to make their pages stand out. Putting your title in ALL CAPS, however, doesn't make your title more noticeable—it just makes it more unreadable. Text in ALL CAPS not only is impolite, but also less readable than regular text. So avoid using ALL CAPS. Don't shout in my ear.

Using the META Tag

The META tag allows you to insert "metadata," or "meta-information," into your Web page. This information describes your Web page and its contents beyond what you can include in the TITLE tag. You can insert multiple META tags to describe the different aspects of your document, such as the name of the author, the modification date, a description, or a list of keywords.

The META tag normally includes two attributes, the NAME (or HTTP-EQUIV) attribute and the CONTENT attribute:

The NAME Attribute

This is the attribute you'll most likely want to use to help identify and describe your page. You include a META tag using the NAME attribute in the HEAD element of your page like this:

```
<META NAME="name" CONTENT="string">
```

You can include multiple META tags here, one for each name item you specify, with the CONTENT attribute being the "content" of what is named. For instance, to identify the name of the author of a document, you might include something like this:

```
<META NAME="author" CONTENT="Callihan, Steven E.">
```

Other names that you might use are "title," "keywords," "description," "owner" (if different than "author"), "publisher," "date" (of creation), "expiry date," and so on. Right now, there is no one scheme for using META names in a Web page header section. There are a few fairly complex schemes, the Dublin Core Metadata scheme, to name just one, that are really more aimed at the need to catalog and organize large numbers of Web documents. Implement a consistent scheme, then meta-data aware software can automate the process of tracking and controlling this information.

The question of what scheme to use, however, is primarily of importance to larger organizations and companies, and really not that relevant to the individual Web publisher. For the purposes of your own internal organization, description, and tracking of your Web pages, feel free to adapt any schemes that already exit freely to your own purposes, mix and match different schemes, invent your own scheme from scratch, or simply skip it.

Using the META Tag To Snag a Search Engine

Search engines such as Alta Vista, Infoseek, the Webcrawler, and OpenText use different techniques and methods for indexing Web pages on the Web. Some search engines, for instance, index every word in your document except comments and then use the first 250 characters or so as an abstract for the page. You can help determine, and in some cases specify, how you would like your document to be indexed and described by including, at minimum, "description" and "keywords" META names and contents.

For instance, here is an example of a document header including a TITLE and two META tags, one for a description, the other for keywords:

```
<HEAD>

<TITLE>Web Page in a Weekend Home Page</TITLE>

<META NAME="description" CONTENT="Home page for the book, Create Your
First Web Page in a Weekend, including resources and information for
Web publishers and authors, listings of affordable presence providers
(Web hosts), and guidance for putting your Web page up on the Web.">

<META NAME="keywords" CONTENT="Web publishing, Web publishing tech-
niques, Web publishing methods, Web publishing resources, Web
authors, basic, intermediate, tutorials, guides, Web hosts, presence
providers, HTML 3.2, hypertext, off-line browsing, Web browsers,
Windows 95, Windows 3.1, Netscape Navigator, Internet Explorer,
Mosaic">

</HEAD>
```

TIP

In creating keywords above, I used the plural rather than the singular form of a word wherever possible. Doing it that way allows me to snag searches for both "tutorial" and "tutorials," for instance. An alternative would be to put in both the singular and plural forms.

I haven't described how to use the HTTP-EQUIV attribute of the META tag because it's really useful only to advanced Web publishers. I also haven't described the other tags, the ISINDEX and LINK tags, that you include in the HEAD tag (the header). In my opinion, you can safely ignore these tags without any detrimental impact whatsoever on your HTML documents.

Additionally, HTML 3.2 specifies two additional header tags, the SCRIPT and STYLE tags. The SCRIPT tag allows you to include scripts, usually JavaScript scripts, in a Web page. Besides Netscape Navigator, which originated this tag, Internet Explorer now also supports it. (For pointers to information on JavaScript available on the Web, see Appendix A.) The STYLE tag, on the other hand, is still up in the air. The release version of Internet Explorer 3.0 has rushed ahead and implemented a version of cascading stylesheets, but whether Microsoft's implementation will be what is finally approved is another matter.

Appendix E:
Putting It Up on the Web

You've created your first Web page, enhanced your graphics, and now you are ready to actually put it up on the Web so the rest of the world can see your handiwork. There are a few things you need to do first before your Web page can open up its doors on the Web.

Finding a Web Host

Before you can put a Web page up on the Web, you need to find a server to host your page. If you are a student, your school may be able to host your pages. If you are a subscriber to one of the online services, such as CompuServe or AOL, for instance, they also may be able to provide some server space. Your local access provider that connects you to the Internet might also be able to provide Web space to you at a nominal cost.

However, if you want to create a commercial Web page, hope to generate a considerable amount of traffic, or maybe want to have access to a fuller range of features and services, you might want to consider finding a Web host that specializes or focuses on providing raw Web space. For a list of affordable presence providers, see my Web site, the Budget Web Host List, at http://www.callihan.com/budget/. It also includes a link to my article, "Web Site on a Budget," which was published in the April '96 issue of *Internet World*.

Transferring Your Web Page to a Server

Your Web host should provide you with FTP access to your Web pages. This means providing you with a User ID and a password, as well as assigning you a directory on their server where you can store your pages. You may also be assigned an account name. This allows you to access your directory (and any directories you create within that directory) through FTP, copying files to or from it, while keeping everyone else out.

A Few Things You Need To Know

Before you can use FTP to transfer Web pages to your Web host's server, you need to know the following information from your Web space provider:

- **Host Name.** The host name of your Web host's server. For instance, the host name of the server on which my Web files reside is "vp2.netgate.net." This must identify a fully qualified Internet host name or IP address that belongs to a real server. It is not the same as a virtual host name, which can't be used here.

- **User ID.** You should have a unique user name that identifies you to your server. Often this is someone's last name.

- **Password.** You need to have a password so that only you, and no one else, can access your Web pages on the server.

- **Account.** You also may need to know the name of your account, although you usually don't have an account name.

- **Directory Path.** This is the directory path to where your files are located on your server. This can be the full directory path from the server's root directory or it can be an "alias" directory. Alias directories are preceded by a tilde—for instance, my alias directory on my server is "/~callihan," which substitutes for my actual, and much longer, directory path.

Using WS-FTP LE

To transfer your Web pages from your local computer to your server, you need to use an FTP program. The CD-ROM that accompanies this book includes two FTP programs, either of which you can use: WS-FTP LE and CuteFTP. The directions I provide below are for using WS-FTP LE.

I am assuming that you have a connection to the Internet, that you have been provided or have rented some space on a Web server to store your Web page, and that you have password protected access to your directory. I'm also assuming that you know the information detailed above under "A Few Things You Need To Know" and that you have installed WS-FTP LE.

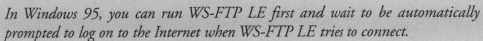

Appendix E: *Putting It Up on the Web*

Even though the two illustrations in this appendix are from Windows 95, the steps detailed befow for using WS-FTP LE are the same for both the 32-bit (Windows 95/NT) and the 16-bit (Windows 3.1) versions.

Run your winsock dialer to log on to the Internet, then after you connect to the Internet, run WS-FTP LE.

> ## NOTE
>
> *In Windows 95, you can run WS-FTP LE first and wait to be automatically prompted to log on to the Internet when WS-FTP LE tries to connect.*

The opening screen of WS-FTP LE is shown in Figure E-1.

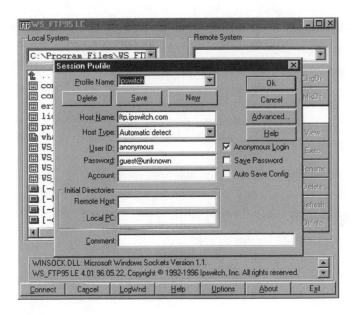

Figure E-1.
WS-FTP LE's opening screen

Do the following to define a new session profile:

1. In the Profile Name box, type a name for your session profile. This can be whatever you want. For instance, you might define "MySite" as your profile name. Just make it something you can remember.

2. In the Host Name box, type the host name of your Web host's server where your Web space is located. This is a fully qualified Internet host name or IP

address. This is not your "virtual" host name, if you happen to have one (for instance, my virtual host name is "www.callihan.com," but that is not the actual host name of my Web host's server).

3. In the Host Type box, leave "Automatically detect" enabled. In most cases, this should work. If it doesn't, you need to select a server type from the list (which may mean you need to send an e-mail query to your Web host to find out your server type).

4. In the User ID box, type your user name.

5. Click in the Anonymous Login check box until it's blank. Enable the Save Password check box.

CAUTION

Enable the Save Password check box only if you are the only user on your computer and no one else has access to your file directories. Although your password is saved here in encrypted form, deciphering it isn't difficult. If you don't save your password here, you must type it in each time you use FTP to log on to your Web server.

6. Type your password in the Password box. If you enabled Save Password, it appears as a row of asterisks.

7. Leave the Account box blank unless your Web host has provided you with an account name.

8. In the Remote Host box, type the actual (full) directory path on your server where your Web pages reside or your directory "alias" provided by your Web host for you to access your directory. A directory "alias" is usually preceded by a tilde. For instance, my directory alias is "~callihan." Thus, in the Remote Host box, to access my directory, I type "/~callihan."

9. Just leave the Local PC box blank (or you can specify a local directory on your PC as the local directory at which you want to start out).

10. Click on the Save button to save your new session profile. Click on the OK button now to log on to your server.

Figure E-2 shows WS-FTP LE's main screen once it has connected with and logged on to your Web server.

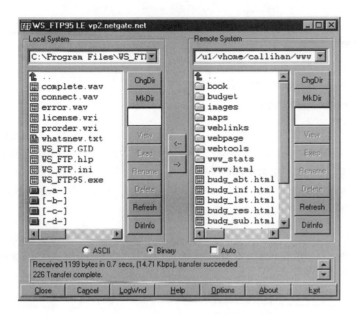

Figure E-2.
WS-FTP LE's main screen.

If this hasn't worked, you'll need to go back to the drawing board. You may need to specify your host type in step 3 (you'll probably have to e-mail your Web host to find out what this is). Make sure the host name of your Web server is correct in step 2. You should double-check that your User ID, password, and account name (if you have one) are correct. Another possibility is that your Web server is using a non-standard port number (other than Port 21) for FTP access; to change this, click on the Advanced button, enter the correct port number in the Remote Port box, and then click on the OK button. If it still doesn't work, under the same Advanced button, increase the Network Timeout amount. If none of this works, check with your Web host to make sure you're using the right user name, password, and so on. Also make sure you have the right directory path or directory alias.

The main screen of WS-FTP LE shows two side-by-side windows. The window on the left shows the starting directory of your local PC that is set by WS-FTP LE (the default is WS-FTP LE's own directory). The window on the right shows your directory on your Web server. Using this screen, you can do the following:

1. You can move up or down the directory structure in either window. Double-clicking on a folder will open a subdirectory. Double-clicking on the two periods ("..") will move you up one directory level. You also can use the ChgDir button in either window to change the directory.

2. You can use the MkDir button to create a directory in either window. You can use the Delete button to delete a directory.

3. To transfer files from the directory on your local PC to the directory on your Web server (you can also do this the other way around):

    A. On your local PC (the window on the left), change to the directory that contains the file or files you want to transfer. Highlight the file or files that you want to transfer.

    B. Check the radio button of the type of file or files you are transferring. If you are transferring an HTML file, click in the ASCII radio button so it is filled. If you are transferring a GIF or JPG graphic, click in the Binary radio button so it is filled. (You also can select the Auto Ratio button to have the file type automatically detected.)

    C. To transfer the highlighted file or files from the local PC directory (the left window) to the currently displayed directory on your Web server (the right window), click on the —> button. (To copy a file the other way, from your Web server to your local PC, you would click on the <— button.)

    Be patient. If you are copying several files, or if any of them are at all large, such as a banner graphic file, for instance, it may take a minute or so before the files have been transferred.

4. Of the remaining buttons, the ones you are most likely to use are the Rename button to rename files that are on your local PC or your Web server, the Delete button to delete either files or directories, and the DirInfo button to get information on the files in a directory (such as size or date).

You should create a directory structure on your Web server that matches the structure of the local directories where you are storing your HTML files and graphics. For instance, I've created a directory, C:\PAGES, in which I've created several directories for storing the files for different Web page projects, as well as a directory for storing all the graphics that are used on my Web pages. On my Web server, inside the directory for my Web pages (/WWW, which is set up by my Web host), I've created exactly the same directories. That way I can dry run my Web pages on my local PC, then when I'm satisfied, simply transfer them from their local to their corresponding directories on my Web server, without having to reset any of the links.

> **TIP**
>
> *In most cases, you shouldn't have to change the file extension of your Web pages from "htm" to "html." Most servers should be able to recognize either extension. In the odd chance that your server doesn't recognize "htm," or you just want to use "html" instead, here's how to have WS-FTP automatically convert the extensions for you:*

1. At WS-FTP LE's main screen, click on Options, click on Session Options, and then check the Convert Extensions check box. Click on OK.

2. Back at the main screen, click on Options, and then click on Extension Conversions. Type the extensions you want automatically to be converted in the Source and Destination boxes. (For instance, to automatically convert "htm" to "html," type the first as the source, the second as the destination.) Click on the Add button to add it to the list. Do the same for converting from "html" to "htm." Your list should now have two entries: "htm=html" and "html=htm".

That's it. After you transfer your Web page or pages up onto the Web using WS-FTP, just click the Close button to log off your Web server. When you log off, click on the Exit button to exit WS-FTP.

Index

BODY tag

Internet Service Providers (ISPs)

Paragraphs

introductory paragraph, creating your, 260
in multi-level outlines, 170-171
Partial URLs
hypertext links using, 124-126
subdirectories, linking to, 125-126
Passwords for FTP, 396
Percentages for height and width, 146-147
Perl Resource Directory, 337
Personal Web page, 223-226
resumes online, 224-226
Planning process, 204-206
Poetry Web page, 241-242
Poker Terms, Glossary of, 235
Pound (#) sign, 113
P (Paragraph) tag, 80-83. *See also* **ALIGN**
attribute
in A (Anchor) tag, 112
BLOCKQUOTE (Block Quote) tag for, 97, 99
multiple P tags to add blank lines, 82-83
PRE (Preformatted Text) tag, 91, 100-102
Project/organization description Web page,
243-244
Promoting your Web page, Resource Directory
for, 314
Publishing information Resource Directory,
321-322

Q

Quarterdeck, 44. *See also* **NCSA Mosaic**
Quotation marks, types of, 92

R

Rand Corporation, 5
RealAudio, streaming with, 113
Reducing image size, 145
Registration signs, 93
Relative font size changes, 189-190
Relative URLs, 13
hypertext links using, 124-126
subdirectories, linking to, 125-126
Reload button, 69
Reserved characters
entity codes, 92
inserting reserved characters, 91-92
Resource Directory. *See also* **Forms; Frames; Image**
maps; Tables; Web browsers
advanced HTML, 339
anti-virus scanners, 369
automated page creators, 356-359
automation tools, 368-369
backgrounds, 308
CGI, 337
character entities, 327-328
clip art directory, 309-312

colors, 307-308
settings, 329-331
utilities, 365-366
copyright information, 315
counters and statistics, 336
example Web pages, 323-324
file managers, 370
FTP software, 367-368
GIF animation, 335-336
glossaries, 339-340
graphics editors, viewers and converters, 359-362
graphics resources, 304-305
HTML converters, 353-356
HTML guides, 316-321
HTML 3.2, 326-327
image size/scaling, 307-308
interlaced GIFs, 305-307
Internet history, 342-343
ISO-8859-1 character set, 327-328
Java/JavaScript, 337-338
legal issues, 315
magazines, online, 340-342
Microsoft extensions, 326
Microsoft-Netscape war, 324
multimedia, 338-339
Netscape extensions, 325-326
Perl, 337
for promoting your Web page, 314
publishing information, 321-322
server, placing your Web page on, 313
site managers, 356-359
software collection sites, 366-369
Telnet software, 367-368
templates, 322-323
text editors, 348-352
transparent GIFs, 305-307
use of, 303-304
for validating your Web page, 314-315
Web authoring sites, 356-359
word processor add-ons, 353
zip utilities, 370
Resumes online, 224-226
Returns, 86-87
RGB hex codes, setting font color with, 194-195
Right-aligned images. *See* **Inline images**
Roman numerals in ordered list, 166
Rows. *See* **Tables**
ROWSPAN attribute, 385

S

SAMP tag, 89
Saving
HTML files, 130
scratch files, 135

Tags

To Order Books

Please send me the following items:

Quantity	Title	Unit Price	Total
_____	_____	$_____	$_____
_____	_____	$_____	$_____
_____	_____	$_____	$_____
_____	_____	$_____	$_____
_____	_____	$_____	$_____

Shipping and Handling depend on Subtotal.

Subtotal	Shipping/Handling
$0.00–$14.99	$3.00
$15.00–$29.99	$4.00
$30.00–$49.99	$6.00
$50.00–$99.99	$10.00
$100.00–$199.99	$13,50
$200.00+	Call for Quote

Foreign and all Priority Request orders:
Call Order Entry department
for price quote at 916/632-4400

*This chart represents the total retail price of books only
(before applicable discouts are taken).*

Subtotal **$**_____

Deduct 10% when ordering 3-5 books $_____

7.25% Sales Tax (CA only) **$**_____

8.25% Sales Tax (TN only) **$**_____

5.0% Sales Tax (MD and IN only) **$**_____

Shipping and Handling* **$**_____

Total Order **$**_____

By Telephone: With MC or VISA, call 800-632-8676 or 916-632-4400,
Mon - Fri, 8:30 - 4:30 P.S.T.

By E-mail: We're on the Web at http://www.primapublishing.com.
Send orders to: sales@primapub.com

By Mail: Just fill out the information below and send with your remittance to:

**Prima Publishing
P.O. Box 1260BK
Rocklin, CA 95677**

My name is _____

I live at _____

City _____ State _____ Zip _____

MC/VISA# _____ Exp _____

Check/Money Order enclosed for $_____ Payable to Prima Publishing

Daytime Telephone _____

Signature _____

Other Books from Prima Publishing, Computer Products Division

ISBN	Title	Price	Release Date
0-7615-0801-5	ActiveX	$35.00	Available Now
0-7615-0680-2	America Online Complete Handbook and Membership Kit	$24.99	Available Now
0-7615-0915-1	Building Intranets with Internet Information Server and FrontPage	$40.00	Available Now
0-7615-0417-6	CompuServe Complete Handbook and Membership Kit	$24.95	Available Now
0-7615-0849-X	Corporate Intranet Development	$40.00	Fall '96
0-7615-0692-6	Create Your First Web Page in a Weekend	$29.99	Available Now
0-7615-0503-2	Discover What's Online!	$24.95	Available Now
0-7615-0693-4	Internet Information Server	$40.00	Available Now
0-7615-0815-5	Introduction to ABAP/4 Programming for SAP	$45.00	Available Now
0-7615-0678-0	Java Applet Powerpack	$30.00	Available Now
0-7615-0685-3	JavaScript	$35.00	Available Now
0-7615-0901-1	Leveraging Visual Basic with ActiveX Controls	$45.00	Available Now
0-7615-0682-9	LiveWire Pro Master's Handbook	$40.00	Fall '96
0-7615-0755-8	Moving Worlds	$35.00	Available Now
0-7615-0690-X	Netscape Enterprise Server	$40.00	Available Now
0-7615-0691-8	Netscape FastTrack Server	$40.00	Available Now
0-7615-0852-X	Netscape Navigator 3 Complete Handbook	$24.99	Available Now
0-7615-0751-5	Windows NT Server 4 Administrator's Guide	$50.00	Available Now
0-7615-0759-0	Professional Web Design	$40.00	Available Now
0-7615-0773-6	Programming Internet Controls	$45.00	Available Now
0-7615-0780-9	Programming Web Server Applications	$40.00	Available Now
0-7615-0063-4	Researching on the Internet	$29.95	Available Now
0-7615-0686-1	Researching on the World Wide Web	$24.99	Available Now
0-7615-0695-0	The Essential Photoshop Book	$35.00	Available Now
0-7615-0752-3	The Essential Windows NT Book	$27.99	Available Now
0-7615-0689-6	The Microsoft Exchange Productivity Guide	$24.99	Available Now
0-7615-0769-8	VBScript Master's Handbook	$40.00	Available Now
0-7615-0684-5	VBScript Web Page Interactivity	$35.00	Available Now
0-7615-0903-8	Visual FoxPro 5 Enterprise Development	$45.00	Available Now
0-7615-0814-7	Visual J++	$35.00	Available Now
0-7615-0383-8	Web Advertising and Marketing	$34.95	Available Now
0-7615-0726-4	Webmaster's Handbook	$40.00	Available Now

License Agreement/Notice of Limited Warranty